EU Expansion to the East

Prospects and Problems

Edited by

Hilary Ingham

Senior Lecturer, Department of Economics, Lancaster University, UK

and

Mike Ingham

Principal, ACOST and Fellow, Lancaster University, UK

Edward Elgar

Cheltenham, UK • Northampton, MA, USA

Published by
Edward Elgar Publishing Limited
Glensanda House
Montpellier Parade
Cheltenham
Glos GL50 1UA
UK

Edward Elgar Publishing, Inc.
136 West Street
Suite 202
Northampton
Massachusetts 01060
USA

Reprinted 2003
Paperback edition 2003

A catalogue record for this book
is available from the British Library

Library of Congress Cataloguing in Publication Data

EU expansion to the East : prospects and problems / edited by Hilary Ingham and Mike Ingham.

p. cm

Includes bibliographical references and index.

1. European Union—Europe, Eastern. 2. Europe—Economic integration. 1. Title: European Union expansion to the East. II. Ingham, Hilary, 1995- III. Ingham Mike, 1953-

HC240.25.E852 E92 2002
337.1'42—dc21 2001056910

ISBN 1 84064 824 4 (cased)
1 84376 520 9 (paperback)

Printed and bound in Great Britain by MPG Books Ltd, Bodmin, Cornwall

EU Expansion to the East

Contents

List of Tables

List of Figures

List of Contributors

George Blazyca is Professor of Economics in the Paisley Business School and Director of the University-wide Centre for Contemporary European Studies. He is a specialist on Polish economic, social and political development and writes regularly on this for, among others, the London based Economist Intelligence Unit Ltd. Edward Elgar has recently published his new book *Poland into the New Millennium*, 2001, co-edited with Ryszard Rapacki of the Warsaw School of Economics.

David Brown is a researcher in Third Pillar matters at the University of Aberdeen. His current work examines the implementation problems involved in European police cooperation and counter-terrorism. Other research interests include the impact of enlargement and immigration.

Martin Dangerfield is Senior Lecturer in Contemporary European Studies in the School of Humanities, Languages and Social Sciences at the University of Wolverhampton. His most recent work has been on subregional cooperation in Central and Eastern Europe and CEFTA. Earlier publications focused on aspects of the Czech transformation process and the external economic relations of Central and East European states.

Hilary Ingham is Senior Lecturer in Economics at Lancaster University. Her research interests are agriculture and rural development, particularly in the light of EU expansion, labour markets in Central and Eastern Europe and spatial spillovers. She has recently co-edited and contributed to *Women on the Polish Labor Market* (CEU Press, 2001, with Mike Ingham and Henryk Domański). Other recent publications on Poland have examined agricultural reform, the regional dynamics of youth unemployment and union membership.

Mike Ingham is the Principal of ACOST consulting and a Research Fellow at Lancaster University. His research interests encompass labour markets and regional and rural development, with particular reference to their European dimension. He co-edited and contributed to *Women on the Polish Labor Market* (CEU Press, 2001) and *The Reform of the Socialist System in Central and Eastern Europe* (Macmillan, 1998).

Ann Kennard is a Senior Lecturer in German at the Faculty of Languages and European Studies, University of the West of England. She has been publishing on border cooperation between Germany and Poland for some years and has more recently broadened the scope of her work to cover the wider Central and East European context of the anticipated of EU enlargement.

Robert McKinlay is Dean of the Faculty of Social Sciences and Professor, Department of Politics and International Relations, Lancaster University. His research interests focus on international studies, with a particular emphasis on international political economy. His published works include *Comparing Government Activity* (Macmillan, 1996), *Third World Military Expenditure* (Pinter, 1989), *Global Problems and World Order* (Pinter, 1986) and *Aid and Arms to the Third World* (Pinter, 1984). He also co-authored *The Recalcitrant Rich* with Helge Bergesen (Pinter, 1982).

Ronald McQuaid is Professor and Director of the Employment Research Institute at Napier University, Edinburgh. His interests inlcude regional and local economic development, transport policy and the implications of expansion of the European Union. He recently co-authored *Entrepreneurial Economics* with Keith Glancey (Palgrave, 2000).

Nick Manning is Professor of Social Policy and Sociology at the University of Nottingham. His research interests include social change and social policy in Russia and Eastern Europe and medical sociology. His latest books are *Work and Welfare in the New Russia* (Ashgate, 2000, with Ovsey Shkaratan and Nataliya Tikhonova) and *New Risks, New Welfare* (Blackwell, 2000, with Ian Shaw). His current projects in the field include a national study of 23 therapeutic communities (funded by the National Lottery Charities Board) and a comparative study of poverty in Moscow, Voronezh and Vladikavkaz (funded by EU INTAS).

Hugh Miall is Reader in Peace and Conflict Research and Director of the Richardson Institute for Peace Studies, Department of Politics and International Relations at Lancaster University. He was previously a Fellow in the European Programme at the Royal Institute of International Affairs. His current research interests lie in conflict resolution and conflict prevention, with an area focus on the wider Europe. He is the editor of *Shaping the New Europe* (RIIA/Pinter, 1993), *Redefining Europe: New Patterns of Conflict and Cooperation* (RIIA/Pinter, 1994) and the author of *Minority Property Rights in Europe: The Scope for a Transnational Regime* (RIIA/Pinter, 1994). He also co-authored *Contemporary Conflict Resolution* (Polity, 2000), with Oliver Ramsbotham and Tom Woodhouse.

Gillian Pascall is Reader in Social Policy at the University of Nottingham. She has worked on social policy and gender in the UK and is the author of *Social Policy: A New Feminist Analysis* (Routledge, 1997). She has current research interests in gender and welfare regimes in the transition countries and has research in progress with Professor Anna Kwak of Warsaw University on 'The Gender Relations of Care: Parents and Social Policy in Poland'.

David Phinnemore is Lecturer in European Integration at the Institute of European Studies, Queen's University Belfast. He has published widely on EU external relations and EU enlargement, most notably *Association: Stepping Stone or Alternative to EU Membership?* (Sheffield Academic Press, 1999). He also works on treaty reform within the EU and is compiling (with Clive Church) *The Penguin Guide to the European Treaties*.

Robert Read is Lecturer in International Economics at Lancaster University and a former Economist with Unilever PLC. His primary research interests are in the fields on EU trade, particularly its banana policy, the single currency and the economics of small states.

Jean-Marc Trouille is Senior Lecturer in German Studies at the University of Bradford, where he also lectures on European Economic Integration as part of the Jean Monnet project funded by the European Commission. He has published widely in the field of Franco-German economic, political, industrial and cultural relations and is a regular contributor to 'Documents - revue des questions allemandes'. He has recently co-authored *France, Germany and Britain: Partners in a Changing World* (Palgrave, 2001), with Mairi Maclean.

Preface

Potential enlargement of the European Union to embrace countries of Central and Eastern Europe introduces enormous challenges, opportunities and threats for parties on both sides. Understanding of the diversity of issues raised by even an experimental expansion is limited and rarely extends beyond the concerns voiced in a particular policy arena. This volume brings together contributions from specialists across the social sciences who consider the possible outcomes of expansion per se, to which countries it might be extended and the future of a Union that continues to be exclusive, but which must advance in the context of the overall march of globalisation.

1. Towards a United Europe?

Hilary Ingham and Mike Ingham[1]

INTRODUCTION

The end of the Second World War heralded a significant, if ultimately temporary, shift in the political complexion of Europe. To the west, sovereign states restored democracy and pursued, to a greater or lesser extent, market-oriented paths to reconstruction and renewed growth. Their endeavours have brought many of these independent nations ever closer to economic, political and social union. To the east, the conditions were created for the rapid emergence of a communist bloc that was to be steered from Moscow for almost half a century. Eventually, however, enforced cooperation could be maintained no longer and, at the beginning of the twenty-first century, the freely created EU faces its hardest challenge to date: assimilating post-communist Central and Eastern European (CEE) countries into membership. The contributions selected for this volume consider in detail the prospects, challenges and problems of an enlargement that would bring the continent the closest it has yet been to a state of voluntary unification.

This opening chapter plots the terrain that has been crossed since the Second World War in order for Europe to arrive at the crossroads at which it is located currently. The following section examines the beginnings of cooperation in the west of the continent, culminating in the establishment of the European Economic Community (EEC) and the European Free Trade Association (EFTA). A very different kind of economic apparatus came into being in the Soviet bloc, the salient features of which are discussed subsequently. Within a decade, the EEC was to evolve into the European Community, thereby establishing the momentum with which to embark upon a far-reaching programme of deepening and widening that would lead a club that had already grown from a membership of six to one of fifteen onto the verge of its most ambitious expansion drive to date. The major landmarks of the preparatory process are described in the fourth section of the chapter.

Relations between east and west were not severed totally between 1945 and 1989 and small, albeit significant, trade flows took place between them. However, the current European Union (EU), like its predecessors, is an organisation for democratic, market-led societies. As such, any vision of the countries of CEE joining its ranks had to await their rejection of communism. Once this began to happen, relations between the two sides took on a more intense character and the fifth section of the work examines how these have developed to the point where formal accession negotiations are now under way with ten CEE states. Nevertheless, desirable and desired as the forthcoming wave of expansion might be, it will not be painless and it is still surrounded by a number of major controversies, with the main economic concerns being elaborated in the sixth section of the chapter. This is followed by an overview of the broader insights provided by the eleven further contributions to the volume.

POST-WAR COOPERATION IN WESTERN EUROPE

The Second World War left most of the continent debt-ridden and with trade patterns between its nations that had been seriously disrupted (Geiger, 1999). However, the major west European economies exhibited impressive growth rates after 1945 as a result of both the need to undertake large-scale reconstruction projects and of the opportunity to avail themselves of the war-driven advances in technology (Postan, 1967).[2] The unwanted consequence was a worsening debt profile through the emergence of large trade deficits, most notably with the USA. In an attempt to redress this situation, America wanted to establish an international trade system based on fixed payments and currency convertibility that it believed would promote intra-European trade and growth. In contrast, Europe wanted reconstruction loans. Having refused at Bretton Woods in 1944 to subsidise European reconstruction (MacBean and Snowden, 1981), America's policy changed in 1947 when the provisions of the Marshall Plan, which followed Truman's Doctrine to Congress, extended direct financial aid to the continent.[3] But such monies, however, came with a price: the aid was conditional upon enhanced intra-European cooperation. This dramatic change in US policy came about for two reasons. First, it saw enhanced cooperation as the best way to avoid any future hostilities; second, and perhaps more importantly, it hoped that the money would bring prosperity and thereby minimise the chance that any west European nation would succumb to the promises of communism.

The European Recovery Program, administered by the European Co-operation Administration (ECA), that emerged from the Marshall Plan financed imports totalling almost fourteen billion dollars during its first five years of operation (Geiger, op. cit.:33). Initially, the majority of these monies were used to fund dollar imports from the USA, which prompted the ECA to establish the Organisation for European Economic Co-operation in 1948 in order to promote intra-European trade. However, the initial payments scheme devised for this purpose was unpopular and failed to achieve its goal and was succeeded by the European Payments Union (EPU) in the middle of 1950. This required deficit countries to pay increasing proportions of their debt, while surplus countries received payment in gold or dollars. Limited convertibility between European currencies was restored and the seventeen participating states retained the freedom to impose duties and quotas on imports from the dollar area.[4] In the first year of the EPU's operation, intra-European trade grew by 41 per cent and had more than doubled by 1956 (ibid.:35). Simultaneously, additional examples of enhanced cooperation were emerging within Western Europe; for example, the Benelux (Belgium, the Netherlands and Luxembourg) customs union.[5] Nevertheless, relations with West Germany remained a major problem for all countries on the continent, but particularly France. Furthermore, the Congress of Europe held in The Hague in 1948 had largely failed in its attempt to establish a European economic and political union.

It is perhaps surprising therefore that the 1950 Schuman Plan, which proposed a supranational authority to integrate Europe's coal and steel sectors (i.e. basic war-making industries) and necessitated a dramatic shift in French policy, secured support. The fact that it did witnessed France, West Germany, Italy and the Benelux countries sign the Treaty of Paris in 1951, which created the European Coal and Steel Community (ECSC). In Messina, in June 1955, the Benelux countries submitted a memorandum that proposed strengthening the ties through measures such as the establishment of a customs union, greater economic cooperation and liberalised factor movements between both the ECSC members and the UK. With the latter remaining sceptical, the ECSC 'six' produced a report, following the deliberations of the 1956 Spaak Committee, proposing a new concept that would become known as the Common Market, encompassing common policies in agriculture, trade, transport and competition. This resulted in the Euratom and EEC treaties (jointly referred to as the Treaty of Rome) being signed in March 1957.[6]

The EEC was therefore designed to be far more than a standard customs union, with its founding Treaty specifying that the common market would be achieved through the harmonisation of an extensive range of policies, to be monitored by an overarching system of supranational judicial review. At the outset, the primary objective of the members was economic; they wanted to create a competitive power to challenge the dominance of the United States (Pelkmans, 1997:19). However, the creation of the Community generated a division within Western Europe, with the UK and the neutral states being unwilling to accept the supranational aspects of the Treaty of Paris. Their preferred alternative was to create EFTA in 1959, initially comprising Austria, Denmark, Norway, Portugal, Sweden, Switzerland and the UK. This enterprise was far less ambitious than the EEC and merely involved the creation of a free trade area for industrial products, with minimal institutional apparatus.

PARALLEL DEVELOPMENTS IN THE EAST

To the east the ravages of the war had been no less serious, but there the similarities with the west ended. In particular, those territories that were effectively ceded to Stalin in the post-war settlement were either absorbed into the Soviet Union or, by 1949, had been transformed into a constellation of communist dictated peoples' democracies whose actions were largely directed from Moscow. This eastern bloc embarked upon a path of reconstruction and development that eschewed market prices in favour of a command system and a policy of central allocation that placed economic management in the hands of bureaucrats. While frequently overlooked, it was this group that undertook the earliest and most profound steps towards European integration through the formation of the Council for Mutual Economic Assistance (CMEA) in January 1949: a move that was greeted with some surprise in the western world.[7] In fact, its creation represented Stalin's reaction to the Marshall Aid Plan of 1947 and the offers made under it to extend assistance to certain east European countries. The founding members of CMEA were the USSR, Bulgaria, Czechoslovakia, Hungary, Poland and Romania. Albania and the GDR were early additional recruits, although the former eventually resigned and allied itself with the Chinese in 1961. The Mongolian People's Republic (1962), Cuba (1972) and Vietnam (1978) represented later additions, while Yugoslavia had associate status from 1962. Eventually, membership was possible for any country willing to abide by the Council's 1959 Charter (Mellor, 1987). While relatively inactive, perhaps even redundant, during the Stalin years, the declared aim of the organisation was to promote the economic development of its members and to facilitate their participation in an international socialist division of labour (Shiryaev and Sokolov, 1977). Nevertheless, there was no stated intention to achieve this through supranational policies and the CMEA's declared respect for national sovereignties was to be reiterated frequently. Within member states, the right to conduct foreign trade was conferred upon state monopolies, with the transactions of these bodies being converted at local prices in the hope of isolating the domestic economy from external influences. In this setting, most trade was a residual, with imports restricted to indispensable commodities and exports being viewed as an outlet for surpluses with which to pay for foreign purchases. The ensuing trade agreements were generally negotiated bilaterally and were quasi-barter in character.

Inter-member trade was in theory based on a five-year average of world prices and, once determined, these were to remain fixed for five years in order to provide stability.[8] In practice, these magnitudes usually constituted simply the basis for negotiating specific contractual prices between each pair of member parties and most trade was based on state determined quota allocations (Brus, 1986). Furthermore, trade settlements were made in a unit of account known as the 'transferable rouble' but, as this was neither convertible nor transferable, most countries tried to avoid accruing surpluses. While some joint ventures between members evolved over time and some degree of specialisation became evident, particularly in response to the creation of the EEC in 1957, this was always limited, both by mistrust and by the difficulties of central plan coordination, notwithstanding the intention to strengthen the latter declared in the 1971 Comprehensive Programme (Shiryaev and Sokolov, op. cit.). Modest as these achievements may have been, they did help to reduce the level of regional inequality prevailing in several of the countries of Eastern Europe. It must be stressed, however, that there was no explicit CMEA regional policy and no investment funds were made available for the purpose. Likewise, manpower flows between member countries were extremely small and generally discouraged. In fact, while the CMEA did much to improve and integrate east European transport networks, the emphasis was normally on the international movement of goods rather than people (Mellor, op. cit.). Above all else, the organisation represented an attempt to further the political aspirations of the USSR, although it simultaneously offered a much-needed ready market for Soviet energy exports, which were paid for by reverse flows of manufactured goods.

Whatever autarkical ambitions may have fuelled its creation, the CMEA was never a self-sufficient grouping and its members always retained trading links with the west, although these ebbed and flowed according to economic cycles and the prevailing political climate. East-west collaboration agreements began to emerge in the 1960s, underpinned to some extent by the links that certain members of CMEA established with GATT (Brus, op. cit.). It now seems somewhat ironic that Romania, along with Hungary, was keenest of the eastern bloc countries to develop such relationships with the west (Matejka, 1986; Trzeciakowski, 1973). As the limitations of the initial extensive growth strategy that the CMEA members had pursued became apparent, they embarked upon a policy of import-led growth in the 1970s. The attempt was, however, mismanaged and they were unable to generate the exports with which to pay for their western purchases. The result was an alarming increase in indebtedness, although particularly so in the case of Poland, and the experiment had to be abandoned. This episode highlighted the serious limitations of the CMEA's capacity to provide 'Mutual Economic Assistance' (Brus, 1986a).

As noted above, the creation of the EEC acted as a spur to the attempts to render the CMEA an effective, operational organisation. Even so, officially it did not recognise the 'capitalist' Community until 1972 (Benavides, 1989). Thereafter, there were various attempts at improving relations between the two, although these always stalled on account of irreconcilable differences (Maslen, 1989). In part, these failures can be traced to complaints from the east European (state-trading) countries about the discriminatory treatment applied to their exports by the Community. Whatever the substance of these allegations, it is certainly true that several anti-dumping cases were brought against CEE states and there were also instances when anti-trust law was applied to them (Maresceau, 1989). Eventually, an EEC–CMEA Joint Declaration was signed on 25 June 1988 which, although not dealing directly with trade, was forecast to 'have a considerable impact on the normalisation of relations between the EEC and Eastern Europe as a whole' (ibid.:4). But by then it was too late and, while the 1990 session of the CMEA decided on an immediate shift to world prices, the organisation was disbanded in the following year.

THE EEC: DEEPER AND BROADER

While cooperation in the east was always more nominal than real, the EEC not only endured, but gained in economic and political significance over time through the parallel processes of deepening and widening. Deepening refers to the evolution of a closer relationship between the member states, as evidenced by the adoption of common policies. An early example of this was provided by the unification of the ECSC, Euratom and EEC treaties in 1965. Widening refers to the dynamics of enlargement, with successive waves bringing in new countries that have transformed the organisation from a club of six to one that currently has fifteen members. Denmark, Ireland and the UK joined in 1973, to be followed by Greece in 1981, Portugal and Spain in 1986 and Austria, Finland and Sweden in 1995.

Although the EEC became a successful international economic power relatively quickly, it was apparent that institutional strengthening was required if this stature was to be matched in other spheres. In particular, its international responsibilities neither reflected its economic weight nor allowed for the effective consideration of the political aspects of its external relations (El-Agraa, 2001). Reform was hampered, however, because its members did not share common views on relationships with extra-Community nations, most notably the USA and the USSR. Nevertheless, foreign ministers of the member states began to liaise in the 1970s and this signalled a move towards greater political cooperation, even if it did not lead to a common foreign policy.

The Community faced major challenges in the 1980s, including recession, high levels of unemployment and concerns regarding its international competitiveness. In the event, these developments were insufficient to prevent the signing of the Single European Act (SEA) at the end of 1986, which became operational on 1 July 1987. The key policy development contained in this Act was the move towards a single market, to be established by the end of 1992, to ensure the free movement of goods, services, capital and labour.[9] Certain commentators argue that this reinvigorated the process of European integration by abolishing all remaining mobility barriers, thereby creating a true common market (Baldwin et al., 1995). At the same time, signs of disintegration within the Warsaw Pact at the end of the 1990s caused the Community to reassess its defence requirements in relation to NATO and the continuing American defence presence on its soil. However, the twelve constituted a far less cohesive group than the original six: while some members championed the idea of political union, others stressed the need for new policies to address changing circumstances.

Another important development within the Community emerged from the Councils held in Maastricht at the end of 1991 and Amsterdam in 1997 that together led to the Treaty on European Union and the formation of the organisation of that name.[10] This was a plan for the future that included economic and monetary union, institutional reform and the development of an international identity, to include political competencies and common defence and foreign policies. The final phase of the single currency was duly adopted on 1 January 1999, although the UK and Sweden declined to join. In addition, Denmark's constitution required that a referendum be held and its electorate subsequently voted against membership. Greece, on the other hand, did not satisfy the so-called convergence criteria, although eventually it was admitted on 1 January 2001.

THE EU'S RELATIONS WITH THE EAST

In the early 1970s, eastern markets were particularly attractive to western firms because many of the communist states were attempting to modernise their industrial infrastructures, a task that necessitated the import of machinery from the first world. In 1975, the first Conference on Security and

Cooperation in Europe, attended by representatives from thirty-four east and west European governments, fostered further trade and cooperation. In quantitative terms, the USSR was a far more important market than the CEE countries. It offered a huge export market for machinery, while it sold commodities that the west needed, such as energy, non-ferrous metals and aluminium. In contrast, the CEE market was much smaller and its exports were dominated by sensitive products such as steel, textiles, chemicals and food: its manufactured goods were not adapted to western tastes and tended to be of low quality. However, increased fear of the risk of payment default by CEE countries in the 1980s, coupled with the loss of international means of payment in the USSR following the collapse of the world oil price in 1986, saw a reduction in east-west trade until the systemic upheavals at the end of the decade.

The fall of the Berlin Wall resulted in the first *de facto* eastern enlargement of the Union when the *länder* of the Democratic Republic were unified with the German Federal Republic in October 1990. Elsewhere, the collapse of communism stoked a similar desire for integration into Western Europe. One provision of the Treaty of Rome states that 'any European country may apply to join the Union' (Article O), although the lack of enthusiasm for eastwards enlargement within the EU meant that the best that the CEE nations achieved initially were the Europe Agreements.[11] The apparent front running nations, namely Poland, Hungary and Czechoslovakia, concluded these at the end of 1991, followed by Bulgaria and Romania in 1993, the Baltic States in 1995 and Slovenia in 1996.[12]

The trade component of the Agreements provided for gradual, asymmetric concessions that would lead to the establishment of a free trade area between each CEE country and the EU in industrial products.[13] In addition, they also contained provisions for technical cooperation. For the transition states, the most important element of the packages was that they contained, for the first time, the explicit commitment that 'the final objective of [the given country] is to become a member of the Community, and that this association, in the view of the Parties, will help to achieve this objective' (cited in Lavigne, 1999:220). However, while accession was recognised as an aim of the associated countries, nowhere in the Agreements is it stated as a goal of the EU. This contrasts with similar documents signed with Greece in 1963 and Turkey in 1964 (Gaudissart and Sinnaeve, 1997).[14]

At face value, the trade provisions appear generous, although this is somewhat misleading. First, many of the concessions merely repeated those already granted in the Generalised System of Preferences or in the trade and economic cooperation agreements that had been concluded with each of the CEE countries from 1988 onwards. Second, the Agreements covered only industrial products; sensitive goods such as agriculture, textiles and coal and steel were not covered, even though they accounted for the dominant share of CEE exports to the west. The actual gains that the CEE countries achieved from these arrangements have therefore been estimated to be limited, at least until 1997, and have been only slightly greater thereafter (Lavigne, op. cit.; Drábek, 1997).

This imposed strain on relations between the two sides in the early 1990s. The issue of CEE exports of sensitive goods caused many problems: the EU won an anti-dumping case against eastern steel producers in 1992 and an agricultural war erupted in 1993, when a ban was imposed on CEE agricultural products after foot and mouth disease in Italy was traced to imports from Yugoslavia, Poland, Hungary, the Czech Republic and Slovakia. On a more positive note, the Copenhagen Council, held in June 1993, contained the statement that 'the associated countries of Central and Eastern Europe that so desire shall become members of the European Union. Accession will take place as soon as an associated country is able to assume the obligations of membership by satisfying the economic and political conditions required' (CEC, 1993). However, no timetable for enlargement was produced.[15] Nevertheless, a decisive pre-accession step was taken in the following year when six of these countries (the Visegrád Four, Bulgaria and Romania) were offered an invitation to attend the Essen Summit.[16] From this meeting emerged a two-dimensional pre-accession strategy that was designed to further both the development of structured relations between the EU institutions and the associated CEE countries as well as the latter's preparation for integration into the single market. While the first element of this strategy was basically a continuation of the Copenhagen decisions, the second was new (op. cit., 1997).[17]

The Madrid Summit in 1995 saw the Union preoccupied with the issues of institutional reform and the furtherance of the conditions for the introduction of the single currency: enlargement was not to the fore of the agenda. It was therefore not until the Amsterdam Summit in 1997 that was it agreed that accession negotiations could be opened with CEE countries in the following year, by which time, frustrated by the EU's lack of commitment to expansion, ten CEE countries had already submitted formal applications for membership.[18] Initially, the EU proposed to open negotiations with five of these (the Czech Republic, Estonia, Hungary, Poland and Slovenia) and Cyprus (collectively known as the Luxembourg Group), provided that they satisfied various entry conditions. These criteria, which were established by the Treaty of Rome and subsequently modified by the SEA and the Maastricht Treaty, followed from the European Councils held in Copenhagen and Essen.

According to the conditions, any European country can apply to join the Union provided that they have:

- a stable pluralist democracy and are committed to the rule of law, the respect of human rights and the protection of minorities;
- a functioning market economy;
- the capacity to cope with the competitive pressures and market forces within the EU;
- endorsed the objective of political, economic and monetary union and are able to assume the obligations of membership, in particular the *acquis communautaire*. As such, they must accept the free circulation of goods, services, capital and labour; the Common Agricultural Policy; the competition policy rules; fiscal harmonisation, and exhibit a commitment towards developing countries.

Lavigne (op. cit.:230) notes that 'These conditions of membership are so broad that they may be considered as met, by and large, and at the same time as unattainable in full for many years'. Also, the terms laid down for the CEE applicants are more stringent than those specified in previous enlargements in certain respects. In particular, any successful applicants will be expected to adhere to the objective of political union and to embrace the single currency.

Determining the degree to which each of the candidate countries satisfies the entry criteria is a complicated process. The Annex to the 1995 White Paper covered 23 'sectors', which the Commission later reinterpreted as 31 'Chapters'. Both of these lists focus on the key tasks to be completed, with each divided into Stage I and Stage II activities, the latter being seen as measures that can only be accomplished satisfactorily once the former have been achieved. This led to a questionnaire, circulated in May 1996 to all candidate countries, with responses required by the end of July in the same year. This represented a considerable hurdle for the potential entrants to climb since the amount of detail required meant that the minimum length of a completed enquiry ran to some two thousand pages (Inotai, 1997). On the basis of these returns, the EU produced an *avis* for each country, along with its recommendations in order that membership could be achieved. Following this exercise, the Commission published Agenda 2000 in July 1997, which was a document that addressed explicitly the issue of the impact of enlargement on the EU budget for the first time. As Mayes (2001:556) notes: 'Somewhat surprisingly, Agenda 2000 suggests that the EU will be able to absorb the budgetary consequences of enlargement reasonably readily'. Additionally, the Agenda outlined the pre-accession funding programmes that would be made available to help the applicant countries prepare for entry.[19] On 31 March 1998, bilateral negotiations commenced with the Luxembourg Group.

On 13 October 1999, the Commission recommended that member states open negotiations with the remaining five CEE applicants and Malta. Members endorsed the recommendation at the Helsinki Summit in December 1999 and the negotiations duly commenced in February 2000. At the same time, Turkey's position in the accession queue was recognised, although there is as yet no timetable for the commencement of formal membership negotiations. Simultaneously, the Union adopted a 'regatta' approach to the membership applications, thereby removing the stark divide between the Luxembourg Group and the remaining countries in the region: admission will be granted in order of adjudged readiness, with the Commission's annual Regular Reports providing an audit of the progress of each aspirant member.[20]

THE PROSPECTS AND THE PROBLEMS

While it is tempting to draw parallels between the proposed current enlargement and those undertaken in the past, in particular the extension of membership to include Greece and the Iberian countries, the admission of CEE states is a far more ambitious project than anything attempted previously. First, the ten have a combined population of 105 million people, or 28 per cent of the current EU-15 total. Second, all of the eastern applicants are far poorer than the existing member states. On average, their GDP per head, at current market prices, is only 18 per cent of the EU average, a figure that only rises to 38 per cent even if a purchasing power parity measure is adopted (Mayes, op. cit.:554–5). This, of course, masks marked differentials within the region: Slovenia's current price GDP is 44 per cent of the EU average, while Bulgaria's amounts to only 7 per cent (ibid.). The CEE economies are also far more agricultural. Thus, while Greece has the highest proportion (17.7 per cent) of its workers engaged in agriculture among current members (Eurostat, 1999), the figure exceeds one-fifth in four of the applicant countries and is almost 40 per cent in Romania (Ingham and Ingham, 2002). Furthermore, a recent world ranking of competitiveness found the combined score of the Czech Republic, Hungary and Poland to be some 27 percentage points behind that of Greece, Portugal and Spain taken together (Salvatore, 2000:42–3).

In addition, Economic and Monetary Union (EMU) has now reached its final stage, with twelve of the fifteen current member states adopting the euro. Admitting new members that realistically cannot hope to adopt this currency, at least in the short-term, would appear to threaten closer financial integration. This is particularly relevant as the euro has not fared well on international currency markets since its introduction and there must be a fear that any extension of its coverage to the east might weaken it yet further. It is also possible to question whether countries that have only recently gained their economic and political independence after nearly half a century of Soviet domination will be keen to surrender some of their new found national sovereignty by foregoing their financial independence.

Any assessment of eastward expansion involves four considerations: the costs and benefits to the east and the costs and benefits to the west (Baldwin et al., 1997). From an economic perspective, it is often suggested that benefits to both parties will flow from the allocation and accumulation effects delivered by the full liberalisation of trade between the two blocs.[21] This would require the elimination of all remaining tariffs and quantitative restrictions and that the new member states adopt the EU's Common External Tariff. However, with the exception of agriculture and certain other sensitive goods, EU-CEE trade has already been liberalised, in particular through the Europe Agreements and, in 1998, the EU accounted for 64 per cent of both exports to, and imports from, CEE countries (EU, 2000). In contrast, only 4 per cent of the Union's imports came from the candidate countries and they absorbed merely 5 per cent of its exports. As a result, the combined CEE trade deficit with the EU reached $24,548 million and this worsening of their current account deficits led certain countries to resort to non-tariff barriers, in direct contradiction of their obligations as World Trade Organization (WTO) members and signatories of the Association Agreements (Fink, 2000).[22] Nevertheless, the Commission pressed ahead with its 'double-zero' agreements, which liberalised trade with the applicants in sensitive products, in the year 2000.

The situation has led certain commentators to conclude that any additional trade gains from eastwards expansion are likely to be limited: 'While these developments will further increase trade links between the EU and the CEECs, they will have – beyond the agricultural sector – a minor impact in comparison to those changes which have already been induced by the opening of the CEECs and the gradual removal of trade barriers following the conclusion of the Europe Agreements' (EU, op. cit.:31). It has been estimated that the benefits that would accrue to seven acceding countries in terms of increases in real income would range from 1.5 per cent under a conservative scenario to 18.8 per cent under an optimistic one (Baldwin et al., 1997:138, 147).[23] The gains to the EU, however, are estimated to be as low as 0.2 per cent, a figure that is invariant to the underlying assumptions behind the estimates (ibid.). In this light, it should be recognised that free trade does not necessarily involve accession: Iceland and Norway, for example, are members of the European Economic Area, which provides them with virtual membership of the Union (El-Agraa, 2001).[24]

Of course, accession is scheduled to bring access to EU budgetary funds to the candidate countries and, as they are considerably poorer than current members on all conventional indicators, they would be net beneficiaries. At current market prices, the poorest member state in 1998 was Portugal, which had a GDP per capita that was only 48 per cent of the EU average. Only Slovenia, with 44 per cent, was comparable to this: no other CEE country recorded a figure that was as high as one-quarter of the Union's average (Mayes, op. cit.:554–5). The Structural Funds, the fastest growing element of the EU budget during the 1990s (Baldwin et al., 1997:151), are transfers to disadvantaged regions throughout the Union designed to promote convergence in per capita income levels. The Cohesion Fund that channels monies towards those member countries with national incomes per capita less than 90 per cent of the EU average – currently Greece, Ireland, Portugal and Spain – is one element of the structural funding package.[25]

Under the current regulations, all CEE regions, with the exception of Prague in the Czech Republic, Bratislava in Slovakia and Közép Magyarország in Hungary would achieve Objective 1 status and thereby qualify for the highest levels of support from the Structural Funds (Eurostat, 2000). In addition, all of the applicant countries would be eligible for support from the Cohesion Fund. The cost of extending these packages to the Visegrád countries and Slovenia has been estimated to be as high as 26.6 billion ECU (Baldwin et al., 1997:153). However, as these authors note, estimates of this magnitude have been criticised on the grounds that CEE governments facing severe fiscal pressure would be unable to provide the required matched funding.[26] On the other hand, the programmes also work on the principle of additionality, which means that potential recipients must convince the Commission that the proposed projects would not have been undertaken without European support. On balance, therefore, Baldwin et al. (1997) produce more conservative figures that estimate the burden to the Structural Funds to be slightly below 13 billion ECU (ibid.:153). Even this calculation could be challenged, however, given that expenditure on the Funds is scheduled to decline under the budgetary plans for the period 2000–06 (CEC, 1999).

A further cause for concern is the burden that admitting new members from the east would place on the Common Agricultural Policy (CAP), the subventions that account for the greatest share of the EU budget. While agriculture remains a significant employer for many countries within CEE, two pose particular problems. Poland, the largest applicant country, has over 27 per cent of its workforce in the sector, while Romania, the second largest applicant, has 38 per cent (BCE, 2000:46). Early estimates of the burden that accession of the CEE-10 would place on the CAP ranged from 9 billion ECU (Slater and Atkinson, 1995) to 55 billion ECU (Brenton and Gros, 1993).

However, the provisions of the CAP have been changing constantly since the MacSharry reforms of 1992, not least because of external pressure from the WTO (Ingham and Ingham, op. cit.). In addition, the EU does not envisage currently that direct payments, which are gradually replacing the price support mechanisms, will be extended to the new member states, although this issue remains a bone of contention between Brussels and the applicants (ibid.). While the future shape of the agricultural support mechanism and whether new members would enjoy the same access to the funds as the EU-15 remain unresolved issues, estimating the cost of expansion is problematic.

When considering the scale of possible transfers to the new member states, it is important not to overlook another aspect of the absorption problem. Although the payments would total less than 1 per cent of the EU budget under current projections, assuming new members were excluded from the income support measures under the CAP, their impact on the budgets of the entrants would be significant, ranging from an increase of 17 per cent for Hungary to 56 per cent for Romania (Rollo, 1997:265). It has been argued that the inflationary pressures induced by transfers of such magnitude would make them untenable, particularly as there would be an additional fiscal impact if CEE governments were forced to increase their own spending in order to match the EU contribution (ibid.).

Although there is no presumption that any of the candidate countries would adopt the euro immediately upon accession, they will have to subscribe to the general principles of EMU. In practice, this would require that they join the revised exchange rate mechanism (ERM II) and that bilateral negotiations between each new member and the EU would establish the value of their respective currencies in terms of the euro. Within ERM II, the new members would have to manage their exchange rates such that they did not breach the +/– 15 per cent band of permissible fluctuation. In the longer term, subject to the fulfilment of the convergence criteria, the new members would be expected to adopt the single currency.[27] Nevertheless, Mayes (op. cit.) contends that the candidate countries are almost keener to get into EMU than they are to assume the obligations of membership, in particular the *acquis*, since it would offer them the macroeconomic stabilisation that has proved so elusive to date and which may continue to be so if the accession costs that the candidate countries must bear have been underestimated.

If the foregoing suggests that the majority of the economic benefits from expansion will accrue to the CEE countries, it must be remembered that enlargement is not solely an economic issue, there are also very important political considerations involved. At the start of the transition, many leaders of CEE governments expressed the desire for a 'return to Europe' (Brabant, 1999). Similarly, it has been asserted that 'We have to base our approach towards enlargement also on political values, on the common historical and civilization links between the countries of all Europe ... there is a vacuum at the heart of Europe, which has preferably to be filled ... by the EU – as quickly as possible' (Saryusz-Wolski, 1997:283). Likewise, 'Eastern enlargement will be a phenomenally good bargain for the incumbent EU15. ...Imagine how eager western Europe would have been in 1980 to pay ECU 18 billion a year in order to free central Europe from communism and remove Soviet troops from the region. ... the Union's primary purpose is to ensure peace and stability in Europe' (Baldwin et al., 1997:168).

However, it would be wrong to equate any supposed return to Europe with EU membership. At the beginning of the twenty-first century, it is difficult to image that the candidate countries will revert to communist rule unless eastward enlargement takes place. The parlous state of the Russian economy rules out its resurgence and, even in Serbia, the Miloševíc regime has been overthrown. While greater economic and political cooperation could be to the benefit of all concerned, it is unlikely that accession will now be permitted on political grounds alone: the economic conditions within the candidate countries will have to improve before they are allowed to join. While early accounts were correct to point to the conflict between the economic and political objectives of the EU in relation to CEE (e.g. Balázs, 1997), the balance has now swung more firmly towards the former.[28]

In November 2000, the Commission published the latest of its Regular Reports on the progress of the candidate countries towards accession. In terms of overall readiness, Hungary is the leading CEE applicant, although it is ranked below both Cyprus and Malta. Amongst the CEE-10, Poland, Estonia, the Czech Republic and Slovenia, respectively, rank next in terms of preparedness for entry. After this, Slovakia is found to be ahead of Latvia and Lithuania, while Bulgaria ranks ninth and, although considered to be some way off being ready for membership, it received praise in the 2000 Report for its progress. Romania is again ranked last of the ten candidate countries: in the view of the EU, it does not have a functioning market economy, there remains a problem with the Roma and institutionalised children, it must fight corruption, de-militarise the police and reform its public administration. In short, there is no prospect of Romania acceding to the Union in the foreseeable future.

In December 2000, the Nice Inter-Governmental Conference (IGC) approved the necessary institutional reforms for enlargement and it seems likely that new members will be admitted from 2004, although CEE governments would like this to be earlier. The Nice Treaty (CEC, 2001) also provides one clue as to how many countries will be admitted in the first wave of expansion. In particular, it addresses the issue of where the European Council should meet when the EU has 18 members (ibid.:85). With major political problems surrounding the application of Cyprus, it seems likely that Malta – a small, economically sound country – may well occupy one of the three slots, which would mean two new CEE members.

THE STRUCTURE OF THE VOLUME

The foregoing account is, of necessity, highly selective and the reader must turn to the voluminous literature that provides fuller accounts, not always consistent, on the topics covered. Before doing so, however, attention should turn to the contributions assembled below, many of which begin to fill in the holes of the historical account while, at the same time, broadening its contemporary perspective. Although the demarcation is necessarily not rigid, the following chapters can be grouped according to four themes. The first four contributions consider issues of general importance to the future configuration of Europe. The second four are concerned with the evolution of the EU's major funding programmes in the context of looming eastern enlargement. These are followed by two country studies, one focusing on a front running candidate for early accession and one examining the issue of enlargement from the perspective of the country regarded as the least likely of the current applicants to be granted membership. However, significant as the European unification project is often regarded, it is being enacted in a world that is subject to even larger, and arguably more powerful, forces of globalisation and this constitutes the concern of the concluding chapter.

Whatever grander ambitions may have been harboured in certain quarters, the seeds of the current EU were sown in a relatively simple free trade area. The number of participants has grown through time, the degree of integration has increased and now a common currency is about to be introduced into circulation. Read assesses the optimality of the Union as both a free trade and a currency area and the impact of enlargement upon this. Significant as these economic concerns are, he is careful to remind us that they must not overshadow the fact that the creation, deepening and widening of the EU are intensely political undertakings. Trouille considers the central influence that France and Germany have exercised in Europe in the past and their ongoing pivotal role in the expansion project. An early enlargement demands that they overcome their mutual suspicions and that Germany relaxes its recently hardened stance towards the admission of its eastern neighbours. Nevertheless, it is evident that the applicant countries are preparing for membership at different speeds and Dangerfield examines the role that the Central European Free Trade Agreement has played in their preparations for accession and its future when some states are successful in their quest while others are not. This brings to the fore the fact that expansion will reconfigure

Europe once again and shift its boundary outwards. Brown explores the vital security implications of this new divide. In particular he considers the ability and willingness of the potential new members to implement the requirements of the Schengen Agreement and the freedom of movement that it permits.

The largest and most contentious of the EU's funding programmes is the Common Agricultural Policy (CAP), which consumes almost 44 per cent of the Community's budget, in spite of the fact that farming employs only 5 per cent of the total workforce. Ingham and Ingham highlight the central features of this unwieldy policy, albeit one that has probably been central to ensuring that the European project could remain on track. First, it has distorted world trade; second, the move from price to income supports seems to have been engineered in a less than rational way; third, it constitutes one of the most difficult issues in the expansion process. The last of these concerns points to the fact that cohesion and convergence are vital if Europe is to retain the consent of its citizens. Enlargement will make this task all the more difficult given the differences in material living standards between east and west. Nevertheless, it is often argued that levels of social support and the degree of equality in the socialist countries carried valuable lessons for the market economies of the west. Pascall and Manning focus upon the impacts of transformation and future accession to the EU on gender equality and child poverty.

Implicit in the work of Pascall and Manning is the fact that inequality is not simply a function of personal characteristics: spatial location would also seem to be a factor. The chapter by Ingham, Ingham and McQuaid details the evolution of EU regional policy and the areas to which it is directed. They also examine the implications of enlargement for cohesion and the policy responses that it has evoked. Their analysis of convergence, both within the existing EU and in Eastern Europe, highlights the enormous challenges that widening will pose to the overall integration project. A regional policy that operated solely on a country-by-country basis, however, would have a fairly evident flaw: it would ignore the fact that border regions within contiguous countries will often face similar problems. This issue has been brought into even sharper relief by the collapse of the divide between the two halves of Europe. Kennard's contribution demonstrates that, however modest, cross-border initiatives in Western Europe have a long history and have proliferated as relations between east and west have improved. She goes on to elaborate how the concept of the cross-border region has evolved to the extent that there are now seven Euroregions, two of which have CEE involvement. While the coordination problems between eastern and western partners are significant and the resources allocated to such projects are small, the portents for a more integrated continent seem clear.

Notwithstanding the opening of accession negotiations with all ten applicant countries from CEE, there is no suggestion that all will join the EU at the same time. Indeed, it seems inevitable that there will be significant lags between their dates of entry, assuming that all eventually succeed in gaining membership. This points to the need for closer examination of the economic and political situation in particular applicant countries and the paths that their accession negotiations have followed. Two such studies are included in this volume. In the first of these, Blazyca examines the progress of Poland, a country that while often regarded as a likely early entrant can also be seen to be one whose negotiations with the Commission have not always proceeded smoothly. Nevertheless, the resolve of its political leadership to gain admission has not faltered, notwithstanding changes of government, and its population are amongst the most committed to membership amongst the countries of CEE. Nevertheless, it is a country that has suffered from the lack of enthusiasm from within the EU for early enlargement. Phinnemore, on the other hand, explores developments in Romania where the commitment to membership is also strong, but where the efforts to comply with the *acquis communautaire* have not always been convincing and have certainly failed to satisfy the Commission. The suggestion that entry will therefore be long delayed leads inevitably to a consideration of whether its population will be prepared to wait and what the alternative scenarios might be for the future.

In the concluding chapter of the book Miall and McKinlay seek to locate the developments in the EU in a wider perspective. In particular, the question they pose is that of whether Western European liberalism is likely to become the model of global governance? Liberal democracy established itself rapidly quickly in Western Europe after the end of the Second World War, while the creation of the EU ushered a new type of political organisation into the arena. Since 1990, liberalism in Europe might appear to have been strengthened by the overthrow of the communist regimes, although the introduction of democracy and free markets in CEE has been less rapid and complete than had been hoped. The EU's attempt to make the CEE states more liberal has met with mixed success, with the tendency to marry nationalism and liberalism in that region leading to major conflicts. However, the evidence suggests that the lure of membership will ultimately align the CEE mode of governance with that of the west. Nevertheless, it cannot be assumed from this that western liberal democracy will become the global model. In the longer term, nation states with non-western cultures are forecast to be likely to predominate.

NOTES

1. The authors would like to thank Maurice Kirby and Robert Read for their comments on an earlier draft of this chapter.
2. There was an early, albeit temporary reversal of the growth trend in 1946–47 when a poor summer and harsh winter led to massive shortages of food and fuel (Deadman, 1996).
3. Truman committed the USA to the worldwide containment of communism by means of aid to counter both internal insurgency and external aggression. Stalin ensured that the countries of CEE did not accept the assistance they were offered.
4. Spain was the largest non-participant in a group that included Turkey; see Geiger (op. cit.:33) for a full list of members.
5. Other examples of cooperation are discussed in Pelkmans (1997).
6. Euratom, which is also known as the European Atomic Energy Community, was the brainchild of the French, although this country was later instrumental in 'placing Euratom in a permanent state of hibernation' (Tsoukalis, 1997:12).
7. Comecon was an alternative term for CMEA coined by western journalists.
8. When it became apparent that fixing prices for such long periods introduced significant economic strains, revisions began to be made annually (Shiryaev and Sokolov, op. cit). Nevertheless, dealing at prevailing world prices did not become an issue until it was apparent that the CMEA had no future.
9. Other provisions of the SEA are discussed in Collins (2001).
10. The Treaty of Rome and the Maastricht Treaty, together with the *acquis communautaire*, formed the initial constitution of the EU. Certain matters were, however, left unresolved and not clarified until the Treaty of Amsterdam in 1997. The EU came into formal existence in November 1993.
11. The Europe Agreements are also known as the Association Agreements.
12. The Agreement with Czechoslovakia was renegotiated with the Czech Republic and Slovakia in 1993. The Baltic States are Estonia, Latvia and Lithuania.
13. The asymmetric nature of the Agreements was supposed in principle to favour CEE countries. They were, for example, able to continue protectionist measures for longer than the EU and were also permitted to impose new tariffs for nascent industries and those undergoing restructuring.
14. Turkey lodged a formal application for membership in 1987 that was simply ignored. In 1996, a customs union between the EU and Turkey was formed, while its position in the accession queue was eventually recognised in 1999. Brabant (1999a) provides an extended discussion of the history of Turkey's relationship with the EU and its predecessors.
15. Associated countries are those that have signed a Europe Agreement.
16. The Visegrád Four are the Czech Republic, Hungary, Poland and Slovakia.
17. Essen set out the broad elements of the task and these were elaborated further in the Commission's White Paper presented to the Cannes meeting of the European Council in June 1995 (CEC, 1995).
18. The applicants were Bulgaria, the Czech Republic, Estonia, Hungary, Latvia, Lithuania, Poland, Romania, Slovakia and Slovenia (the CEE-10).
19. These were the continuation of Phare (Poland, Hungary Assistance to the Restructuring of the Economy) and the introduction of two new instruments ISPA (Instrument for Structural Pre-Accession Aid) and SAPARD (Special Aid Programme for Agriculture and Rural Development). Full details can be found at http://www.europa.eu.int/enlargement.
20. Balzás (1997) called the initial EU approach to expansion a 'crawling strategy', which was subject to 'banalization' (p. 369) as discussions widened beyond the Visegrád Group, who themselves were angered by the associated reduction in the speed of the CEE-EU dialogue.
21. Allocation and accumulation effects have replaced the traditional creation and diversion effects in modern trade theory (see, for example, Baldwin and Venables, 1995). Allocation effects capture the way in which integration induces changes in economic efficiency through resource and expenditure reallocation while accumulation effects focus on the

channels through which trade can alter the level of national resources, especially capital, rather than merely serve to reallocate the existing stock of resources.

22. Fink (2000) discusses only the Czech Republic, Hungary, Poland, Slovakia and Slovenia. But, of these, all bar Slovenia adopted this protectionist stance.
23. Baldwin et al. (1997) consider only Bulgaria, the Czech Republic, Hungary, Poland, Romania, Slovakia and Slovenia.
24. While EEA members enjoy access to the single market, agriculture is excluded from the agreement (Mayes, op. cit.).
25. Measured in terms of purchasing power parity, Ireland became the EU's fourth richest member in 1999 (BCE, 2000a). When eligibility for the Cohesion Funds is reassessed, the country will lose its current status.
26. From 1999, the maximum EU contribution from the Structural Funds was 40 per cent of the total eligible costs in the regions covered by Objective 1 (GDP per capita less than 75 per cent of the EU average); although an extra 10 per cent is available for the Cohesion countries (CEC, 1999).
27. For details on the convergence criteria see El-Agraa (2001:143).
28. Economically, the EU would prefer to minimise its risks and costs, which favours limited expansion. Politically, stabilization of the whole eastern European area might be seen to demand the admission of as many former communist states as possible.

REFERENCES

Arndt, Sven, Heinz Handler and Dominick Salvatore (eds) (2000), *Eastern Enlargement: the Sooner, the Better?*, Vienna: Austrian Federal Ministry for Economic Affairs and Labour.

Balázs, Péter (1997), 'Globalization: Symptoms and Consequences', in: Marc Maresceau (ed.), pp. 358–75.

Baldwin, Richard and Anthony Venables (1995), 'Regional Economic Integration', in Gene Grossman and Kenneth Rogoff (eds), *Handbook of International Economics*, vol. 3, Amsterdam: North-Holland, pp. 1597–1644.

Baldwin, R.E, J.F. Francois and R. Portes (1997), 'EU Enlargement: Small Costs for the West, Big Gains for the East', *Economic Policy*, **12** (24), pp. 126–76.

Baldwin, Richard E., Pertti Haaparantha and Jaakko Kiander (1995), 'Introduction', in: Richard E. Baldwin, Pertti Haaparantha and Jaakko Kiander (eds) *Expanding Membership of the European Union*, Cambridge: Cambridge University Press, pp. 1–21.

BCE (Business Central Europe) (2000), 'Off to Market', July/August, pp. 45–52.

BCE (Business Central Europe) (2000a), 'The Model for Success', September, available at http://www.bcemag.com.

Benavides, Pablo (1989), 'Bilateral Relations Between the European Community and Eastern European Countries: The Problems and the Prospects of Trade Relations', in Marc Maresceau (ed.), pp. 21–37.

Brabant, Jozef M. van (1999), 'Introduction', in Jozef M. van Brabant (ed.), pp. 1–12.

Brabant, Jozef M. van (1999a), 'The Impact of Widening on Outsiders', in Jozef M. van in Brabant (ed.), pp. 183–210.

Brabant, Jozef M. van (ed.) (1999), *Remaking Europe*, Maryland: Rowman and Littlefield Publishers, Inc.

Brenton, P. and D. Gros (1993), 'The Budgetary Implications of EC Enlargement', CEPS Working Document No. 78, Centre for European Policy Studies, Brussels.

Brus, Włodzimierz (1986), 'In Search of Balanced Development', in Michael Kaser (ed.), pp. 71–138.

Brus, Włodzimierz (1986a), 'Normalization and Conflict', in Michael Kaser (ed.), 139–249.

Collins, C. Doreen E. (2001), 'History and Institutions', in Ali M. El-Agraa (ed.), pp. 25–48.

CEC (Commission of the European Communities) (2001), 'Treaty of Nice', Official Journal of the European Communities, C80/1, Brussels: CEC.

CEC (Commission of the European Communities) (1999), 'Council Regulation (EC) No. 1260/1999 of 21 June 1999 laying down general provisions on the Structural Funds', Official Journal of the European Communities, L161/1, 26 June 1999, Brussels: CEC.

CEC (Commission of the European Communities) (1995), 'Preparation of the Associated Countries of Central and Eastern Europe for Integration into the Internal Market of the Union', COM(95) 163 final, 3 May, and COM(95) 163 final/2 (Annex), 10 May, Brussels: CEC.

CEC (Commission of the European Communities) (1993), *Bulletin*, 6-1993, part I-13, Brussels: CEC.

Deadman, Martin J. (1996), *The Origins and Development of the European Union 1945-1995*, London: Routledge.

Drábek, Zdenek (1997), 'Regional and Sub-Regional Integration in Central and Eastern Europe: An Overview', in: Jan J. Teunissen (ed.), pp. 11–77.

El-Agraa, Ali M. (2001), 'European Monetary Integration', in Ali M. El-Agraa (ed.), pp. 124–48.

El-Agraa, Ali M. (ed.) (2001), *The European Union: Economics and Politics*, 6th edition, Harlow: Pearson Education.

EU (European Union) (2000), *The Impact of Eastern Enlargement on Employment and Labour Markets in the EU Member States*, Final Report, Brussels: EU, available at http://europa.eu.int/comm/dg5/employment_social/key_en.htm.

Eurostat (2000), 'Regional Gross Domestic Product in Central European Candidate Countries', *Statistics in Focus*, Luxembourg: Office for Official Publications of the European Communities.

Eurostat (1999), *Labour Force Survey: Results 1998*, Luxembourg: Office for Official Publications of the European Communities.

Fink, Gerhard (2000), 'Trade Protection in Five EU Member Candidate Countries by Exchange Rate Adjustment, Customs Tariffs and Non-Tariff Measures', in Sven Arndt, Heinz Handler and Dominick (eds), pp. 133–48.

Gaudissart, Marc-André and Adinda Sinnaeve (1997) 'The Role of the White Paper', in Marc Maresceau (ed.), pp. 41–72.

Geiger, Till (1999), 'Reconstruction and the Beginnings of European Integration', in: Max-Stephan Schulze (ed.), *Western Europe: Economic and Social Change since 1945*, London: Longman, pp. 23–41.

Ingham, Hilary and Mike Ingham (2002) 'EU Expansion to the East: The Problem of Agriculture', this volume, pp. 110–33.

Inotai, András (1997), 'Prospects for Joining the European Union', in Jan J. Teunissen (ed.), pp. 200–35.

Kaser, Michael (ed.) (1986), *The Economic History of Eastern Europe 1919–1975, Volume III, Institutional Change Within a Planned Economy*, Oxford: Clarendon Press.

Lavigne, Marie (1999), *The Economics of Transition*, 2nd edition, Basingstoke, Macmillan Press.

MacBean Alasdair I. and Nick Snowden (1981), *International Institutions in Trade and Finance*, London: Allen and Unwin.

Maresceau, Marc (ed.) (1997), *Enlarging the Union*, Harlow: Addison Wesley Longman.

Maresceau, Marc (1989), 'A General Survey of the Current Legal Framework of Trade Relations Between the European Community and Eastern Europe', in Marc Maresceau (ed.), pp. 3–20.

Maresceau, Marc (ed.) (1989), *The Political and Legal Framework of Trade Relations Between the European Community and Eastern Europe*, Dordrecht: Martinus Nijhoff.

Maslen, John (1989), 'European Community-CMEA: Institutional Relations', in Marc Maresceau (ed.), pp. 85–92.

Matejka, Harriet (1986), 'The Foreign Trade System', in Michael Kaser (ed.), pp. 250–88.

Mayes, David .G (2001), 'Enlargement', in Ali M. El-Agraa (ed.), pp. 548–62.

Mellor, Roy (1987), 'Comecon', in: Andrew Dawson (ed.), *Planning in Eastern Europe*, London: Croom Helm, pp. 293–323.

Pelkmans, Jacques (1997), *European Integration: Methods and Economic Analysis*, Harlow: Addison Wesley Longman.

Postan, M. M. (1967), *An Economic History of Western Europe 1945–1964*, London: Methuen & Co. Ltd.

Rollo, Jim (1997), 'Economic Aspects of Enlargement to the East', in Marc Maresceau (ed.), pp. 252–75.

Salvatore, Dominick (2000), 'Narrowing the Structural Gap in Transition Economies', in Sven Arndt, Heinz Handler and Dominick Salvatore (eds), pp. 30–55.

Saryusz-Wolski, Jacek (1997), 'Towards a Single Perspective. Economics and Politics of Eastern Enlargement', in Marc Marescu (ed.), pp. 276–86.

Shiryaev, Y. and A. Sokolov (1977), 'The Division of Labour Among CMEA Countries: Problems and Prospects', *International Labour Review*, **116** (3), 289–301.

Slater, J. and N. Atkinson (1995), 'The Common Agricultural Policy and EU Enlargement to the East', London: UK Ministry of Agriculture, Fisheries and Food.

Teunissen, Jan J. (ed.) (1997), *Regionalism and the Global Economy: The Case of Central and Eastern Europe*, The Hague: FONDAD.

Trzeciakowski, Witold (1973), 'Foreign Trade: A Retrospective View', in Adam Bromke and John Strong (eds) *Gierek's Poland*, New York: Praeger, pp. 71–89.

Tsoukalis, Loukas (1997), *The New European Economy Revisited*, Oxford: Oxford University Press.

2. Monetary Union and Eastward Expansion of the EU

Robert Read

INTRODUCTION

The eastward expansion of the European Union (EU) will include many, if not eventually all, of the former Soviet Bloc and/or their successor states. Enlargement therefore has a critical strategic dimension, but there are also important economic implications for both existing EU member states and the acceding countries. These encompass principally the interaction between the effects of trade and economic growth. Latterly, however, a key theme of EU policy has been macroeconomic convergence and policy coordination, leading to the introduction of the euro in January 1999 and the elimination of national currencies in euroland in 2002. To date, there has been very little consideration of the conjunction between eastward enlargement and its implications for monetary union, specifically the single currency.

This chapter provides an overview of the major issues relating to the prospective incorporation of the countries of Central and Eastern Europe (CEE) into the euro area. It considers the economic structures of the applicant countries in terms of their production and trade flows in the context of insights and issues relating to economic theories of monetary union. The first section outlines the key structural characteristics of the economies of the ten CEE applicants and their evolutions since 1989 when they emerged from almost five decades of central planning and essentially autarkic growth processes. Economic, political and social transition to western norms is therefore only a recent phenomenon and very much an ongoing process. This gives rise to a consideration of whether the CEE countries are appropriate economic partners for the EU in the light of the theory of economic integration. There then follows a summary of the principal approaches to the economic theory of monetary union and the issues that arise in the context of CEE, including a brief discussion of the insights to be gained from German unification. Following this, the fourth section addresses macroeconomic policy issues for the CEE economies with respect to convergence and policy coordination, given their anticipated membership of the single currency. The final section considers the prospects of euroland membership for the applicant countries in the light of the preceding theoretical and structural discussion.

THE ECONOMIC STRUCTURE OF THE CEE-10

Analysis of monetary union and the implications of the introduction of a shared currency between countries relies upon comparative data relating to the structure of economic activity and patterns of consumption within the potential member states such as that provided in this section. The economies under discussion are Bulgaria, Czech Republic, Estonia, Hungary, Latvia, Lithuania, Poland, Romania, Slovakia and Slovenia. Further, it considers their prospective membership of the EU in the context of the economic theory of integration.

Population, GDP Growth and per capita Incomes, 1989–99

In 1999, the CEE-10 had a combined population of just under 105 million, little more than a quarter of that of the current EU-15 (see Table 2.1). Their demography since 1989 has generally been characterised by low rates of population growth or even decline, as a result of migration and low rates of replacement, and their aggregate population has hardly changed since transition began. The economic performance of the ten has been very mixed. Average annual real GDP growth rates between 1989 and 1994 were negative in all of them, with very significant declines in the Baltic states, Bulgaria, Romania and Slovakia. The period from 1995 to 1999, however, witnessed general improvement and a strong recovery in some of the applicants. Nevertheless, the conflict in Kosovo had a dampening effect on growth, particularly in Bulgaria and Romania, where negative GDP growth persisted, while the effects of the 1998 Russian economic crisis affected the Baltic States adversely. Overall, the data in Table 2.2 indicate that only Hungary, Poland, Slovakia and Slovenia enjoyed any real improvement between 1989 and 1999.

There are several explanations for this poor economic performance, although the principal determinant was undoubtedly the process of economic and institutional transition necessitated by their structural transformation from centrally planned, command-based economies to ones that are more

Table 2.1 Population, area and GDP in CEE, 1999

	Population (million)	Area (km^2)	GDP (billion euro)
Bulgaria	8.211	110 910	11.6
Czech Republic	10.283	78 866	49.8
Estonia	1.442	45 227	4.8
Hungary	10.068	93 030	45.4
Latvia	2.432	64 589	5.7
Lithuania	3.700	65 300	10.0
Poland	38.654	312 685	146.0
Romania	22.458	238 390	31.9
Slovakia	5.395	49 035	18.5
Slovenia	1.986	20 273	18.7
Total CEE-10	104.629	1 078 305	342.4
Total EU-15	375.0	3 245 000	3625.0

Source: CEC (2000).

market-oriented. This has involved a reduction in the role of the state through privatisation, the drastic reduction or complete withdrawal of subsidies to loss-making ventures, the reorganisation and retraining of management and the introduction of market prices and contracts for both factor inputs and outputs. The net effect was to reduce aggregate domestic economic activity, at least in the short-run. In addition, the collapse of the Council for Mutual Economic Assistance trading system, coupled with economic transition in Russia and the rest of the Commonwealth of Independent States (the former Soviet Union), closed many of the established export markets of the CEE-10. The intrinsic lack of competitiveness of many of their exports, however, meant that they had difficulty in taking immediate advantage of opportunities elsewhere, especially in the EU and the US. Nevertheless, the poor growth performance of the EU economies in the 1990s was also important since they had become a target export market. In short, sluggish aggregate demand, the extremely deflationary impact of the Maastricht convergence criteria and the restructuring engendered by the introduction of the single market all combined to inhibit the potentially beneficial demand-pull effects of the EU on CEE-10 exports.

Table 2.2 Growth and per capita incomes in CEE, 1989–99

	GDP Growth[a] (%)		Income per capita ($ PPP)			GDP per capita (% EU av.)
	1989–94	1995–99	1989	1995	1999	
Bulgaria	-3.8	-1.9	5 000	4 480	4 812	22.0
Czech Republic[b]	-2.1	1.4	8 600	11 001	12 498	59.0
Estonia	-5.5	4.4	8 900	5 608	7 682	36.0
Hungary	-2.4	3.3	6 810	8 119	10 705	51.0
Latvia	-6.2	3.0	8 590	4 288	5 786	27.0
Lithuania	-4.6	3.2	6 430	4 856	6 169	29.0
Poland	-1.3	5.8	5 150	5 664	7 806	37.0
Romania	-3.8	-0.9	3 470	-	5 798	27.0
Slovakia[b]	-2.9	5.0	7 600	-	10 255	49.0
Slovenia	-1.9	4.2	9 200	11 324	14 964	71.0
CEE-10 Average						35.0
EU-15						100.0

Notes:

a GDP growth rates are at constant prices in national currencies.

b Figures for the Czech and Slovak Republics are the same for 1989 and 1990.

Source: CEC (2000), EBRD (1996), IMF (2000) and World Bank (1997).

The evolution of incomes per capita at purchasing power parity (PPP) in the CEE-10 has not been as gloomy as might be expected from the performance of their GDPs. Table 2.2 indicates that per capita incomes have increased in six of them – significantly in the cases of the Czech Republic, Hungary, Romania and Slovenia – and declined marginally in three, but only significantly in Latvia. However, caution should be exercised when attempting to compare the GDP and income data, as they are drawn from different sources with potentially conflicting methodologies. Furthermore, estimates of PPP incomes in the CEE-10 prior to transition are notoriously problematic. Nevertheless, the underlying trends may well be robust given that the data measures real standards of living and excludes the government sector, the share in GDP of which declined significantly.

The Structure of Economic Activity and Employment, 1989–99

The command-based system of central planning placed undue emphasis upon a relatively autarkic development process that favoured large-scale heavy industries. The allocation of non-resource based industrial activities, both between countries and sub-national regions, as well as their output and prices, were determined by political rather than economic criteria. The structure of economic activity and employment by 1989 was thus related only incidentally to the fundamental pattern of international comparative advantage and adjustments to this have been a critical element of the transition process. This structural transformation is intended to improve the stability and robustness of the CEE economies as well as enhancing their international competitiveness.

In this context, it is important to compare activity and employment in the CEE-10 with that in the EU. From Table 2.3 it is clear that the share of agriculture in both was significantly greater in the former in 1999, with gross

Table 2.3 The structure of gross value added and employment in CEE

	Gross Value Added (%)				Employment (%)			
	Agriculture		Industry		Agriculture		Industry	
	1995	1999	1995	1999	1995	1999	1995	1999
Bulgaria	15.4[a]	17.3	25.9[a]	23.1	24.4	26.6	27.3	25.1
Czech Republic	4.7	3.7	33.3	34.3	6.6	5.2	32.7	30.8
Estonia	7.9	5.7	23.1	19.9	10.5	8.8	28.7	25.3
Hungary	6.8	5.5[b]	26.3	28.2[b]	8.0	7.1	26.7	27.4
Latvia	10.8	4.0	28.1	20.0	17.4	15.3	23.1	20.1
Lithuania	11.7	8.8	26.1	23.3	21.0	20.2	20.9	20.7
Poland	6.9	3.8	31.7	27.7	22.6	18.1	25.9	24.6
Romania	20.7	15.5	34.5	30.9	40.3	41.7	26.8	23.9
Slovakia	5.7	4.5	31.6	29.3	9.2	7.4	30.3	29.5
Slovenia	4.5	3.6	32.6	31.4	10.4	10.2	37.9	32.8
CEE-10 Average[c]	8.2	5.8	31.0	28.8	22.3	20.7	27.2	25.5

Notes:
a 1996 data.
b 1998 data.
c Gross value added and employment weighted by 1999 GDP and population, respectively.

Source: CEC (2000).

value added averaging 5.8 per cent compared with less than 4 per cent in the EU. Nevertheless its share in the five 'fast-track' applicants – the Czech Republic, Estonia, Hungary, Poland and Slovenia – was more or less comparable with Ireland, Portugal and Spain and very much lower than for Greece. There is, however, a greater dissimilarity in the sectoral distribution of employment, with the CEE-10 possessing an average of 20.7 per cent of their workforces in agriculture in 1999 compared with the EU-15 average of around 5 per cent. The share of agricultural employment was below 10 per cent in only the Czech Republic, Estonia, Hungary and Slovakia. The decline in the share of industrial gross value added and employment in most CEE economies between 1995 and 1999 can be attributed directly to the impact of transition.

The Structure and Pattern of CEE Trade, 1989–99

The pattern of international trade of the CEE-10 underwent significant structural change between 1989 to 1999 in terms of principal trading partners, volume, value and commodity structure. In part, this was the outcome of the Europe Agreements (EAs) and the trade and aid compacts signed between the EU and the transition countries, but it was also a reflection of domestic structural transformation and increasingly outward orientation of the CEE economies. In addition, they were pressed by the EU to form their own free trade agreement (CEFTA), as described in Dangerfield (2002).

It is evident from the data in Table 2.4 that nearly all of the ten exhibited a significant growth in the nominal euro value of both their imports and exports between 1995 and 1999. Only Bulgaria experienced negative growth in its exports. The growing importance of international trade to them is also reflected in their openness, as measured by the share of trade (exports + imports) in GDP, which tended to increase significantly, with only Lithuania registering a marked decrease. However, the trade balance data reveals the magnitude of the deficits accumulated over the period, with only Bulgaria amassing one of less than one billion euro. This is unsustainable since the deficits constitute a substantial proportion of annual GDP and without sufficient external financing, in the form of either direct investment (FDI) or foreign loans, a significant readjustment in the balance of trade will be required in the near future. If not, a rapid deterioration of the foreign exchange position of the CEE-10 economies can be expected relative to the euro and US dollar. However, at least part of the growth in imports is likely to have been composed of capital goods (machinery, technology and know-how), which will improve the fundamental competitiveness of their output through increased productivity.

Table 2.4 The growth of trade and openness in CEE, 1995–99

	Growth of Trade (%)[a]		Openness (Trade/GDP) (%)		Trade Balance Accumulated
	Exports 1995–1999	Imports 1995–99	1995	1999	1995–1999[b]
Bulgaria	-1.17	3.40	91.0	96.0	-762
Czech Republic[c]	8.75	6.99	112.0	128.8	-15 653
Estonia	12.19	11.65	152.8	159.5	-4 133
Hungary	15.68	13.99	75.1	107.6	-9 811
Latvia	11.11	12.91	96.2	104.3	-3 792
Lithuania	7.37	10.41	117.8	89.9	-4 924
Poland	5.24	13.37	48.4	58.9	-40 600
Romania	5.70	4.41	60.8	64.4	-8 258
Slovakia[d]	7.84	9.60	117.8	128.4	-6 947
Slovenia	4.82	5.18	112.0	109.4	-3 882

Notes:

a Average annual rates calculated from euro data at current prices.
b In million euro.
c Calculated from balance of payments data in million euro at current prices.
d 1999 balance of payments data unavailable, calculations based on external trade data.

Source: Own calculations from CEC (2000).

Table 2.5 highlights the growing importance of the EU-15 as key trading partners of the CEE-10 economies and the significant increase in both exports and imports between 1995 and 1999 in all countries except Poland and Slovenia. Even though this came about during a time when there were substantial increases in the overall value of international trade in virtually all of the CEE-10 economies, the EU is now responsible for more than half of all their trade, with the minor exceptions of Bulgarian and Lithuanian imports. The pattern of export specialisation of the CEE economies to the EU in 1989 was characterised by the above average representation of labour and energy intensive industrial commodities. Significant changes have since taken place in Hungary and, to a lesser extent Poland and the Czech Republic, with growth witnessed in their exports of capital and skill intensive outputs. In Bulgaria and Romania, on the other hand, reliance on labour and energy intensive exports has actually increased (see Landesmann, 2000).

Table 2.5 The share of the EU in CEE trade, 1995 and 1999 (%)

	Share of EU-15 in Exports		Share of EU-15 in Imports	
	1995	1999	1995	1999
Bulgaria	37.6	52.6	37.2	48.6
Czech. Republic	60.9	69.2	61.1	64.0
Estonia	56.7	72.7	67.4	65.0
Hungary	62.8	76.2	61.5	64.4
Latvia	44.0	62.5	49.9	54.5
Lithuania	36.4	50.1	37.1	49.7
Poland	70.0	70.5	64.6	64.9
Romania	54.1	65.5	50.5	60.4
Slovakia	37.4	59.4	34.8	51.7
Slovenia	67.0	66.0	68.8	68.6

Source: CEC (2000).

ISSUES IN THE THEORY OF ECONOMIC INTEGRATION

The preceding discussion of the structure and pattern of economic activity in the CEE-10 raises important issues relating to the potential impact of their EU accession in the context of both economic and monetary integration. The primary condition for a successful monetary union, incorporating a single currency, between sovereign countries is that the members are already part of a common market incorporating free trade and the free movement of the factors of production. Otherwise, only a pseudo-monetary union is possible in which one or more countries utilise another country's currency in order to 'free-ride' on its greater macroeconomic policy discipline and monetary credibility. This is tantamount to 'dollarisation', when governments with weaker currencies deliberately choose to adopt a harder one, as in the case of Ecuador's recent switch to the US dollar, or when economic agents seek refuge in a harder currency, such as during the hyperinflations in Latin America and, paradoxically, Poland in the 1980s.

It follows that any discussion of the likely effects of monetary union on the CEE-10 when they accede should consider the extent to which they are appropriate economic partners. The legislative depth of economic integration already achieved in the existing EU extends beyond the creation of a common market, but is currently somewhat short of a full economic union. By the time that the first wave of CEE countries enter, the EU will have moved rather closer to economic union, with the introduction of the single currency scheduled for 1 January 2002 and increasingly centralised macroeconomic policy coordination in at least twelve member states under the auspices of the European Central Bank.

The underlying motivation for the formation of a customs union between two or more countries is the expectation that internal free trade will generate economic benefits for all of its members. Several sources of this potential gain are identified by standard economic theory. These can be split into static gains (once-and-for-all effects arising from the move to internal free trade) and dynamic gains (long-run effects of integration on internal production and trade). The principal static gains are: increased market size, which promotes economies of scale in research and development, production and distribution; improved specialisation, resulting from the reorganisation of production and trade according to comparative advantage; increased competition, which erodes the market power of national monopolies and oligopolies and reduces *x*-inefficiency within firms and industries and increases consumer surplus through downward pressure on prices; and improved international terms of trade and bargaining power, which increase the customs union's power over import and export prices and gives its members greater weight in international policy making. The dynamic effects relate to the fuller realisation of the potential gains generated by the complete liberalisation of internal free trade and include its impact on investment flows and international competitiveness in the customs union. Both the static and the dynamic effects lead to improved economic efficiency and increased economic activity in the member states and result in greater consumer welfare within the territory of the union.

It is evident, however, that the relative magnitude of the potential gains for member states will vary according to the appropriateness with which partner countries are chosen. Customs unions have been seen as a 'second-best' outcome of the trade liberalisation process, which generate both economic efficiency gains in the form of trade creation (the benefits of internal free trade) and economic efficiency losses from the trade diversion that occurs as a result of the protective trade barriers that are erected between the customs union and the rest of the world (Viner, 1950). This approach provides a means by which to identify the relevant factors in the selection of appropriate members of a customs union through the optimisation of the likely resultant gains and losses.

Static and dynamic efficiency gains arise from the interaction between trade and production; hence the first condition is that exchange must take place between member states. The greater the intensity of inter-member trade, the greater the potential for efficiency gains. Trade intensity is influenced partly by transport costs, with the gains being greater for members in close geographic proximity. Clearly, both of these conditions are satisfied in the case of the potential accession of the CEE-10 to the EU, as indicated by Table 2.5.

Maximising static net gains also depends upon the magnitude of the protective barriers between the prospective partners prior to integration and the protectionist stance assumed by the customs union after its formation. The greater the prior protection, the greater will be the likely benefits from its removal (trade creation) and the more liberal the stance of the union towards the rest of the world, the lower will be the likely losses (trade diversion). The CEE-10 already have relatively free access to the EU market, subject to the EAs, and enjoy limited asymmetric protection against EU imports and will continue to do so during their transition periods following accession. The implementation of free trade after they join may have little effect on the spatial structure of production in the enlarged EU, except to the extent that the EAs have protected sensitive products in the declining industries of current members. The EU's external trade stance remains relatively liberal, with the notable exception of some specific sectors such as agriculture, and is governed by the rules of the General Agreement on Tariffs and Trade and the World Trade Organization.

The more members there are of a custom union, the greater the likelihood that low cost competitive producers of a wide range of goods and services are included. The logical extension of this argument is that the world is the optimal customs union; that is, global free trade. The argument can be refined by explicit reference to supply and demand factors. The greater the degree of overlap in production structures, the greater the likely benefits from specialisation and trade to take account of initial cost differences in the production of competing products. On the demand side, the greater the similarities in income levels, tastes and patterns of consumption, the greater will be the imperative for inter-member trade. While the accession of the CEE-10 clearly satisfies the simple condition of increasing the number of members, the issue is rather less clear-cut in terms of the similarity of production structures, incomes and consumption patterns. This suggests that they may be inappropriate candidates for EU membership (particularly Bulgaria and Romania) and that their accession should be delayed until they are able to satisfy the similarity conditions more fully.

This conclusion may be modified by dynamic considerations insofar as membership itself will promote the more rapid convergence of the transition economies to the levels of the EU. This is a similar argument to that applied in the case of the southern enlargement, with the accession of Greece in 1981, and Portugal and Spain in 1986. Nevertheless, the magnitude of the income disparities between the EU-15 and the CEE-10 are significantly greater than was the case in previous enlargements. It will therefore take a considerably longer period of time for the new entrants to converge and, in the meantime, they will continue to be a drain on EU budgetary resources. Indeed, analysis of the impact of trade liberalisation on the structure of EU-Visegrád exchange suggests that there is likely to be structural divergence, with the CEE economies increasingly specialising in low quality, low technology, low value added products (Gabrisch and Werner, 1999).

It is necessary, however, to extend the discussion beyond the confines of pure economic analysis in order to incorporate political considerations, which have driven the move towards enlargement on both sides. The EU, and the US, have been concerned with the shape of Europe in the aftermath of the collapse of the Soviet Union and the end of the Cold War and with the strategic need to establish and provide guarantees for the success of the new democracies in the east. Once again, there are echoes of the southern enlargement and the desire to foster and guarantee democracy in post-dictatorship Greece, Portugal and Spain. The task, however, is substantially greater in the present case because of the highly sensitive strategic issues involved and the need to create functioning market economies from first principles. It was for pressing political, rather than economic, reasons that almost immediate EU accession for the CEE countries was proposed soon after the collapse of the old regimes, although it is notable that the principal advocates of rapid enlargement tended to be those in favour of the broadening of the EU and opposed to its deepening, such as the UK. In the event, enlargement was delayed, with the exception of the unification of Germany, to enable the EU to complete the single market project and introduce the single currency. In fact, the case for the accession of the CEE-10 to the EU on economic grounds alone is hard to support (Baldwin, 1994). This can be expected to have important implications for the extension of monetary union after their accession.

ISSUES IN THE THEORY OF MONETARY UNION

This section considers the range of critical issues regarding the impact of enlargement identified by the economic theory of monetary integration.

The Benefits and Costs of a Single Currency

A variety of benefits arise from the use of a single currency between economies previously reliant upon exchange rates. The most straightforward of these results from the elimination of currency transaction costs between economic agents in the different member countries, including the elimination of the risk rationale for hedging. These gains are generally greater for smaller economies because of the higher proportion of trade in their GDPs, but limited ability to benefit from the economies of scale in foreign exchange trading. Prior to the 1996 enlargement, it was estimated that these gains were worth around 0.2 per cent of the Union's GDP (Emerson et al., 1992). However, the elimination of transaction costs has two secondary effects. A single currency means that prices within a monetary union are transparent and that economic agents are better informed about comparable prices, costs and rates of return. This means that there is greater scope to capture the efficiency gains arising from free trade. Further, there is a reduction in the scope for price discrimination between markets formerly distinguished by different currencies. A single currency area also increases monetary stability since uncertainties associated with exchange rate fluctuations between member states are eliminated, which reduces the risks associated with trade and capital movements.

A second group of benefits arises from the macroeconomic policy implications of a single currency. International trade between members of a monetary union has no impact on the national balances of payments and therefore does not affect the exchange rate. Only the balance of payments of the union as a whole with the rest of the world is important since external imbalance will affect the international value of the single currency. Because foreign currency reserves are therefore only necessary for external transactions, they can be pooled and their overall magnitude reduced. Further savings on foreign reserves arise from the likelihood that member states generally will not have simultaneous external deficits, thereby lowering its aggregate total. The adoption of a single currency and the absence of exchange rate fluctuations eliminate risk premia between the currencies of member states and may also reduce the risk premium on the single currency. This will enable interest rates in the monetary union to be set at a lower level than under multiple exchange rates, so raising the rate of investment. If the single currency also becomes an important international reserve currency, third country reserves provide effective seigniorage gains in the form of interest free loans.

The economic costs associated with the adoption of a single currency are principally losses of macroeconomic policy autonomy. The most obvious of these is the removal of an independent exchange rate. Loss of the exchange rate as a policy instrument means that alternative and less efficient policies have to be found. These are likely to be less easy to target and may generate possible secondary distortions. For example, deflationary adjustment based upon higher interest rates is more cumbersome than devaluation, when all foreign prices change at a stroke, and leads to higher unemployment in achieving the same policy objective. An independent exchange rate also enables countries to choose their own domestic rate of inflation, which gives rise to seigniorage gains through the erosion of nominal government debt. Under a single currency, any government deficits will have to be financed through higher taxation.

The losses to member states associated with the introduction of a single currency also have a non-economic dimension, relating to the loss of sovereignty and national monetary identity. However, these nebulous concepts are hard to quantify in any meaningful way. The loss of sovereignty is closely related to the loss of an independent exchange rate, but is concerned more with the loss of a critical potential source of political and social, rather than purely economic, independence. The term 'sovereignty' itself is hard to define and, given the rapid pace of globalisation, no country or economic bloc has complete policy independence any longer on international foreign exchange markets. Similarly, the impact of the loss of national monetary identity is hard to assess, but it was an important issue in the Danish Referendum campaign of 2000 and a critical element of the Save the Pound campaign in the UK. The loss arises where a currency that is regarded as a cogent symbol of national identity is threatened with being subsumed into something that is more universal. The loss of national monetary identity might be important to the CEE-10, given the recent restoration of independence, although there may still be strong lingering preferences for a hard currency.

Ultimately, the economic cost-benefit approach to monetary union is inconclusive and a more in-depth approach is required to generate clear inferences concerning the appropriateness of the CEE-10 as prospective members of the EU single currency area.

The Theory of Optimal Currency Areas

The theory of optimal currency areas is concerned with the identification of those factors that promote or discourage the use of a single currency over a specific geographic area in order to determine the boundary between currencies. There are similarities with the approach adopted to economic integration with one critical exception; the world is not an optimal currency area.

As already noted, economic integration should be viewed as a necessary precondition for monetary integration and the necessary structural similarities between members mean that there is only limited potential for asymmetric shocks to create severe disequilibria between regions of the currency area that would otherwise require exchange rate adjustment. Further, the economic structures of the members of a currency area should be relatively diversified, which provides insulation against the excessive impact of the sector-specific shocks that might arise with the existence of dominant economic activities. These two criteria appear to favour more developed, larger economies such as France, Germany and Italy in euroland, rather than smaller ones such as Belgium and Luxembourg. Smaller economies, however, can be regarded as being equivalent to additional sub-national regions of the larger member states such that they enhance both the structural similarity and diversity requirements. Membership of a currency area is therefore a means for smaller economies to overcome their critical lack of diversification and so reduce their exposure to external shocks.

The optimality of a currency area is enhanced the greater the extent of economic integration between its members and the greater their openness to trade. Free trade and factor mobility between member states facilitates a smoother response to internal disequilibria by means of direct adjustment through the goods and labour markets without the need for exchange rate adjustment. Nevertheless, the speed of adjustment within a single currency area, involving the movement of goods and factors, is slower than under exchange rates, when it is virtually instantaneous. Thus, economic integration, at least to a common market allowing free trade and free factor mobility, is a pre-condition for an effectively functioning currency union.

The final requirement for an optimal currency area is that its member states should experience synchronous business cycles such that it will not be subject to cyclical disequilibria. This argument has been used as a reason for the UK continuing to remain outside the euro area. Business cycles, however, can be expected to be correlated with economic integration and the greater the extent of trade and factor mobility between countries, the faster the likely convergence of their respective business cycles. It is too early to analyse the pattern of business cycles within the CEE-10, but the rapid switch of their trade towards the EU and the increasing openness of their economies suggests that they are evolving towards the EU-15.

The Adjustment Problem

The adjustment problem arises as a consequence of an asymmetric shock that affects two countries in different ways and was first outlined by Mundell (1961). Under a system of exchange rates, the policy implications are straightforward, but they are not as simple if the shock occurs between members of a single currency area. Under the former, an exogenous shift in aggregate demand away from Country A towards Country B results in A running a current account deficit and B a surplus. In addition, A experiences rising unemployment and deflation while B encounters tightening in its labour market and inflationary upward pressure on domestic wages and prices. The problem can be solved by the exchange rate as the sole policy instrument. Devaluation relieves A's deflationary pressures by increasing its international competitiveness and therefore the demand for its output, particularly exports. The appreciation of B's currency reduces aggregate demand and relieves domestic inflationary pressures through cheaper imports.

Within a single currency area, however, adjustment can only be achieved through wage flexibility and/or labour mobility. In the case of wage flexibility, unemployment in A caused by the asymmetric shock imposes downward pressure on wages while inflationary pressures in B lead to higher wages. Relative wage levels in the two countries therefore bear the burden of adjustment, leading to a change in relative prices and the restoration of equilibrium. In the case of labour mobility, increasing wage differentials lead to the migration of workers from A to B, so alleviating unemployment in the former and inflationary pressures in the latter to restore equilibrium. If wages are inflexible and labour immobile, however, the problem can still be resolved through fiscal transfers from B to A, raised by increased taxation in B, such that aggregate demand falls in B and rises in A.

An understanding of the adjustment problem highlights two critical issues relating to optimal currency areas. First, that close adherence to the structural criteria – similar but well-diversified economic structures – means that the adjustment problem can largely be avoided. Second, if the structural criteria are not met, economic integration, wage flexibility, factor mobility and appropriate regional transfer mechanisms to relieve disequilibria are critical.

Is the EU an Optimal Currency Area?

The preceding discussion raises the inevitable question of whether the existing EU-15, or even the euroland EU-12, currently satisfy the optimal currency area criteria. The answer has important implications for the effective functioning of the monetary union completed when the EU-12 national currencies were replaced by the euro at the beginning of 2002.

The EU has made significant progress towards economic integration and the intensification of its internal trade, half of which is between the member states, and it is effectively a single market for most goods, services and factors. The original six members, the UK, Austria, Finland and Sweden have relatively similar economic structures, albeit with different degrees of diversity, partly reflecting economic size. Ireland, Greece, Portugal and Spain are more similar in structure to each other, but to varying extents remain substantively different to the rest of the EU. However, the UK business cycle appears to be closer to that of the US than the EU (Artis and Zhang, 1995) and labour mobility in the EU is estimated to be only 20 to 30 per cent of that in the US. Further, wages in many member states are inflexible downwards for historical and institutional reasons. The strong inference is that the EU in total does not constitute an optimal currency area, as discussed further in De Grauwe (1997). Nevertheless, a subset of core member states (France and Germany plus Belgium, Luxembourg and the Netherlands) is. There is also some empirical support for a further five states – Austria, Ireland, Italy, Portugal and Spain – joining them, as discussed in De Grauwe (ibid.). This group therefore has virtually the same membership as the current EU-12.

A single currency encompassing the EU-15 and CEE-10 would clearly fail to satisfy the optimal currency area criteria because of both the significant real economic divergence between them and also, to a lesser extent, within the CEE-10 itself. It can be argued, however, that labour market flexibility in CEE may be similar to, if not greater than, that in the EU because economic transition has eliminated many institutional barriers. Nevertheless, the ten alone, whether as a whole or split into sub-groups, are very unlikely to satisfy the optimal currency criteria because of the limited extent of trade and integration between themselves, in spite of the creation of CEFTA and the Baltic Free Trade Agreement (Dangerfield, op. cit.). Thus, while the economic structures of the CEE-10 are not identical, they are generally exporting similar products, hence the critical importance of the EU as the region's principal trading partner. Even critical subsets of the ten, such as the four Visegrád members or the five 'fast-track' countries, could still be expected to fall well short of optimal currency areas. Nevertheless, further trade and integration is likely to lead to increasing convergence, both between them and with the EU, although structural divergence may persist (Gabrisch and Werner, op. cit.).

The Different Approaches to Achieving Monetary Union

The economics literature identifies three main approaches to the achievement of monetary union with a single currency: immediate, step-by-step and currency competition. Each has its strengths and weaknesses, determined partly by macroeconomic conditions and economic heritage, with the first two representing the monetarist and Keynesian approaches, respectively.

The monetarist approach is immediate, irrevocable and underpinned by the assumption of a vertical long-run Phillips Curve. Monetary integration is rapid and decisive, thus eliminating any macroeconomic uncertainty and instability associated with a slower transition process. Under this approach, monetary integration can take place independently of the prevailing macroeconomic conditions in member countries. After integration, the rate of inflation will be determined by the credibility of the central bank and the natural rate of unemployment in each member state, as determined by the effectiveness of supply side policies implemented to solve regional problems. The monetarist approach would therefore appear to be straightforward and relatively costless. However, the potential conflict between the primacy attached by monetarists to national monetary policy and the need for it to be transferred to the central bank of a (federal) monetary union remains problematic.

The more cautious Keynesian approach is based upon there being some long-run inverse trade-off between a country's rate of inflation and unemployment. In this case, step-by-step monetary integration is necessary to minimise the deflationary impact of a single, relatively low inflation rate in the monetary union on unemployment in those member states with a previously high inflation–unemployment trade-off. Gradual macroeconomic convergence, particularly of inflation and the margin of exchange rate fluctuations, between the candidate economies therefore replaces immediate integration. The power of the Keynesian approach has, however, been undermined by theoretical developments regarding the role of expectations in inflation determination. Also, problems arise in relation to the choice of magnitudes for the convergence criteria, especially the inflation rate. The cost to national policy makers is the loss of both the exchange rate as a policy instrument and a nationally determined target rate of inflation or unemployment.

The currency competition approach to monetary integration differs to the extent that it is not driven by ideology. It proposes that national currencies should compete against each other for primacy. Economic agents demonstrate their preferences by choosing to use the least risky currency for their transactions, leading to the gradual abandonment and withdrawal of others. Under this approach, the chosen single currency is introduced in parallel to national currencies and used as an alternative vehicle for transactions. An initial proposal for the introduction of the European single currency was that a 'hard ECU' should circulate in parallel with national currencies and gradually replace them. While currency competition may be more a controversial approach to monetary integration, it has featured in several economies: during the hyperinflations of the 1980s in Argentina, Brazil and, surprisingly, in Poland (Shaffer, 1992) and on Ascension Island where four different currencies (the UK pound, the US dollar, the St Helena pound and the Falkland Island pound) circulate in parallel.

In the event, the EU adopted the Keynesian approach to monetary integration in order to ensure macroeconomic convergence prior to the final locking of exchange rates on 1 January 1999 and the full introduction of the euro in 2002, with five convergence criteria being agreed by member governments. First, national currencies were to remain within the narrow, absolute 2.25 per cent band of the Exchange Rate Mechanism (ERM) for at least two years prior to start of the third and final stage of integration without any devaluation or severe tension. Second, the average rate of consumer price inflation in the twelve months preceding integration was not to exceed the three best performing member countries by more than 1.5 percentage points. Third, average nominal interest rates on long-term government bonds, or comparable securities, were not to exceed those of the three best performing member states by more than two percentage points. Fourth, government budgetary positions were not to exhibit 'excessive' deficits, with actual or planned annual shortfalls not to exceed 3 per cent of GDP. Fifth, accumulated long-run public debt should not exceed 60 per cent of GDP. These convergence criteria were not based on the original EU-12 member state averages, but were agreed variations around their lowest levels. Controversy regarding the final exchange rates for the single currency was avoided by the creation of the ERM as part of the European Monetary System in 1979, which provided a relatively stable matrix of currencies with reference values against the ECU, albeit with some notable exceptions.

Lessons for the EU and CEE-10 from German Monetary Integration

It was widely expected that Germany would be the policy leader in European monetary integration and determine the key benchmark macroeconomic indicators. In practice, the performance of the German economy was adversely affected by the problems generated by the process of unification. Monetary unification between East and West Germany took place on 1 July 1990 and formed an integral part of the overall unification process completed in October 1990. Not surprisingly, it was decided that the West German Deutschmark (DM) would replace the East German Ost Mark (OM). The exchange rate chosen for the two currencies was one to one, the choice of the government of Chancellor Kohl, rather than the rate of 1 DM = 2 OM preferred by the Bundesbank. This exchange rate greatly overvalued the Ost Mark, with the unofficial market price at the time being around 1 DM = 6 OM and the true (PPP) rate somewhere between 2 and 3 OM. The decision to overvalue the Ost Mark exchange rate was a political one designed to maintain the Deutschmark value of Ost Mark savings, particularly of East German pensioners, subject to maximum thresholds.

The economic impact of the overvalued Ost Mark was to make East German real wages grossly uncompetitive because of the low productivity of labour. In the first twelve months after monetary integration, output in East Germany almost halved. This resulted in a massive increase in unemployment in the east, rising social problems and aroused fears of substantial migration to West Germany. In order to stem this threat, while stimulating the recovery of the eastern economy, inflationary fiscal transfers to the value of 140 billion DM were made by West Germany, financed by increased taxation, together with substantial emergency inflows of Structural

Funds from the EU. The deteriorating state of Germany's macroeconomic performance forced the Bundesbank to deflate by raising domestic interest rates. This in turn destabilised the other EU currencies in the ERM through upward pressure on the DM in the international currency markets and led to deflation across the EU, just as the European Monetary Union (EMU) convergence process was beginning.

East and West Germany did not fulfil the optimal currency area criteria. The extent of economic integration between them prior to unification was low, while the east had a low level of structural diversification and there was a policy preference in the west for capital over labour mobility. While unification was immediate, the ensuing economic dislocation cannot be ascribed to a failure of the monetarist approach, but rather to the fact that the east was in the process of simultaneously switching from central planning and exposing its market to external competition. While the overvaluation of the unification exchange rate reduced immediate pressures on migration from east to west, it was instrumental in the deteriorating performance of the German economy. However, the reasons underlying rapid monetary unification and the overvaluation of the exchange rate were primarily political, so the economic consequences should be regarded as the price that Germany was willing to bear to meet its avowed objective of national reunification.

CEE-10 IN THE EURO ZONE: ISSUES AND PROSPECTS

The prospective accession of the CEE-10 countries to the EU is anticipated to culminate in their eventual participation in the euro zone as full members of the single currency, which raises a number of economic issues.

Cost-Benefit and the Optimal Currency Area Criteria

The cost-benefit approach to assessing the prospects for a single currency area, provides little in the way of quantifiable evidence. The balance of the argument depends upon the values attached to a number of subjective variables, notably policy autonomy over the exchange rate, national sovereignty and identity. In the case of the CEE-10, however, the issues are perhaps more clear-cut than for some EU member states. The adoption of the euro specifically, as opposed to a single currency generally, would be highly attractive because of the switch it involves from relatively weak currencies operating in thin foreign exchange markets to a much harder and more credible one. The benefits in terms of greater monetary stability, certainty and investment, together with lower risk premia and interest rates, can therefore be regarded as rather more important than the lesser gains from greater price transparency and lower trade costs. These gains appear to be overwhelming in comparison with the possibly low value attached to the loss of policy autonomy.

Although membership of the euro zone might appear to be of potential substantial benefit to the CEE-10 economies, the optimal currency criteria introduce a considerable degree of ambiguity. Under them, the adjustment of real economic magnitudes relies critically upon economic integration and labour market flexibility. While accession will lead to a greater degree of economic integration and convergent business cycles, the current economic structures of the ten differ greatly from those of the EU-15. Until differences between patterns of production and consumption (incomes and tastes) can be eliminated, or at least greatly reduced, a monetary union would be subject to persistent asymmetric shocks and disequilibria. Further, wage rather than labour flexibility would be the favoured means of internal adjustment because of the preference of existing members for the movement of capital over the possibility of labour migration from CEE.

There can be little doubt that accession will lead to an acceleration in the rate of economic convergence between the CEE-10 and the EU-15, although the length of the process will depend upon the progress of transition and economic integration in the CEE-10, as well as the magnitude and effectiveness of regional policy expenditure under the EU Structural Funds. Convergence will reduce the potential exposure of an expanded euro zone to asymmetric shocks and assist it to satisfy the optimal currency area criteria. Findings of increasing structural divergence between the EU-15 and the Visegrád economies (Gabrisch and Werner, op. cit.), however, confirm that convergence is unlikely without appropriate policy action.

The Macroeconomic Performance of the CEE-10 During Transition

Before considering the process of monetary integration through which the CEE-10 can be expected to join the euro zone, it is useful to review their recent macroeconomic performance. This is undertaken with specific reference to the variables identified in the Maastricht Treaty as the critical convergence criteria for the EU single currency.

The key macroeconomic indicators for the CEE-10 economies are presented in Table 2.6. It is evident that the performance of the ten is manifestly worse than that of the EU-15, primarily because of the effects of the transition process. This has required the CEE economies to switch from central planning to a market system, open up to external competition and locate new export markets while on a steep institutional and policy-making

Table 2.6 Macroeconomic indicators for CEE, 1999

	Inflation		Interest Rates on Deposits	Government Deficit[b]	Government Debt[b]
	1999	1989–99[a]			
Bulgaria	2.6	68.4	3.2	0.9	-
Czech Republic	2.1	7.8	4.5	0.6	16.0
Estonia	3.3	24.3	4.2	4.7	-
Hungary	10.3	19.7	12.6	3.7	-
Latvia	2.4	35.1	5.0	3.8	13.9
Lithuania	0.8	41.0	7.4	7.5	28.1
Poland	7.3	49.2	10.4	3.5	-
Romania	45.8	76.1	47.6	3.5	-
Slovakia	10.6	14.3	14.4	3.4	-
Slovenia	6.6	12.9	7.2	0.6	24.6

Notes:
a Average annual rate.
b Expressed as a percentage of GDP.

Source: CEC (2000), IMF (2000, 2000a).

learning curve. The economic health of their principal trading partner (the EU) has also been relatively weak throughout this period because of the deflationary effects of the Maastricht convergence criteria.

The inflation record of the CEE-10 has been very poor, with only the Czech Republic having enjoyed an average rate of less than 10 per cent. Further, five economies with rates of price increase above 25 per cent have experienced what is considered technically to be hyperinflation. The most recent data for 1999, however, indicates substantial improvement for all ten economies, although Romania continues to suffer from hyperinflation. The principal reason for the inflationary conditions has been the shock impact of successive rounds of price liberalisation necessitated by the transition process. This has required the lifting of extensive price controls on a wide range of previously regulated domestic goods and services in the face of supply side rigidities.

Tax reform has also been necessary, particularly with respect to changes in indirect taxation and the introduction of VAT, so as to bring tax structures more into line with those in the EU. In spite of rapidly depreciating currencies, the increasing preference for the consumption of higher value imported products instead of domestic output, particularly of consumer goods, in the wake of trade liberalisation exacerbated domestic inflationary pressures.

The exchange rate stability of the CEE-10 economies is closely related to their inflation performance since they have needed to devalue their currencies substantially against the US dollar and the major EU currencies. Domestic inflation, however, has tended to be greater than nominal depreciation, reflecting tight monetary policies accompanied by inflation targeting, reduced price indexation and the pursuit of policy credibility (Orlowski, 1999). This real appreciation has reduced some domestic inflationary pressure, but resulted in the erosion of international competitiveness in the CEE-10. This has been aggravated by the role of the US dollar as an important component in the exchange rate policies of some transition economies, whether as a nominal peg or in a weighted currency basket, during a period of significant dollar appreciation.

Exchange rate policies in the CEE-10 remain relatively interventionist and most are still some way short of being fully flexible and based upon full currency convertibility and the development of properly functioning domestic foreign exchange markets. At the start of the transition process, most of the economies abandoned their fixed exchange rate regimes in favour of various types of exchange rate peg against the major currencies. Only the Czech Republic, Hungary and Poland have moved towards complete currency convertibility, with the full liberalisation of portfolio investment flows in 1999, and only Poland to a free float (in April 2000). The Czech Republic, after major devaluations in 1990 and 1991, fixed the koruna within tight bands against a DM/US dollar basket until it was floated in 1997. Hungary adopted an adjustable peg for the forint from 1990 until 1995 when a crawling peg based on a 70:30 weighted euro/US dollar basket was introduced after a devaluation. This was changed to a 100 per cent euro weight in 2000. Poland adopted a weighted crawling peg for the złoty in 1991, but the failure to reduce domestic inflationary pressures led to the recent shift to a free float. Slovenia has operated a managed float since the introduction of the tolar in 1991. Bulgaria, Estonia and Lithuania have used currency board arrangements to peg their currencies. The Bulgarian lev continues to be pegged to the euro, the Estonian kroon has remained pegged to the DM since 1992, while the Lithuanian litas is currently pegged to the US dollar, but is expected to shift to a euro peg in the second half of 2001. The Romania leu and the Slovakian koruna have weighted pegs linked closely to the euro and the Latvian lat has been pegged to a special drawing rights basket within narrow bands since 1994, but is expected to switch to a euro peg in the near future.

Interest rate trends in the CEE-10 reflect the poor macroeconomic situation of many of the economies together with problems relating to imperfections in their poorly developed domestic capital markets. Several of the economies have recently suffered banking crises, primarily because of poor lending policies and a high share of non-performing loans. This problem has caused particular problems in the Czech Republic where the substantial losses of the state-owned Konsolidacni Banka adversely affected the 1999 government deficit. Nevertheless, nominal interest rates have been falling in Bulgaria, the Czech Republic, Estonia, Hungary, Latvia and Slovakia, but are well adrift of the Maastricht target. Higher interest rates in Poland and especially Romania are a reflection of domestic inflationary conditions. The small size of the financial sectors in Lithuania and Slovenia and lack of effective power of the central banks over interest rates have exposed both economies to interest rate volatility, although of a much greater magnitude in the former country. The economic problems of the CEE-10 countries, together with the poor state of development of their domestic financial systems, means that the interest rate is not a particularly effective policy tool in most cases.

The performance of some of the transition economies with respect to government deficits and accumulated government debt would appear to bear favourable comparison with the Maastricht criteria and the performance of some EU member states. There is, however, a problem concerning the use of appropriate statistical definitions and methodologies such that the data, particularly that for government deficits and long-run debt, is not harmonised and therefore not directly comparable with that for the EU. All of the CEE-10 economies are currently running government deficits, although the apparent magnitudes are generally within or close to the Maastricht criterion of 3 per cent. Bulgaria's annual budget deficit has declined significantly, from 12 per cent in 1996 to just 0.9 per cent in 1999, reflecting falling expenditure and improved revenues. The 1999 deficit in the Czech Republic was just 0.6 per cent, but this excludes the losses of Konsolidacni Banka and includes substantial revenues from privatisation (CEC, 2000). Slovenia has had a well-managed and cautious fiscal policy throughout the transition period, with its government deficit continuing its downward trend to reach 0.6 per cent in 1999. The government deficits of the remaining economies are rather higher and are the result of uncertain economic conditions on budgeted revenue and expenditure, the economic impact of the Kosovo conflict and the Russian economic crisis, as well as loose fiscal policy. The accumulated government debt figures, however, are reasonably good according to the Commission's Regular Reports and generally fall well within the Maastricht criterion of 60 per cent of GDP. The two exceptions are Bulgaria and Romania, both of which have experienced significant budgetary problems in recent years.

The current macroeconomic performance of the CEE-10 is significantly out of line with even the weakest of the EU economies, particularly since

Greek membership of the EU-12 in January 2001, and does not come close to satisfying most of the Maastricht convergence criteria. The current divergence in macroeconomic performance between the ten and the EU is a matter of critical concern, regardless of whether monetary union between them would be beneficial and whether the optimal currency criteria would be satisfied. From its analysis of Bulgaria's economic situation, the Commission appears to be taking the view that macroeconomic convergence by the CEE-10 economies prior to accession might constrain domestic policy choices unnecessarily (CEC, 2000). That is, the transition process and achieving macroeconomic stability in the CEE-10 economies are currently more important priorities than convergence. Nevertheless, the economic performance of the CEE-10 can be expected to show signs of improvement and increasing macroeconomic stability as the transition process is completed and the nascent economic structures mature.

ERM II AND THE CEE-10 IN THE EURO ZONE

The conditions for the accession of the CEE-10 and their eventual membership of the euro zone are set out in the 1993 Copenhagen Treaty and the Agenda 2000 Programme. Progress on meeting these conditions is subject to periodic monitoring and assessment by the Commission. This section provides a brief overview of the means by which monetary integration between the ten and the EU might be achieved and the likely timetable for their ultimate admission to the euro zone.

CEE-10 Accession and ERM II

Under Article 109k of the Maastricht Treaty, a condition of EU membership is that countries acceding after the commencement of Stage 3 of EMU (i.e., after January 1999) accept monetary union in principle and are committed to membership of the euro zone. A derogation under Article 122 of the Copenhagen Treaty, however, permits the CEE-10 economies to accede to the EU without joining the single currency immediately. Instead, they will be included in ERM II along with those existing members remaining outside the euro zone, currently Denmark, Sweden and the UK. ERM II is a successor arrangement to the original, now defunct, ERM linking non-euro zone currencies to the euro via fixed, but adjustable, exchange rates with 15 per cent margins of fluctuation.

For the CEE-10, ERM II therefore represents an intermediate stage in the process towards their eventual membership of the euro zone. In addition, it will also provide a means for them to gain some of the benefits of monetary union through the linking of their currencies with the euro, in spite of the wide margin of permitted fluctuations. These will include increased policy credibility, greater exchange rate certainty, lower risk premia and possibly greater inflows of investment. While there are already explicit links between some CEE-10 currencies and the euro, membership of ERM II will impose additional policy constraints on their economies in the form of tighter fiscal and monetary policies consistent with the stabilisation requirements of Agenda 2000. This may involve a later narrowing of the margins of fluctuation within the exchange rate bands to improve the effective management of inflation. Accession, coupled with membership of ERM II, marks the onset of macroeconomic convergence for the ten and is designed to lead to eventual membership of the single currency. It is therefore conceivable that the EU will attempt to delay the accession of particular countries where there are severe concerns about their macroeconomic performance under the rigorous application of the Copenhagen criteria and Agenda 2000 requirements.

CEE-10 Macroeconomic Convergence and Euro Zone Membership

The convergence process for the CEE-10 economies in preparation for their membership of an enlarged euro zone, possibly comprising as many as 17 members – including Denmark, Sweden, the UK, Cyprus and Malta – can be expected to begin immediately upon their accession and membership of ERM II. Given that eastern enlargement of the EU is likely to take place in at least two stages, this suggests that convergence will be a ‘two-track’ process, possibly with both narrow and wide exchange rate bands within ERM II. The convergence criteria for the CEE-10 economies can be expected to use the original Maastricht conditions for EU monetary integration as reference values applied to the actual macroeconomic performance data of the euro zone. The Maastricht criteria are nominal and are based upon price relationships rather than upon the convergence of real economic variables, notably of incomes and productivity. One empirical analysis of nominal and real convergence in the CEE-10 since 1989 found that nominal convergence may take place in spite of real divergence (Andreff, 1999). This focus on real rather than nominal convergence is important because of its emphasis on the optimal currency area criteria and therefore the economic robustness of an enlarged euro zone.

It is clear that real convergence of the CEE-10 economies with the existing EU member states is likely to take substantially longer than nominal convergence, given the significant disparities in income and productivity that currently exist between them. A critical issue for the EU is therefore the extent to which their premature entry into monetary union may destabilise the smooth functioning of the euro zone. In addition, the extent of any adverse deflationary impact on the economies of the ten needs to be considered in the context of its implications for the ultimate success of the transition process in delivering sustained growth. In the light of the uneven performance of the currency in the two years since its introduction, the EU can be expected to be rather more circumspect regarding the possible premature admission of up to ten CEE countries to the euro zone. While there may be compelling strategic arguments for accelerated EU membership for the CEE-10 that override economic considerations, such issues are not relevant to their participation in the monetary union. Although the timetable for the admission of the CEE-10 to the euro zone remains a matter for speculation at this moment in time, it is not inconceivable that the EU will defer entry until there has been significant progress in real economic convergence.

REFERENCES

Andreff, Wladimir (1999), 'Nominal and Real Convergence – At What Speed?', in Jozef M. van Brabant (ed.), pp. 111–38.

Artis, M. and W. Zhang (1995), 'International Business Cycles and the ERM: Is There a European Business Cycle?', CEPR Discussion Paper, no. 1191.

Baldwin, Richard E. (1994), *Towards an Integrated Europe*, London: CEPR.

Brabant, Jozef M. van (ed.) (1999), *Remaking Europe: the European Union and the Transition Economies*, London: Rowan and Littlefield

CEC (Commission of the European Communities) (2000), *Regular Reports from the Commission on Progress towards Accession by each of the Candidate Countries*, available at http://europa.eu.int/comm/enlargement/report_11_00/index.htm.

Dangerfield, Martin (2002) 'Integrating the "New" Europe: What Role (if any) Does CEFTA Have?', this volume, pp. 65–88.

De Grauwe, Paul (1997), *The Economics of Monetary Integration*, 3rd revised edition, Oxford: Oxford University Press.

Emerson, Michael, Daniel Gros, Alexander Italianer, Jean Pisani-Ferry and Horst Reichenbach (1992), *One Market, One Money: an Evaluation of the Potential Benefits and Costs of Forming an Economic and Monetary Union*, Oxford: Oxford University Press.

EBRD (European Bank for Reconstruction and Development) (1998), *Transition Report, 1998: Economic Transition in Central and Eastern Europe, the Baltic States and the Commonwealth of Independent States*, London: EBRD.

EBRD (European Bank for Reconstruction and Development) (1996), *Transition Report, 1996: Economic Transition in Eastern Europe and the Former Soviet Union*, London: EBRD.

Gabrisch, Hubert and Klaus Werner (1999), 'Structural Convergence – Through Industrial Policy?', in Jozef M. van Brabant (ed.), pp. 139–61.

IMF (International Monetary Fund) (2000), *International Financial Statistics, Annual 2000*, Washington DC: IMF.

IMF (International Monetary Fund) (2000a), *World Economic Outlook*, Washington DC: IMF.

Landesmann, Michael (2000), 'Narrowing the Structural Gap: Structural Change in the Transition Economies, 1989 to 1999', in Sven Arndt, Heinz Handler and Dominic Salvatore (eds) *Eastern Enlargement: the Sooner, the Better?*, Vienna: Austrian Federal Ministry for Economic Affairs and Labour, pp. 58–103.

Mundell, R. (1961), 'A theory of optimal currency areas', *American Economic Review*, **51** (4), 657–65.

Orlowski, Lucjan T. (1999), 'Exchange rate regimes and monetary policies for EU candidates', in Jozef M. van Brabant (ed.), pp. 93–110.

Shaffer, M. (1992), 'The Economy of Poland', Centre for Economic Performance, Discussion Paper No. 67, LSE.

Viner, Jakob (1950), *The Customs Union Issue*, New York: Carnegie Endowment for International Peace.

World Bank (1997), *World Development Report, 1997*, Washington DC: World Bank.

3. France, Germany and the Eastwards Expansion of the EU: Towards a Common *Ostpolitik*

Jean-Marc Trouille

INTRODUCTION

At the beginning of the new millennium, the European Union (EU) is facing two major challenges: the consolidation of monetary integration and the enlargement of the Union towards former communist countries in Central and Eastern Europe (CEE). Both of these could potentially bring great success, but also severe drawbacks for the European project. The inauguration of European Monetary Union on 1 January 1999 is leading Europe towards increased integration, not least in the fields of monetary and budgetary policy, but also in a range of other areas where harmonisation appears increasingly necessary, such as fiscal and social policies. The opening of the EU to new members from 'the other Europe' bears with it, however, the potential threat of diffusion, especially if the expansion is not consolidated sufficiently by a thorough review of existing institutions.

Both challenges require crucial reforms that may lead gradually towards political union. The European currency needs to be reinforced by a coherent political project in order for it to gain full international recognition and to be able to compete against the dollar. Enlargement will increase multiplicity in the EU to an unprecedented scale. Twenty-one member states in 2004, and nearly thirty a few years later, could be a great strength for Europe on the world scene, provided that the large-scale accession is accompanied by the necessary structural reforms. Alternatively, expansion has the potential to become the Achilles' heel of the entire European construction project.

In this context, France and perhaps more importantly Germany, the two leading countries in the Union, whose special relationship has been very much at the heart of the European blueprint from its inception in the 1950s, have a special responsibility towards the new democracies of CEE. Neither country would want an enlarged EU to become a mere free trade zone. Both of them have a strong interest in implementing what will be the largest ever wave of Union expansion as smoothly and efficiently as possible. After the Soviet withdrawal from CEE, it soon became clear that an enlargement of the European Community eastwards was indispensable and unavoidable. But, in the face of the obstacles that have to be overcome, both in the east and in the west, it has so far constantly been postponed to better days. This contribution examines the changing positions of France and Germany on the issue of enlargement and their degree of compatibility with the views of other member states.

PREVIOUS ENLARGEMENTS AND THE ISSUE OF PARITY

Admitting new members to the Community, latterly the Union, was always a possibility inherent in the very idea of Europe as a 'realistic utopia' (Duhamel, 1999:25), as defined by Jean Monnet. Indeed, four successive enlargement rounds have taken place already, or even five if German unification is included. These enlargements happened in three waves, in the 1970s (Britain, Ireland and Denmark), in the 1980s (Greece and then the Iberian countries) and in the 1990s (Austria, Finland and Sweden). Each of these expansions raised delicate political issues in terms of the balance of power between the different member states, but in particular between France and Germany, the two major continental players. Britain's accession in 1973, for instance, had taken ten years to materialise, primarily due to France's desire to consolidate her privileged position before inviting her close neighbour to join. In the 1980s, when the Community was extended southwards to Mediterranean countries, West Germany was concerned about a shift of the centre of gravity towards Southern Europe. On the other hand, when the first *de facto* eastern enlargement of the Community happened in 1990 with the unification of Germany, it was an expansion without accession, undertaken in order to facilitate the integration of the former German Democratic Republic. Fears were expressed at that time, in both France and other neighbouring countries, about what was perceived clearly as a strengthening of Germany's central geo-political position on the European continent (Trouille, 1996:53–64).

This was followed, just a few years later, by the admission of three European Free Trade Association countries from Northern and Central Europe – Austria, Finland and Sweden – all of which are economically, culturally and geographically much closer to Germany than to France.[1] This raised the thorny question of the balance of power once again in a country that had just come to terms with German unification. However, what the French policy makers interpreted as a shift of the EU's centre of gravity to the north and the centre-east was seen in Germany as nothing more than a righting of the balance following the expansion southwards in the 1980s. Therefore, like previous enlargements, the eastern expansion of the EU threatens the parity on which Franco–German leadership in Europe has been based, whilst at the same time creating a need, as well as an opportunity, for the two partners to overcome their respective basic misapprehensions and divergences.

Although France and Germany have developed a unique partnership and built up an exemplary relationship during the last fifty years, the two sides of the Rhine often find it difficult to operate on an equal footing. As soon as the equilibrium of the Franco–German axis is threatened, relations between the two countries suffer as a direct result. When Germany and the European continent were divided by the Iron Curtain, France enjoyed a comfortable geo-political position in the east-west confrontation. In addition, France was able to play a leading role on the Franco–German axis and therefore in the Community. Whilst the former was the dominant political partner on the axis, West Germany was the dominant player in the economic sphere, but without enjoying the status of a sovereign country: no fewer than nine different armies (seven foreign and two German) were based on its soil during the Cold War.[2] Under this scenario, West Germany needed her French ally in order to exert an influence on the European scene. The events of 1989 saw Germany regain her unity and her sovereignty and become the strongest power in Europe, with France's status as an atomic power enjoying a permanent seat at the United Nations Organization's Security Council tending to have less weight than during the Cold War. To a certain extent, the political re-balancing in favour of Germany that took place during the course of the 1990s has also been accompanied by some economic re-balancing between the two partners (Leblond, 1997). Nevertheless, divergences persist between Berlin and Paris and it is frequently in the field of foreign and security policies that these tend to be the most acute (Pedersen, 1998).

As soon as an initiative was taken in Eastern Europe during the years immediately following the end of the Cold War, each of the two partners was quick to suspect the other of having a hidden agenda, notwithstanding Germany's frequent attempts to reassure her partners about her international ambitions, and also despite an apparent willingness to share her leadership in Europe with the French. However, since then a more consensual attitude has emerged across the Rhine. Whereas Paris was reluctant to embrace the enlargement initially, it then advocated the opening of negotiations with all candidates for accession. As such, the French position moved gradually closer to the German one, which was favourable to a limited wave of accession in the first instance, comprising Poland, the Czech Republic and Hungary. While this change was probably motivated by political concerns, particularly the desire not to weaken even more the strained French–German partnership, financial considerations also played their part, especially that of dispersing the tremendous budgetary burden that enlargement will unavoidably generate.

DIFFERENT POLICIES IN CEE

The French and the Germans tend to have different relationships with CEE countries and these sometimes entail different agendas, priorities and interests. Although Berlin and Paris would in principle both favour a common approach to a region that stretches from the Baltic down to the Black Sea, the partners have often adopted contrary positions in their foreign policies towards the area. The ex-Yugoslavia conflict is quite revealing as an illustration of the contrasts: initially, French political leaders were favourable to the Serbs, old allies of their country since the beginning of the First World War, while Germany regarded them as aggressors. Instead, the Germans considered Slovenia and Croatia, both of which used to be part of the Austro-Hungarian Empire, as allied countries and they officially acknowledged the independence of those former Yugoslavian territories on 23 December 1991, despite French attempts to dissuade Bonn from doing so. Paris perceived this unilateral initiative over hastily as a sign that Germany was once again willing to go her own way in European foreign policy.

In the case of the Bosnian conflict, France was sending Blue Helmets to the area as early as 1992, while Germany was aware of the fact that domestic as well as international public opinion would not look upon her military intervention favourably and chose to step back. This non-intervention seemed to increase relative French influence in the region. When it came to lifting the weapons embargo and to protecting Muslims in Bosnia, France and Germany were once again unable to speak with one voice. It was only on 8 November 1993 that a common Franco–German initiative led by Alain Juppé and Klaus Kinkel, the then foreign ministers of their respective countries, allowed some convergence between their positions. The Dayton Agreement marked the end of the war in Bosnia on 21 November 1995, but was due primarily to the role played by the United States, with France and Germany having only minor roles: the French by resisting Serb pressure and the Germans by accepting large numbers of war refugees. More recently, the Kosovo conflict offered an opportunity for tighter diplomatic and military cooperation between France,

Germany and other Western European powers against Serbia: the ultimate pay-off to which was the recent demise of the Miloševíc regime.

FRENCH VIEWS ON ENLARGEMENT

In the early 1990s, French attitudes on enlargement were very cautious and far less assertive than those of the Germans. The possibility that Germany would look again towards the east, as was frequently the case in the past, and that its new role could become a continuation of the old one, has been an underlying fear that explains the dilemma facing the French political leadership. Large-scale expansion of the Community towards the centre and the east of the continent would appear to be beneficial largely to Germany after reunification. In an enlarged and possibly more diffuse Europe, Germany might be tempted to go her own way and play a leadership role in *Mitteleuropa* and perhaps even to replace this by domination. Under such an unlikely scenario, France would invariably be marginalised. But open French opposition to the enlargement after German unification could have been fatal to the Franco–German entente and would also have had serious effects on France's international image. Consequently, she seemed to follow Germany in this tremendous venture only through lack of any alternative. At first, the official position was that France was 'not fundamentally opposed to the principle' of enlarging the Community to include Eastern Europe.[3] In November 1991, however, François Mitterrand committed a serious psychological mistake, for which he was severely criticised by Vaclav Havel, then president of the former Czechoslovakian Republic, by declaring in Prague that the newly independent nations of Eastern Europe would have to 'wait for several decades before joining the European Community'.[4] This was only two years after Mitterrand's failed attempts to go against the stream of German unification.

At first, Mitterrand even refused to consider the deepening of the European institutions, which is now regarded by France, Italy, Belgium and more recently by Germany as the prerequisite for further progress. It was only in 1993 that both countries agreed in principle on the enlargement of the Community, but even this did not give birth to a joint approach, let alone a Franco–German *Ostpolitik*. Whether the fears of the French political elites were justified or irrational, they still largely explain France's current strong desire to deepen EU institutions before carrying out the enlargement towards CEE. In addition, she views implementation of the enlargement without prior consolidation of the European institutions as leading towards a mere free trade zone in which coalitions and imbalanced relationships between states could soon reappear. This would be incompatible with the interests of France, which regards the EU as a potential superpower, a view that presupposes political independence and cohesion.

FRENCH INFLUENCE IN THE EAST

Contrary to Germany, where Willi Brandt's *Ostpolitik* was launched in the early 1970s, France has never had a coherent long-term policy in the east (Schreiber, 2000). Nevertheless, and very early after the fall of the Iron Curtain, France was anxious not to let Germany fill the new power vacuum resulting from the demise of communism and the independence of CEE states. Indeed, she was far from indifferent to the upheavals affecting 'the other Europe' at the end of the Cold War and several attempts were made in order to increase her influence. For instance, France initiated the Phare programme, geared towards economic reconstruction and spearheaded the drive to establish the European Bank for Reconstruction and Development (EBRD), even though lack of coordination with Germany has since prevented the Bank from playing a key role in CEE on more than one occasion.[5]

However, despite these useful and commendable initiatives, French influence in this vast zone has been weaker as a result of the attraction that Germany holds for eastern Europeans. For both historical and cultural reasons, France traditionally has had good relations with Poland and Romania, which have links with the *Francophonie*. Other countries like the Czech Republic, whose relationship with Germany is extremely complex, could possibly also see France as an alternative western partner. Aware of these facts, as well as of the advantageous geo-political and economic situation of Germany in the heart of the continent, Jacques Chirac paid several state visits to Central Europe, accompanied each time by a delegation of French top industrialists, in an attempt to gather momentum, to advocate closer cooperation and to offer an ally other than Germany (Deloche-Gaudez, 2000).

GERMAN VIEWS ON ENLARGEMENT

As far as Germany is concerned, widening the EU towards her eastern neighbours is primarily a question of vital national interest, with a tightly integrated structure perceived as the best way to protect the region from political turbulence whilst extending German economic and commercial interests eastwards. Kohl frequently underlined his belief that 'The German–Polish border (the Oder–Neiße Line) should not remain the eastern border of Europe' (Pedersen, op. cit.:189). Since 1990, and for the first time ever in her history, Germany has enjoyed peaceful relations with all of her numerous neighbours. Preserving political and economic stability at her doorsteps is therefore of crucial importance, even more so than for any other western partner. Indeed, Germany tends to feel threatened by conflicts taking place on the continent, while France is more concerned about stability in the Mediterranean. In addition, the post-war generation in Germany grew up with the idea that their country would have to assume some of the moral responsibility for the fate of *Mitteleuropa*. For all these reasons, it is not surprising that the German commitment to bind CEE to the west was unequivocally stronger than that exhibited by any other EU member, at least during the Kohl chancellorship, even though there were clear signs of a weakening of this position towards the end of his government's term of office.

The election of a new German federal government on 27 September 1998 reinforced the emerging less enthusiastic attitude towards enlargement. However, the change of government did not, at first, mark an improvement in the overall relations between Bonn and Paris. These were overshadowed by divergences on nuclear cooperation, by French anxieties about the first, aborted merger attempt between Dasa and British Aerospace, then also by the severing of industrial cooperation in the telecommunications industry and by attempts to merge the Frankfurter Börse and the London Stock Exchange. Schröder's initial desire to include Britain within some sort of trilateral axis with the French also did not please Paris. Notwithstanding these difficulties, Joschka Fischer, the new Federal Minister for Foreign Affairs, underlined the belief that the eastern enlargement was a political imperative in a speech to the French *Assemblée Nationale* on 20 January 1999, although one that would materialise only after a thorough reform of community institutions. The German view had thus come considerably closer to the French position regarding the deepening of EU structures. Nevertheless, Chancellor Schröder appeared to be less dedicated than his predecessor to the enlargement on several occasions. In the run-up to the Berlin Summit of March 1999, for instance, he declared that a lower German contribution to the EU budget would be a pre-condition for the enlargement process to carry on. This confrontational way of launching the debate was in contradiction to Germany's initial pledge to open the EU to new members from the east. At first sight, the country's new position appears paradoxical: on the one hand, Germany supports enlargement in her prime long-term interest; on the other, she is not prepared to pay the price for the gigantic venture. Indeed, the German government's emphasis lies on employment and social policies, with the declared intention being to give priority to national interests and to be more assertive on the international scene.

Clearly, the German approach to European enlargement is now less dogmatic than during the Kohl chancellorship. For Kohl and his post-war generation, German support for a rapid integration of the new candidates for accession was a moral duty, but cost is the key issue for Schröder. During the German presidency of the EU in the first half of 1999, Schröder did not succeed in his attempt to revisit the issue of his country's contributions to the Union. In view of the lack of budgetary freedom, Schröder wants to postpone the inevitable financial burden that enlargement will cause at some stage. Despite her weight, Germany cannot, and does not want to, solve the economic and political problems of CEE countries on her own: she is still paying a high price for unification with the former East German communist state and is fully aware of the costs that expansion will generate.

GERMAN INFLUENCE IN THE EAST

Germany would appear to be in a very strong position to benefit considerably more than any other European country from enlargement. The Germans are more acquainted with Central European mentalities and business cultures than their French, British or Italian counterparts and German businesses enjoy a qualitative competitive advantage in this vast area, where their language is understood and used more widely than French or even English. Very soon after the fall of communism, German businesses started to look towards the east, and the country soon became the leading trade partner of virtually all the new democracies of CEE.[6] Thus, between 1989 and 1995, the volume of German exports to the region increased from 36.05 to 51.43 per cent of all exports to these countries (Grabbe and Hughes, 1998; Pedersen, op. cit.).[7] In the same period, the French share of overall exports to these markets fell from 9.83 to 5.84 per cent. A similar trend was noticeable for Britain, with her share of total exports to CEE going down from 7.79 to 5.47 per cent. In 1997, German exports to the whole of CEE, including Russia and the former Soviet Republic, rose by 28 per cent to a record DM 91.6 billion, or 10.5 per cent of German exports by volume. Imports from this area were up 19 per cent to DM 75 billion, that is, 9.5 per cent of German imports by volume.[8]

Germany also leads the way in terms of direct investment, which amounted to 21 per cent of the total inflows to Poland, the Czech Republic and Hungary in 1995, compared to 7.1 per cent emanating from France and 4.5 per cent from Britain. German direct investments tend to flow to areas of Poland like Gdańsk, Katowice, Wrocław, Kraków and Łódż and to Central Bohemia in the Czech Republic, regions with a longstanding industrial tradition and which used to have close industrial and cultural links with, or belong to, Germany prior to the Second World War (Bafoil, 1997). It must be said, however, that German investments in CEE still tend to be considerably lower than those she undertakes in south-east Asia. Despite comparatively limited French financial commitment, it is noteworthy that her largest direct investments in Central Europe have been made in East Germany, where French companies have become the leading foreign investors, trailing only Germany itself (Leblond, op. cit.:210).

Can it be deduced from the previous figures and comments that Germany is on the brink of dominating the countries of CEE economically, if not politically, as some French political leaders still seem to believe? Such a view reveals limited knowledge of modern Germany and also neglects the fact that Germany's influence in *Mitteleuropa* has clear limitations, of which she is very well aware. The extermination during the Second World War of five million Polish people by the Nazis, of which three million were Jews, has left very deep scars. German–Polish reconciliation dates back only to 1991 and is still extremely fragile, with the Poles being very much concerned about any sign or prospect of economic or political domination by her neighbour. Not surprisingly, Poland attaches considerable importance to the strengthening of trilateral cooperation involving France as well as Germany. German occupation during the War also left bad memories as far away as the Caucasus and the Black Sea. Relations with the Czech Republic are still highly sensitive, despite an amicable solution to the question of the *Sudetendeutschen*, the German people who were expelled from the Sudetes at the end of the War, having been found. The past is a very powerful psychological handicap that German politicians and industrialists must take into account in all of their negotiations with their eastern counterparts.

THE WEIMAR TRIANGLE[9]

One of the very few countries of CEE with which France and Germany have established a common policy of cooperation is Poland. So far, the results have been constructive, albeit rather limited in view of Polish expectations of early EU accession. In May 1991, the foreign ministers of the three countries met in Weimar and agreed on the principle of holding regular talks and each year a trilateral summit is organised by turns in one of the three countries involved. Warsaw saw an opportunity to deepen contacts with the west in these regular consultations whilst developing a strategic partnership with the Franco–German tandem, which has been the motor of European construction for several decades. In the attempt to normalise their relationship with their former enemy, the Poles can also learn from the French, who followed a path of reconciliation with Germany after the end of the Second World War. One of the concrete results of these trilateral talks was the Franco–German proposal to grant Poland associated status to the EU with effect from 1994. In addition, on 17 June 1991, Bonn and Warsaw signed a good neighbourhood treaty that included the establishment of a German–Polish Youth Office designed along similar lines to the Franco–German Youth Office, founded in 1963 as part of the Elysée Treaty. This new bi-national institution organises and subsidises exchange programmes that allow young Germans and Poles to meet and know each other better. Since 1991, youths from CEE have also been offered opportunities to take part in Franco–German exchange programmes.

At the end of 1998, the new German Federal Government reiterated that particular attention would continue to be devoted to relations with Poland and to the strengthening of cooperation within the Weimar Triangle. However, Polish hopes of rapid EU-membership have faded and, like its co-applicants, the largest accession candidate, with 39 million inhabitants, is weary of making the painful reforms required by Brussels only to see the promised rewards constantly recede into the future as negotiations fail to be concluded. In spite of (or due to) numerous promises about possible early accession, strong suspicions gradually emerged, not only in Poland, that France as well as Germany could be stalling the increasingly unpopular enlargement process intentionally until well after the French presidential and German federal elections, both to take place in 2002. The new notional date for the first wave of enlargement is now 2004.

THE COSTS OF THE ENLARGEMENT

France has consistently insisted on the need to adapt and reform EU institutions beyond the limited results achieved by the 1997 Treaty of Amsterdam (Trouille, 1997:457–65), which initially was conceived precisely as a response to the challenge of eastern enlargement. However, despite some occasional progress, the question of this indispensable deepening remains unresolved. The fifteen-member Union, as created by the Maastricht Treaty in 1992, functions with arrangements established initially for a Community of six or nine members and, notwithstanding the limited adjustments made by the Amsterdam Treaty, and the more consistent ones made by the Nice Treaty, current decision-making procedures are no longer sufficient or appropriate. The EU also needs a common foreign policy that would include security and defence. Former Chancellor Brandt's well-known words comparing pre-unification Germany to 'an economic giant, but a political dwarf' are certainly applicable to the EU. Kissinger's *bon mot* on the fact that 'when you call Europe there is nobody on the line' is a sad reflection of this situation.

Internal policies have to be adjusted to prevent unbearable pressure on already over-strained national budgets. The Structural Funds and the Common Agricultural Policy (CAP) have to be streamlined further, with the latter alone still costing about 40 billion euro per year, that is, 42 per cent of the EU budget.[10] Clearly, if the CAP were to remain unreformed, the next enlargement would make its financing unbearable, while a reduction in its scale and consequent lowering of the German contribution would be a serious set-back for French (and southern European) farmers. Potentially, for Germany, the so-called 'paymaster' of Europe, financing the eastward expansion is not only a highly sensitive political issue, but also an acute financial headache and, since 1996, she has been demanding a revision of her contribution. More recently, on 10 December 1998, Schröder declared unequivocally to the German Bundestag: 'We cannot and do not want to solve the problems of Europe with the German cheque-book'.[11]

None of the EU member states would dispute the fact that the CAP needs adjusting, nor would anyone contest the fact that Germany is a major net contributor to the EU budget: in 1998, the difference between her payments into and receipts from the account amounted to 10,940 billion euro.[12] Although France is the second major gross contributor to the budget, she receives far more than Germany in return: as a result, her net contribution amounts to only 781.1 million euro, which is fourteen times less than that of Germany. Clearly, this blatant disparity is a potential source of contention between the two partners. The second largest net contributor, far behind Germany, is the Netherlands, with 2.2 billion euro. At the European Summit of Berlin in March 1999, which took place during the German Presidency, with the budget of the EU from 2000 onwards as its main agenda item, Germany did not succeed in her struggle to reduce her contribution. It was also agreed that the integration of new members would only take place gradually, that eastern European agriculture would only be partially funded by the CAP and that the current budgetary limit of 1.27 per cent of the EU's GDP would remain (Charpin, 1999). It can, however, be argued that Germany will benefit more than anyone else from enlargement, both in terms of political stability and economic gain, and that therefore she should be willing to pay the price. Amongst others, French political leaders enjoy pointing out that while Germany pays DM 22 billion to Brussels each year, her annual trade surplus with her European partners amounts to DM 95 billion.[13]

THE CURRENT DEBATE

The debate surrounding the next enlargement of the EU has to be seen not only in the light of the new geo-political situation in Europe after the end of the Cold War and the subsequent unification of Germany, but also in the context of the current debate on the future shape of the Union and on how to share the so-called 'instruments of solidarity' with the newcomers. Although existing members have agreed in principle to the next enlargement, it is likely to prove a very costly and an extremely complex operation. The ten small member states express concern about their reduced weight in an enlarged Union and maintain their right to have an individual Commissioner in Brussels. The southern European member states, in particular, fear that they could become the losers from this unprecedented wave of accession; especially in relation to the benefits they draw from the CAP and the Structural Funds. In addition, by no means all of the applicants to accede meet all of the conditions that were imposed at the Copenhagen Summit. The current fifteen member states failed, at both the Amsterdam and the Berlin Summits, to sort out new financial arrangements for agricultural payments and the Structural Funds. New entrants could not just be excluded from the benefits of these, but existing members, notably Germany as the leading paymaster, are increasingly unwilling to cede high net contributions to the EU budget.

In spite of these delicate issues, a number of recent initiatives taken by German and French political leaders just prior to, or at the beginning of, the French EU presidency indicated a strong Franco–German willingness to achieve concrete results on institutional reforms. A speech in May 2000 by German Foreign Minister Joschka Fischer at the Humbolt University in Berlin placed strong emphasis upon the possibility of enhanced integration amongst certain member states in order to advance towards political union. French President Jacques Chirac subsequently used the term 'pioneer group' in a speech to the German Bundestag in Berlin. Both interventions spurred further discussion on the future shape of Europe in the run-up to the French presidency and the European Council Summit in Nice.

France, Belgium, Italy and, more recently, Germany have insisted that the purpose of the inter-governmental conference (IGC) on institutional reforms, which commenced in February 2000, was to find a solution to the difficult design questions that remained unresolved at the Amsterdam Summit (McCarthy, 1999:1–57), but were crucial if the EU was to absorb a dozen new members while simultaneously not undermining the possibility of decision-making. The first task of the IGC was therefore to replace the unanimity requirement in the Council of Ministers by extending qualified majority voting. With the national veto being a prerogative of each member, reaching unanimity has become an increasingly awkward political exercise with each new wave of members. The forthcoming enlargement would make it practically impossible for EU institutions to work. Greater scope for majority voting was therefore seen as absolutely indispensable, although the deal reached at the Nice Summit only allows for a small increase in its use.

The future size and composition of the Commission and the weighting of the votes of member states in the EU's decision-making Council of Ministers were other major outstanding reform issues. A re-weighting of votes in favour of larger countries was agreed in Nice, but decision-making procedures will be more complicated: the larger member states will still be able to nullify decisions, either by using their national veto or through a 'blocking minority'. This re-weighting of votes was, however, a complex issue. Germany, for instance, with 23 million more inhabitants than France, Britain or Italy, asked for this discrepancy to be taken into account, while Spain was seeking parity with Italy. The Netherlands, with 15 million citizens, sees itself as 'the smallest of the big member states', rather than the biggest among the small ones, and hoped to have more say. In the event, France's insistence in Nice on retaining political parity with Germany in EU decision-making illustrated the difficulty that the Franco–German alliance faces in adjusting to a more assertive and unified Germany. It also reflects France's unease in the face of further enlargement.

The thorny issue of enhanced cooperation was a last bone of contention that remained unresolved after Amsterdam. This was strongly advocated by Germany, France and the Benelux countries to enable small groups of member states to forge ahead with deeper integration in specific policy areas, despite differing speeds of integration among the fifteen and without the agreement of all. Previously, crucial disagreements were solved by the traditional mechanisms of power-broking, bargaining and package deals at EU summits. In fact, the situation had become *de facto* a *fait accompli* since not all member states are part of the euro zone or of the Schengen convention, for example, while the Nice Summit formally sanctioned groups of nations 'enhancing' cooperation on particular areas of common interest.

The outcome of the Nice Treaty is more modest than it had been hoped, and decision-making in the EU will be more complicated than ever before. However, the Treaty achieved some quite substantial progress that will allow the European Union to go forward with the eastern enlargement. At the moment, twelve countries are in a phase of pre-accession and half of them might be admitted in 2004, at the earliest, depending on their ability to meet the EU's economic requirements, on the one hand, and its ability to carry on reforming her structures beyond Nice, on the other. The six other accession candidates should follow at a later stage.

In order to meet this unprecedented challenge, the EU now has to improve its institutional framework and to find a consensus on the so-called 'instruments of European solidarity': agricultural subsidies and the Structural Funds. The initial enthusiasm about the re-unification of Eastern and Western Europe soon gave way to more down-to-earth concerns. The divisions of the Cold War will only be overcome once Eastern and Western Europe are united. In view of this historic challenge, the bilateral Franco–German approach will still, perhaps more than ever before, be an essential prerequisite in tomorrow's enlarged Union. However, if this requirement is undeniably necessary, it may not be sufficient in an EU of 27 member states. Leadership may have to be carried out by more than two nations and this will only be possible with strong political voluntarism and with a radical change of attitude by both larger and smaller European players.

NOTES

1. One of the countries is German-speaking while the other two share their Protestant ethics with Northern Germany.
2. The *Bundeswehr* was the West German army and the *Nationale Volksarmee* was based in the GDR.
3. 'Contradictions de la Grande Europe', *Le Monde Dossiers et Documents*, January 1998.
4. *Le Monde*, 6 September 1994, p. 2.
5. Phare – Pologne-Hongrie: Aide à la Reconstruction Economique. EBRD – Banque Européenne pour la Reconstruction et le Développement.
6. German businesses and investors concentrated their efforts particularly on the Visegrád-group: Poland, Hungary, the Czech Republic and Slovakia, neighbouring economies that were quicker than others to rebuild their economies.
7. These figures cover the three Baltic States, Poland, the Czech Republic, Slovakia, Hungary, Romania and Bulgaria.
8. Poland and the Czech Republic were the most important markets in this area for German exporters (Economic report from the Embassy of the Federal Republic of Germany in London, 24 April 1998).
9. The Weimar Triangle consists of Poland, Germany and France.
10. *Le Point*, 30 January 1999, p. 67.
11. *Le Point*, 27 February 1999, p. 32.
12. *Le Monde*, 12 December 1998, p. 2.
13. *Le Monde*, 4 June 1999, p. 9.

REFERENCES

Bafoil, François (1997), *Les stratégies allemandes en Europe Centrale et Orientale. Une géopolitique des investissements directs*, Paris: L'Harmattan, Coll. Pays de L'Est.

Charpin, J. (1999), 'L'élargissement de L'Union Européenne à L'Est de L'Europe', Report from the Commissariat Général du Plan, La Documentation Française.

Deloche-Gaudez, Florence (2000), 'Les Réactions de la France à L'élargissement à L'Est de L'Union Européenne', in Edith Lhomel (ed.), *L'Europe Centrale et Orientale*, Paris: Notes et Études Documentaires No 5108–09, La Documentation Française, pp. 51–68.
Duhamel, Alain (1999), *Une ambition française*, Paris: Plon.
Grabbe, Henry and Kirsty Hughes (1998), *Enlarging the EU Eastwards*, London: Pinter/Royal Institute of International Affairs.
Leblond, Laurent (1997), *Le couple franco-allemand depuis 1945*, Paris: Le Monde-Editions.
McCarthy, Patrick (1999), 'France, Germany, the IGC and Eastern Enlargement', in: Douglas Webber (ed.), *The Franco-German Relationship in the European Union*, London: Routledge Research in European Public Policy, pp. 41–57.
Pedersen, Thomas (1998), *France, Germany and the Integration of Europe: A Realist Interpretation*, Pinter: London.
Schreiber, Thomas (2000), *Les actions de la France à l'Est, ou les absences de Marianne*, Paris: L'Harmattan.
Trouille, Jean-Marc (1996), 'The Franco-German Axis since Unification', in: Tony Chafer and Brian Jenkins (eds), *France – From the Cold War to the New World Order*, New York: St Martin's Press Inc., pp. 53–64.
Trouille, J.M. (1997) 'Europe after the Intergovernmental Conference – The French View', *Modern and Contemporary France*, **5** (4), 457–65.

4. Integrating the 'New' Europe: What Role (if any) Does CEFTA Have?

Martin Dangerfield

INTRODUCTION

This chapter assesses the contribution that subregional economic cooperation in the Central European Free Trade Agreement (CEFTA) has been making to the endeavours of its member states to join the European Union (EU).[1] It also addresses some wider issues concerning the potential future role of CEFTA in the context of the various complications attaching to the EU's enlargement to the east. Although the various subregional groupings that have emerged in post Cold War Europe are all to some extent linked to wider integration processes, for example through generic contributions to security and improved levels of political understanding, CEFTA clearly has the most explicit connections to the EU. Indeed, as Dwan (1999:230) noted: 'CEFTA was not created as a subregional integrative group per se but rather as a tool for accelerating integration of the member states into the EU'. The various attributes that distinguish it from other groupings in terms of links to the enlargement process include the 'hard' and more clearly defined nature of the cooperation (trade liberalisation), which is restricted, at least formally, to the economic sphere. This is in contrast to the more broadly based and more loosely defined cooperation agendas of undertakings such as the Central European Initiative or Black Sea Economic Cooperation. Also, CEFTA membership is restricted to Central and East European (CEE) states, whereas most other groupings have mixed memberships of CEE and EU countries. Furthermore, unlike the other subregional organisations, CEFTA must legally cease to exist when all of its member states have entered the EU and its rigidly enforced joining criteria exclude countries not yet at the same stage as its current members in their relations with the EU.[2]

The first part of the chapter includes an overview of the major features of CEFTA and a discussion of the main ways in which it has been a factor in the pre-accession process. It will show that, although the organisation has tended to maintain a low profile, it has nevertheless played a useful role in the transition from integration in the Council for Mutual Economic Assistance (CMEA) to (anticipated) integration into the EU and, in so doing, has had positive effects on subregional economic and political affairs in general. The second part of the chapter focuses on the future of CEFTA. Since its members are close to completing the integration agenda set out in the Kraków Treaty and its various amendments, the main issues here would seem to be concerned with how much longer the organisation will be in existence and whether the member states will engage in any additional EU-compatible cooperation before it has to be disbanded. Nevertheless, the uncertainties surrounding the eastward enlargement mean that the fate of CEFTA is not straightforward to predict. At a minimum, as some of its members, notably Bulgaria and Romania, will wait much longer for accession than others, it seems certain that a diminished CEFTA will continue to exist for an as yet indeterminate period of time. The picture is further complicated by the fact that additional CEE countries, including Croatia, Former Yugoslavian Republic of Macedonia (FYRM), Ukraine and Moldova, are interested in joining the group. What could such an expanded membership imply for the future role of CEFTA, especially as the centre of gravity would shift to areas where EU accession prospects are at best long-term? Consideration of this question connects obviously to another highly pressing issue on the European agenda, namely the need to re-activate trade and integration amongst the west Balkan states. Should CEFTA be a model or a player in the development of the subregional cooperation that the EU is demanding as a condition of offering Stability and Association Agreements to that region?

SUBREGIONAL COOPERATION IN CEFTA

As the countries of CEE were latecomers to both economic globalisation and the mainstream process of European integration, their post-communist transformation strategies were based on the assumption that becoming capitalist was not just about reforming the domestic economy, but had an equally important external dimension. While the trends of regionalism and simultaneous globalisation during the 1990s have seemed somewhat contradictory to many, in central Europe at least the link was clear:

> Joining Europe, as seen from Poland or Hungary, is not just joining a dynamic form of *regional* integration (the EC) in place of the defunct

> CMEA but integration into the *international* economy after forty years of involuntary seclusion. For these countries, Europe is not so much a continent distinct from America or Asia as one of the centres of a global economy previously blocked to them by the CMEA structure. (Köves, 1992:93)

The role of subregional economic cooperation in the reconstruction of foreign relations was, however, less clear. In fact, the 'reintegration or re-orientation' debate of the early post-communist phase was less to do with the most appropriate model for post-CMEA collaboration than whether in fact it was actually necessary at the multilateral level.

On the one hand, certain eminent western specialists, alarmed by the rapid and large-scale decline in trade between the former CMEA states, argued the case for a gradual abandonment of regional trade biases and advocated a Central and East European Economic Union (CEEU) that combined a preferential trade regime with multilateral clearing arrangements.[3] On the other hand, experts from the CEE countries who opposed the reintegration approach argued that it was not justified, since the politically driven over-trading within the CMEA – mainly with the ex-USSR – had been a major cause of economic failure that therefore had to be jettisoned. Neither was it feasible, since the CEEU proposal could not influence the principal cause of the collapse of intra-CMEA trade, which was the Soviet economic crisis of 1990–91. As one author observed, the:

> phenomenon called the collapse of the CMEA must, therefore, be carefully used as a general explanation to the developments in the dynamics of intra-regional trade within the CMEA. The economic disruptions in Soviet and post-Soviet markets must be separated from problems related to the complete overhaul of the trading regime, and subsequent dissolution of the CMEA. (Toth, 1994:16)

The debate was somewhat more open as far as small scale – that is, excluding the USSR – post-CMEA economic cooperation was concerned. Nevertheless, as well as the complication of significantly different degrees of progress in economic reform among the 'five', there was a general aversion to multilateral cooperation with former socialist allies, usually referred to as the 'CMEA syndrome'. Furthermore, the economic case for such an endeavour was not compelling since the USSR had dominated the CMEA and it was felt that the trade potential of the area was limited because of a relatively small and impoverished collective market and the close similarities in the economic structures and factor endowments of the countries involved.

It was also the case that the internal pressures on CEE governments were increasingly against re-opening markets to former CMEA partners:

> Domestic producers had already been complaining about the liberalisation of regulations on imports coming from the EC countries, which had resulted in a number of factory closures ... state-owned firms, citing high unemployment figures, were by no means eager to confront still more competition as a result of the new free trade zone. (Okolicsanyi, 1993:21)

However, two factors in particular combined to bring about the creation of CEFTA. First, it was made clear to the CEE states during their negotiations for Europe Agreements (EAs) that subregional economic cooperation was a pre-condition for further integration with the EU, and the need to bring mutual trading conditions into line with those in place with the Union and EFTA was accepted. Second, Czechoslovakia, Hungary and Poland had already been coordinating their eastern and western foreign policies through the 'Visegrád Group' and this provided the governments of the three most advanced transforming countries with a framework on which to discuss and activate mutual economic cooperation. As the political agenda of this Group seemed to reach its conclusion at the end of 1992, attention was transferred to the economic sphere with the signing in Kraków, in December 1992, of the treaty that established CEFTA. In sum, the activation of post-CMEA economic cooperation had its roots in Visegrád and the EU's preference for aspirant members to work together as a forerunner to accession. The formation of CEFTA was driven essentially therefore by a political rather than an economic rationale.

Aims and Objectives

The life of CEFTA began on 1 March 1993, having been created according to the Kraków Treaty to support the signatories' 'intention to participate actively in the process of economic integration in Europe ... and preparedness to cooperate in seeking ways and means to strengthen this process' (CEFTA:1). The agreement provided for a free trade area for industrial products to be put in place by the beginning of 2001. It also included a range of concessions for intra-CEFTA agricultural trade, with details of the tariff removal schedules worked out on a bilateral basis for both industrial and agricultural goods. The overall liberalisation timetable and the contents of the general provisions of CEFTA were modelled on the EAs, although the lack of reciprocity in the latter was a notable difference. CEFTA itself has no implications for trade arrangements with third parties since it incorporates no common external trade policy. Nevertheless, the need not to drift out of alignment with the EU's external trade relations has exerted an indirect harmonisation effect. As for other aspects of integration, while the CEFTA Treaty contained a clause that allowed for the parties to discuss the further development of economic cooperation, no objectives beyond trade liberalisation were included and it has been commonplace for officials in member countries to stress that the organisation is 'not an integration but a mere free trade agreement'. It is also important to note that, in its original formulation, CEFTA contained no provision for the intake of additional members, demonstrating that the founders were thinking initially only of a Visegrád free trade area and not in terms of a wider CEE economic grouping.

CEFTA has evolved in two main ways since its inception. First, there has been a shortening of the transition period to complete liberalisation of industrial goods trade, with the removal of most tariffs and quotas being achieved by the beginning of 1997, some four years ahead of the original schedule. However, a small percentage of products – the so-called Lists of Exceptions – still qualify for protection (see Dangerfield, 2000b). [4] Advances were also made in the scope and speed of liberalising trade in agricultural products. The original CEFTA preferential arrangements covered some one-third of traded agricultural products but, following the last major amendment, agreed in Warsaw in December 1995 and elaborated in Additional Protocol Number 3, which came into force on 1 January 1996, about 80 per cent are now covered, many of which are duty free.[5] The complete liberalisation of agricultural trade was also envisaged in the 1995 Warsaw amendment, but it was suspended in August 1998 in the context of serious disputes, mainly over wheat.[6] The second major development has involved the enlargement of CEFTA. While the switch from a closed to an open organisation was in line with the EU's preference for a wider subregional economic grouping, the CEFTA countries soon recognised that their national economic and political interests were served by the enlargement of their organisation and that, more importantly, their EU membership ambitions were not compromised by it. The necessary amendment – Article 39a, approved at the September 1995 meeting of CEFTA Prime Ministers – stated that the group was open to countries that were World Trade Organization (WTO) members; had signed association, or free trade, agreements with the EU and had signed bilateral free trade agreements with all the existing CEFTA states; and had the approval of all existing members. The accessions of Slovenia (1 January 1995), Romania (1 July 1997) and Bulgaria (1 January 1999) mean that CEFTA is now a market of some 98 million people.

Structure

CEFTA has no permanent institutions: even the seemingly innocuous step of establishing a secretariat to carry out the basic coordination functions, for which the Slovaks pushed hard in the early years of the organisation's existence, proved unacceptable to other members, especially the Czechs and Hungarians. The latter were deterred by the costs, influenced by recent memory of the excessively heavy and ineffective CMEA bureaucracy, while also being sensitive to any developments that might give the impression that a new economic 'bloc' was developing in post-communist Europe.

Government officials of the member states undertake the implementation and monitoring of the free trade agreement within a three-level framework. At the apex is the annual summit of the Prime Ministers of the CEFTA states, which convenes to review and evaluate cooperation to date and to approve the activities to be carried out in the twelve months before the next meeting. Regular sessions of the CEFTA Joint Committee, comprising ministers in charge of foreign economic relations, precede the summits and prepare most of the work for, and reach decisions for formal approval at, them. The agenda usually includes matters connected with the implementation of the CEFTA Treaty and any major disputes that have arisen, applications from interested countries and proposals to extend the extent of cooperation. Meetings must take place at least once per year, although additional sessions can be convened for extraordinary purposes; for example, to approve and sign accession treaties for new members. The third tier of the administrative machinery consists of groups of experts, usually from a department for multilateral trade or department for European integration. They are responsible for the detailed and technical aspects of cooperation and, during years when their country holds the presidency, organising the main CEFTA annual meetings and preparing a report on the functioning and implementation of cooperation during their year of office. In essence, the organisation operates a rolling secretariat principle, as well as a rolling presidency. Finally, CEFTA works in strict inter-governmentalist fashion, with unanimous decisions required at all times.

Developments in Intra-CEFTA Trade

The development of intra-CEFTA trade between 1993 and 1999 provides conclusive evidence of its success in the rebuilding and rationalisation of its participants' mutual trade flows, as shown in Table 4.1. The period to 1995 was essentially one of recovery as the mutual trade of the four founder members returned to 1989 levels (see Richter, 1997; Dangerfield,

Table 4.1 Intra-CEFTA trade, 1993–99 ($US million)

	1993	1994	1995	1996	1997	1998	1999	Index 1999/93 =100
CZECH REPUBLIC								
Total CEFTA:								
Export	3 489	3 258	4.348	4 944	4 816	5 199	4 709	135.0
Import	2 746	2 718	3 883	3 886	3 622	3 657	3 901	142.0
Excluding Slovakia:								
Export	655	925	1 343	1 824	1 927	2 392	-	365.0[a]
Import	497	594	900	1 236	1 369	1 581	-	317.8[a]
HUNGARY								
Export	462	565	757	1 163	1 387	2 039	1 961	424.0
Import	655	900	982	1 254	1 378	1 766	2 025	309.0
POLAND								
Export	680	823	1 245	1 481	1 659	2 026	2 227	328.0
Import	682	919	1 624	2 161	2 585	2 974	3 070	450.0
ROMANIA								
Export	-	-	-	294	342	369	597	202.0[b]
Import	-	-	-	541	642	1 040	928	171.0[b]
SLOVAKIA								
Total CEFTA								
Export	2 716	3 057	3 778	3 656	3 357	3 397	3 027	111.0
Import	2 483	2 226	2 757	3 225	2 915	3 122	2 641	106.0
Excluding Czech Republic								
Export	406	555	767	918	999	1 223	-	303.7[a]
Import	208	268	424	543	563	732	-	351.9[a]
SLOVENIA								
Export	-	-	403	451	480	588	622	154.0[c]
Import	-	-	634	616	688	725	844	133.0[c]

Notes:

a Index 1998/93.

b Index 1999/96.

c Index 1999/95.

Source: *CESTAT Statistical Bulletin*, Dangerfield (2000b).

2000b). Intra-CEFTA trade has continued to grow relatively rapidly since that time and tended to outpace increases in overall exchange (see Tables 4.2–4.4).[7]

Table 4.2 Intra-CEFTA trade as per cent of total trade, 1995–98

	Export 1995	Import 1995	Export 1996	Import 1996	Export 1997	Import 1997	Export 1998	Import 1998
Czech Rep.*	6.2	3.4	8.3	4.5	8.6	5.1	9.1	5.5
Hungary	5.9	6.4	7.4	6.9	7.3	6.5	8.9	6.9
Poland	5.4	5.6	6.1	5.8	6.4	6.1	7.2	6.3
Romania	-	-	-	-	4.1	5.7	4.4	8.8
Slovakia*	8.9	4.8	10.4	4.9	11.3	5.5	11.6	5.6
Slovenia	-	-	5.4	6.5	5.7	7.4	6.5	7.2

Notes: * Excludes Czech/Slovak trade.

Source: *CESTAT Statistical Bulletin*.

Table 4.3 Total and intra-CEFTA exports, 1995–98[a]

	To CEFTA 1995	Total 1995	To CEFTA 1996	Total 1996	To CEFTA 1997	Total 1997	To CEFTA 1998	Total 1998
Czech Rep.[b]	145.2	110.3	135.8	101.2	105.7	101.0	124.1	115.7
Hungary	134.5	121.5	124.1	122.0	119.9	117.7	147.0	120.5
Poland	151.3	132.8	115.5	106.7	111.7	105.0	122.1	109.6
Romania	-	-	-	-	-	-	108.0	98.4
Slovakia[b]	138.2	119.0	119.7	102.3	108.8	102.2	123.4	129.3
Slovenia	-	-	117.7	99.9	103.9	99.1	122.6	108.1

Notes:
a Previous year =100.
b Excludes Czech/Slovak trade.

Source: *CESTAT Statistical Bulletin*; Dangerfield (2000b).

Of course, the significance of intra-CEFTA trade remains fairly minor compared with its members' transactions with the EU, although this is only to be expected since there was never any question of the former market being anything other than a supplement to the latter.

Table 4.4 Total and intra-CEFTA imports, 1995–98[a]

	From CEFTA 1995	Total 1995	From CEFTA 1996	Total 1996	From CEFTA 1997	Total 1997	From CEFTA 1998	Total 1998
Czech Rep.[b]	151.5	139.5	137.2	109.7	110.7	98.0	115.4	106.1
Hungary	109.1	106.3	127.6	117.3	109.8	117.0	128.2	121.1
Poland	176.9	134.7	133.0	127.8	119.7	113.9	115.0	111.2
Romania	-	-	-	-	118.5	98.6	162.9	104.8
Slovakia[b]	158.2	132.7	128.1	126.8	103.7	92.3	130.0	126.3
Slovenia	-	-	97.2	99.2	111.8	99.4	105.4	107.8

Notes:

a Previous year =100.

b Excludes Czech/Slovak trade.

Source: *CESTAT Statistical Bulletin*; Dangerfield (2000b).

Though all of the CEFTA states have reaped the benefits of the subregional trade liberalisation through an expansion of exports, some imbalances have been evident, with the Czech Republic and Slovakia maintaining strong surplus positions, while Poland, Slovenia and, more recently, Romania have consistently been the deficit countries. So far, the most significant structural change in this respect concerns the position of Hungary, which had gradually reversed its deficit position by 1998 to achieve a more or less balanced account. Obvious contributory factors to this development were the admission of Romania, the strong export orientation of the economy, relatively fast progress in transformation and the high levels of foreign direct investment (FDI). The advantages of agricultural trade liberalisation have also been important for Hungary, given its relatively efficient farms and high levels of involvement of foreign capital in the sector. However, its higher dependence on agricultural trade makes Hungarian exports to CEFTA vulnerable to short-term fluctuations.

Turning to the commodity structure of intra-CEFTA trade, it must be remembered that the organisation was formed in the context of 'the dramatic decline in mutual trade of sophisticated products while the mutual trade of raw materials, foodstuffs, energy and chemical products strongly increased.

Table 4.5 Commodity structure of intra-CEFTA trade: the Visegrád 4, 1994 and 1997

	0	1	2	3	4	5	6	7	8	9[a]	Total
1994											
Czech Republic	185.4	60.0	105.9	372.2	21.1	532.0	873.9	828.9	288.7	0.5	3 268.6
Hungary[b]	70.4	25.6	35.6	26.4	19.5	135.6	87.9	63.4	38	0	502.4
Poland	47.8	1.4	60.7	190.6	0.1	113.9	215.5	126.2	66.9	0.2	823.2
Slovakia	171.6	43.7	188.8	235.3	4.4	487.5	632.5	583.2	266.4	2.2	2 615.6
Total	475.2	130.7	391.0	824.5	45.1	1 269.0	1 809.8	1601.7	660.0	2.9	7 209.8
% of total exports	6.59	1.81	5.42	11.44	0.62	17.6	25.1	22.2	9.15	0.04	
1997											
Czech Republic	274.2	95.6	135.2	330.4	19.5	700.2	1 390.3	1 482.6	432.6	4.5	4 865.1
Hungary[b]	321.4	16.7	69.4	111.3	37.8	292.0	240.7	259.3	93.8	0	1 442.4
Poland	145.5	0.8	58.6	258.3	1.1	229.5	504.2	293.9	166.8	0	1 658.7
Slovakia	144.9	45	167	339.5	8.5	532.3	1 218.3	666.6	237.8	0.9	3 360.8
Total	886.0	158.1	430.2	1 039.4	66.9	1 753.9	3 353.4	2 702.4	931.0	5.4	11 327.0
% of total exports	7.82	1.40	3.8	9.18	0.59	15.5	29.6	23.9	8.22	0.05	
Index 1997/1994	186.5	121.0	110.0	126.1	148.6	138.2	185.3	168.7	141.1	186.2	157.1

Table 4.5 Continued

	0	1	2	3	4	5	6	7	8	9[a]	Total
Weighted Index 1997/1994[c]											
Czech Republic	8.3	3.1	3.6	6.0	0.4	18.9	45.5	54.5	13.3	0.81	
Hungary	101.7	0.8	9.4	32.5	5.1	43.6	45.7	73.5	16.1	-	
Poland	26.7	0	3.4	21.1	0.8	27.9	71.1	41.3	25.1	-	
Slovakia	3.6	1.4	4.4	14.6	0.5	17.3	69.8	22.7	6.3	0.1	
Total	14.6	1.7	4.2	11.6	0.9	21.4	54.9	40.3	11.6	0.09	

Notes:

a 0=food and live animals; 1=beverages and tobacco; 2=crude materials, except fuels; 3=mineral fuels, lubricants, related materials; 4=animal and vegetable oils, fats, waxes; 5=chemicals and related products; 6=manufactured goods, classified chiefly by materials; 7=machinery and transport equipment; 8=miscellaneous manufactured items; 9=others.

b The Hungarian data is based on import data of Czech Republic, Poland and Slovakia.

c The formula for the Weighted Index is, for any country or in total: (Index 1997/1994) x (% of total exports in 1997).

Source: Tables 4.1 and 4.2, Dangerfield (2000b).

Again, an especially sharp decline was noticed in the trade of machinery and industrial consumer goods' (Rudka and Mizsei, 1995:5). Looking at the dynamics of the composition of intra-CEFTA trade over the first five years of its existence, Table 4.5 reveals that it was predominantly industrial and concentrated heavily in SITC groups 5, 6 and 7.[8] Hungary was the main exception to the general pattern, with food and agricultural goods being both the most important exports to CEFTA in 1997 and those that had registered most growth (1997/1994 index = 456.6). The positive effects of the liberalisation of trade in agricultural goods were also important for Poland, the other Visegrád country with a significant agricultural sector, and it registered an index for 1997/1994 of 304.4.

Second, a weighted index of 1997 over 1994 trade, which takes into account the relative importance of each commodity group in the total trade of each country, reveals that the greatest gains in exports were in SITC categories 6 and 7, with other sectors some way behind.[9] For all four countries, growth in the sales of SITC7 items in CEFTA was evident, while overall sales of SITC8 also grew healthily. Therefore, although exchanges of the more traditional, basic industrial products covered by SITC6 continued to play an important part in CEFTA trade and exhibited a strong growth dynamic, exports of machinery and equipment have also registered a significant increase and are indicative of positive trends in the overall commodity structure of intra-CEFTA trade. These developments were recognised within the member countries themselves: analysts in Prague, for example, found that, during 1997, Czech exports to CEFTA were characterised by 'a strengthening of an already significant position in machinery and transport equipment (SITC7) which moved to the foremost place in the export structure' (Czechtrade, 1998:75). Also, Polish analysts had already concluded in 1996 that:

> the primitive model of trade typical of the early nineties was put further behind. One of the most notable developments in this sphere was the fact that electro-engineering exports grew faster than exports in general ... Similar improvements were recorded in exports of the chemical, wood and paper and light industries, that is branches characterised by high value-added. There was a marked decline in the share of the metallurgical and mineral industries, that is ones with the highest percentages of raw materials and low value-added products. (Perczyński, 1996:191–2)

Third, certain differences within the CEFTA group should be noted. The growth of sales of SITC7 was far less pronounced in Slovakia than elsewhere while its sales of SITC8 actually declined. Although free trade arrangements allow certain comparative advantages to assert themselves, the dynamic changes to the export commodity profiles of individual countries depend on a range of supply side factors. In the case of countries in CEE, this means progress in reform and restructuring and their degree of success in attracting FDI. The analysis of trade by commodity structure shows clearly that Slovakia stood out in terms of its reliance on traditional industrial exports to the CEFTA market and this corresponds closely with the relatively low inflows of FDI received by the country (see Table 4.6). This in turn implies that any trends towards a decline in Slovakia's overall standing in the CEFTA market will be difficult to overturn in the short term.

Table 4.6 Cumulative FDI inflows to CEFTA states, 1997

	$US billion	As % of GDP
Poland	26.0	15
Hungary	22.5	39
Czech Republic	8.0	11
Romania	2.8	8
Slovenia	2.4	14
Slovakia	1.0	5

Source: *Business Central Europe*, November 1998, p. 18.

CEFTA AND THE EU PRE-ACCESSION PROCESS

Before discussing the various aspects of CEFTA's role in the preparations for EU entry, it is worth noting that there have been important differences in the way that its member countries have themselves viewed their relationship, and that these alternative perspectives help to explain why the organisation's pre-accession function has had clear limitations. In 1997, the then Under-Secretary of State in the Polish Ministry of Foreign Economic Relations, wrote that, despite the various developments in CEFTA cooperation which were under consideration, the intention 'of the CEFTA governments is not to detract from the original design of the grouping, which is transitional in nature and whose principal aim is to better prepare its members for negotiations of their entry in the European Union and for the future membership itself' (Kaczurba, 1997:15).

The Czech and Slovak sides did not quite share this interpretation of CEFTA's principal aim, however, and were in general less convinced that pre-accession preparation was the only *raison d'être* for the group. These different interpretations of the CEFTA-EU accession relationship can be traced back to debates that took place at the time that the organisation was formed. Although all of the Visegrád countries adhered to the baseline agreement that subregional economic cooperation should not be a substitute for the main objective of EU membership, the initial discussions about the nature of that cooperation included the suggestion, mainly associated with Poland, that CEFTA could be accompanied by other measures (for example, common approaches to important components of constructing functioning market economies) that would support and help to synchronise moves towards integration with Europe. The outcome of this debate was consistent with the 'Czechoslovak approach which rejected a close, also politically based cooperation, while it fervently supported, in concert with the Czech government's liberal credo, the creation of a free trade area' (Richter, 1997:2).

During the early years of CEFTA's life, the Hungarians and Poles called regularly for closer coordination of the members' approaches to the EU, although the Czech government consistently rejected these. From its neo-liberal perspective, free trade was held as the logical state of affairs for all capitalist economies and the existence of CEFTA was therefore independent of relations with other regional integration frameworks. In the case of Slovakia, as the prospects for keeping pace with the progress of other Visegrád states in their efforts to join the EU and the North Atlantic Treaty Organization (NATO) diminished during the Mečiar era, the idea that CEFTA could be upgraded and develop as an alternative to the EU gained credence and influenced Slovak policy towards the organisation accordingly. Given these different perceptions of subregional economic cooperation and the general tendency for the CEE states to be competitive rather than cooperative as far as their EU accession endeavours were concerned, it is obvious that there was little chance that CEFTA would conclude a formal joint EU accession strategy, even before its own enlargement in the context of the 1997 Agenda 2000 decisions made it an inappropriate forum for such a purpose.

Pre-accession Contributions

The first, and rather obvious, contribution of the Visegrád group's willingness to form CEFTA was that they were able to meet the EU requirement that future members should be taking steps to further their own integration. In this connection, it has been noted that 'the pressure from the Central European countries on the Community mounted following the signature of the CEFTA agreement, as if to stress that the CEFTA countries had fulfilled a precondition' (Lavigne, 1995:199). There was a feeling in

CEE that the stance of the EU was aimed at the creation of a new 'bloc' in their region and was therefore a device to forestall accession, but in fact it has been a long-standing element of the EU's 'classical' method of enlargement (see Preston, 1997). In any case, the EU's insistence on the end of subregional trade discrimination had a clear practical purpose, which was to advance the process of putting in place the market integration that would be the platform for accession to the Union. As discussed above, intra-CEFTA trade has developed accordingly.

Second, the implementation of CEFTA has stimulated further inflows of FDI, which make important contributions to the economic restructuring, development and competitiveness that are a vital part of the preparation for coping with the threats and opportunities of full integration into the single market. The argument that the formation of regional and subregional economic associations with a free trade base leads to increased FDI is widely accepted in the general literature and, in the case of CEFTA, various studies have shown that subregional trade liberalisation has been an important factor in the decision-making of certain investors (Rudka and Mizsei, 1995; Elteto and Sass, 1998). Of course, the attraction of the subregional market does not in itself mean that each participating state will automatically gain in terms of FDI inflows. Companies choose a location from which to supply a market and countries where the general climate for inward investment is perceived negatively are likely to miss out: Slovakia, as noted earlier, has been a case in point.

The third dimension of CEFTA's pre-accession function involves subregional political relations. In their general evaluations of the impact of Europe's new subregionalism, various scholars have emphasised the contributions that such groupings can make to 'soft' security issues (such as environment, organised crime and terrorism, developing economic interdependence) and their subtle influences on political relations and stability within and beyond their particular territory (see, in particular, Cottey, 1999; Bailes, 1997). As well as the more obvious fostering of deeper interdependence between the member states, CEFTA cooperation has provided a forum for dialogue at the highest level and created a need to upgrade and maintain good channels of communication.[10] There is also the benefit that CEFTA candidacy is an incentive to maintain good relations with the existing member countries and to settle any problems that could compromise admission: the need for Bulgaria to clear its socialist era debts to Poland and Hungary being a good example. Clearly, its influence will be limited in the case of serious bilateral disputes but, in all the above ways, CEFTA can help to cement improved political relations in CEE. Further, the organisation has served as a 'holding operation' for political cooperation during the dormant phase of the 'Visegrád Group', since CEFTA summits were the only occasions when the leaders of all four countries came together on a regular basis. Once the agents representing the main obstructions to its revival were no longer in office, it was through the CEFTA forum that agreement to re-activate the Visegrád Group was reached.[11]

Another political aspect of CEFTA's operations is the 'practical experience of the modalities of voluntary multilateral cooperation' that it has generated (Cottey, 1996:21). This aids preparations for operating in organisations with bigger and more complicated agendas and, it is supposed, demonstrates suitability to join them on the basis that 'a good record of cooperation at subregional level will help, not handicap, states which otherwise meet the conditions for membership, reflecting as it does the qualities of maturity, stability and good-neighbourliness which are central to the NATO and EU *acquis*' (Bailes, 1997:30). Though this factor can be seen as a potential product of all the post Cold War European subregional groupings, it can be argued that CEFTA has had a higher profile in this respect due to its focused, accession-oriented agenda, shaky early foundations and potential to generate really testing problems (viz. the 1998 agricultural trade disputes).

Finally, CEFTA has been serving the more mature stages of the pre-accession process by providing a forum for the discussion of EU-compatible cooperation at the subregional level. The parameters of this have to a large extent always followed the state of play in the relations of its member states with the EU. Thus, free trade as the centrepiece of CEFTA cooperation reflected the trade dimension of the EAs and, following the publication of the 1995 White Paper on EU enlargement to the east, the questions of free movement of capital, liberalisation of trade in services and even free movement of labour were brought to the table.[12] The CEFTA provisions also include a commitment to tackle a range of non-tariff barriers, as a result of their duplication of EA articles and the need to harmonise state-aid policies and to open public procurement contracts to all CEFTA companies by the deadline of 2001 has been occupying the CEFTA agenda recently.

FUTURE PERSPECTIVES ON CEFTA

For the existing members, mutual economic cooperation can continue during the run-up to full membership of the EU. Integration can develop through the trade expansion that should be possible in the context of economic growth, further economic development and restructuring, growing inflows of FDI, the erosion of the last tariffs on the items that have been classified as most sensitive and the ongoing opening of the markets of the newer members of CEFTA. The member states can make further progress by attending to other trade-enhancing activities covered by the present framework of their organisation that are, at the same time, consistent with their adaptation to the rules and regulations of the EU's single market. Prominent examples of this include the certification and mutual recognition of test results for agricultural produce; mutual opening of state procurement contracts; and perhaps even some degree of harmonisation of agricultural support systems as the CEFTA states grapple with the problem of how to revive the objective of fully freeing agricultural trade in the context of their preparations for incorporation into the Common Agricultural Policy. The staggered enlargement of the EU will, of course, have implications for subregional cooperation outside the CEFTA framework, which may well be disrupted.[13]

Any assessment of the longer-term picture for CEFTA is complicated by two factors. On the one hand, much hinges on whether CEFTA will enlarge further during the next few years, although the arguments for it to do so are unconvincing and it seems rather doubtful at present. On the other, in terms of its members' place in the EU enlargement process, the organisation is already a diverse grouping and, with countries that may be up to thirty years away from Union membership in the CEFTA accession queue, this heterogeneity may increase and create new agendas. Such uncertainties feed a variety of hypotheses about the organisation's future trajectory.

First, assuming that the close link between CEFTA membership and EU integration means that it will not prove possible to enlarge membership beyond the present group of EA countries, the organisation could wither, as with EFTA.[14] Alternatively, as some CEE officials have suggested, it could follow the example of other subregional groupings within and around the EU, such as Benelux and the Nordic Council, which have become consultative bodies that focus on the special interests of the players in their area (see Grela, 1997; Paleckis, 1997). Obviously, the main problem with the latter scenario is that the CEFTA countries are not slated to enter the EU simultaneously and there are other subregional groupings that are potentially better candidates for such a consultative role, including the now revived Visegrád Group.

Second, there is the prospect that CEFTA may undergo some further enlargement and continue as a bridge to the EU, but with a more pan-European identity, thus helping to make the European integration process less exclusive. Given that the predicted date for the first phase of the EU's eastward enlargement is receding continually and that certain CEFTA members, namely Bulgaria and Romania, face a long wait for EU membership anyway, this scenario seems to have some credibility. At present, four countries can be considered to be in the CEFTA accession queue (Croatia, FYRM, Ukraine and Moldova) and their status is shown in Table 4.7. Although Croatia certainly seems to have been on a fast track to membership since the key political developments at the end of 1999, accession before the end of 2001 would appear to be optimistic and the point of entering the group at this stage has to be questioned seriously.[15] For one thing, the core CEFTA countries will be that much closer to leaving the organisation and joining the EU. Also, the organisation's agenda will have been completed and new entrants will therefore face a considerable catching-up task that will necessitate periods of transition. All this points to the argument that the best strategy would be to avoid the complications of CEFTA and settle for a more flexible approach based on bilateral

Table 4.7 Past and possible future enlargements of CEFTA

Country (Years invited as guest at CEFTA summit)	Date of accession to CEFTA	Date of WTO accession	Date of signing of EA	Bilateral free trade agreements with CEFTA states?
Slovenia (1994)	1.1.96	30.7.95	10.6.96	
Romania (1995, 1996)	1.7.97	1.1.95	4.10.93	
Bulgaria (1995, 1996, 1997)	1.1.99	1.2.96	4.10.93	
Croatia (1997)		30.11.00		Slovenia (12.12.97)
FYR Macedonia (1997)		[a]	[b]	Slovenia (1.7.96)
Ukraine (1996, 1997)		[a]	[c]	
Moldova (none)		[a]	[c]	Romania (15.2.95)

Notes:

a WTO applications currently being considered by accession working parties.

b FYR Macedonia's 'Trade and Cooperation' Agreement with the EU entered into force on 1 January 1998.

c EU relations are on the basis of 'Partnership and Cooperation' Agreements which contain a provision for the two parties to discuss the establishment of a free trade area. So far this is not on the agenda.

Source: Dangerfield (2000b).

arrangements that can then be smoothly transferred to the EU context when enlargement takes place. In fact, the real significance of full CEFTA membership has been overstated because some non-EA countries have been able to gain access to the CEFTA market through bilateral free trade agreements with individual member states. Croatia and Macedonia, for example, have free trade agreements with Slovenia. Though the need to ensure that trade arrangements with third parties stay in line with EU requirements has undermined further extension of '*de facto*' participation in CEFTA over the last two years or so, the Stability and Association Agreements (SAAs) now in the pipeline for the west Balkans as part of the EU's post-Kosovo approach has re-opened the door, at least for certain CEFTA candidates.[16]

The third hypothesis is for CEFTA to develop a more independent role as an alternative integration framework for CEE countries that face, or opt for, long term exclusion from the EU. Like scenario two, this development path assumes enlargement to the south and east, but also takes into account the possibility that the members of a reconfigured CEFTA, or a significant group of them, could either fail to become engaged in the EU accession process or, in line with the potential consequences of '*de facto* satellisation' (Phinnemore, 1999), downgrade their relations with the EU. In these circumstances, having shifted its centre of gravity further towards Europe's eastern and southern periphery, CEFTA could develop into something beyond a component of the broader pan-European free trade complex. It is hard to imagine how this could come about in practice: to develop as a genuine alternative, economic cooperation would have to proceed beyond free trade to more advanced forms of integration. CEFTA would, however, consist of less transformed, less developed and economically relatively weak post-communist states that will lack the necessary geographic contiguity and other important cohesive characteristics. Moreover, the members would still vary in terms of their relations with the EU. The more likely development is that once the core of CEFTA has acceded to Europe, it would come to resemble the rump EFTA and be composed of a group of countries that lack the prerequisites to further their own integration, but who will have free trade amongst themselves and will be, or will become, linked to the extended pan-European free trade area. Individual countries would be free either to opt for the free trade *status quo* indefinitely or to attempt to upgrade their integration into the European Economic Area, and then perhaps to seek full EU membership.

CONCLUSIONS

CEFTA has proved to be a useful instrument for assisting the transition to integration with the EU, with pre-accession roles that have included preliminary market integration and the chance to explore other avenues of EU-compatible cooperation, practical experience of operating as equals in international integration exercises and attempts to enhance the political credentials of its members. The fact that it has been possible to combine what are these days 'Luxembourg' and 'Helsinki' groups of countries in a collective EU pre-accession exercise should also be interpreted as a clear advantage of the CEFTA model.[17] From the perspective of certain CEE countries looking in from the outside, CEFTA has succeeded in embodying a concept of Central Europe and, as such, of representing a 'club' whose members are pre-destined for EU membership.

Notwithstanding its successes, there are also clear constraints on both the present, and potential future, roles of CEFTA. It has never been a device to coordinate CEE approaches to the EU actively, even before the Agenda 2000 proposals split its membership into 'in' and 'pre-in' applicants. So far, coordination of accession strategies has occurred as and when particular issues demanded it and, logically, as part of initiatives other than CEFTA; for example, during the coordination meetings of the key officials of the Luxembourg Group and the reconvened Visegrád Group. Unfortunately, the idea that CEFTA may evolve in such a way that it can help to compensate for the new divide in Europe runs into a number of difficulties. Its enlargement is still beset by delays, especially for those candidates who do not meet its accession criteria. Even Croatia, which could accede relatively early, faces the prospect of joining something that could be seriously dismembered shortly thereafter, while it must also find formulae to deal with the problems of joining CEFTA at such an advanced stage of its development. A more flexible network of bilateral economic agreements between CEFTA members and the other CEE states seems to be a more logical development. This may occur at the expense of the opportunity for CEFTA to operate as an alternative for CEE countries that seem to be excluded long-term from the EU. The reality, however, is that by the time the relevant countries could engage independently in advanced economic integration the logic for excluding them from EU membership will probably have long disappeared.

The conditions of the SAAs for the west Balkan states stress the need for them to engage in subregional cooperation and the CEFTA experience may represent an appropriate model for other areas. In the west Balkans, however, the lack of cohesive foundations and, as yet, the exclusion of its main economic hub (Serbia) mean that ideas of emulating the CEFTA model may be too ambitious in the short term, with less rigid models of cooperation being needed. As for the wider picture, not only is the EU unable to rely on subregional cooperation as a potential substitute for an inclusive EU enlargement strategy, there is also some way to go in ensuring that the requirements of the enlargement process do not undermine existing subregional relations. Associate EU membership for the west Balkan states is a step forward in this respect, but countries to the east of CEFTA need to be included in the process as well, notwithstanding the enormously disruptive potential of the looming expansion of the Schengen area. It is vital therefore that due attention is paid to the subregional implications of the EU enlargement process.

NOTES

1. The CEFTA member states are the Czech Republic, Hungary, Poland and Slovakia, who were the founder countries, and Slovenia (acceded on 1 January 1996), Romania (1 July 1997) and Bulgaria (1 January 1999). Though not usually regarded as a fully-fledged subregional grouping, CEFTA's smaller 'cousin', the Baltic Free Trade Area (BFTA), is a parallel pre-accession instrument for Latvia, Lithuania and Estonia. The CEFTA and BFTA economic spaces are linked to each other via the network of bilateral free trade arrangements in place between each of the CEFTA and BFTA countries.
2. This refers to the prevailing international agreement with the EU and not to the state of play in the accession process. In the CEFTA case, prospective members must have Europe Agreements or free trade agreements with the EU.
3. See, for example, Brabant (1991).
4. Including exports of automobiles to Poland, for example.
5. See Kiss (1997) for more details of the CEFTA agricultural provisions.
6. To illustrate the fluidity of the agricultural trade situation in CEFTA, it can be noted that, two years on from the 'wheat wars' of 1998, it was announced at a meeting of the recently convened CEFTA sub-committee for agricultural trade that 'The greatest barrier to agro-trade among the CEFTA countries is no longer protective tariffs, but whether or not the drought-stricken exporter countries can produce enough to trade' (Hungarian News Agency (MTI), 22 June 2000).
7. Presenting the data in the national currencies of the CEFTA countries would reveal higher rates of growth of exports and imports between the members, albeit in nominal terms. However, given that exchange rates movements have reflected the higher levels of inflation in the CEFTA countries, the trade data are based on $US values, which gives a better indication of the real changes.
8. See notes to Table 4.5 for a key to SITC codes. The importance of SITC 7 – machinery and transport – in exports is usually regarded as a principal indicator of the degree of sophistication of the export structure.
9. The formula for calculating the weighted index is given with Table 4.5. When comparing the growth of particular SITC single-digit categories, total intra-CEFTA sales in SITC9 ('others') grew by 86.2 per cent according to the normal index while SITC6 grew by 85.3 per cent. However, in 1997 SITC9 accounted for 0.05 per cent of total intra-CEFTA sales while SITC6 accounted for 29.6 per cent. The weighted index, therefore, is an attempt to standardise the changes in values of sales of the various commodity categories by factoring in the relative significance of particular product categories in intra-CEFTA exchanges. The weighted index figures for SITC6 and SITC9 were 54.9 and 0.09, respectively.

10. The Prime Ministers of the CEFTA countries meet annually at CEFTA summits. In the case of certain countries (the Czech Republic and Slovak Republics during large parts of the Klaus and Mečiar regimes, for example) CEFTA summits were the only occasions when their leaders were guaranteed to come face to face.
11. At the 1998 CEFTA Summit in Prague, the Czech government suggested that CEFTA could 'develop some political dimensions along the lines of the Visegrád Accord' (RFE/RL Newsline, 177, 2, 14 September 1998) and although Slovak Premier Mečiar refused to endorse the idea, the change of government in Slovakia in the following month paved the way for the reconvening of the Visegrád Group in May 1999. For a discussion of the results of 'Visegrád 2' to date and its future prospects see Handl (2000).
12. Proposals for all three were tabled at the 1995 CEFTA Summit in Brno. The Polish proposal for the free movement of labour was rejected, while working parties were convened to investigate ways of implementing the free movement of capital and services. The membership concluded eventually that these developments would have to be activated in the context of EU accession.
13. The potential abolition of the Czech-Slovak customs union, for example, along with the possible partial reversal of agricultural trade liberalisation and disruptions to general trade and cross-border investment caused by the extension of the Shengen area to new members.
14. Obviously, the EFTA parallel only goes so far. Unlike the rump EFTA, the countries of the remaining CEFTA will not be staying out of the EU on account of their own policy preferences.
15. Croatia was admitted to the WTO on 30 November 2000 and the process of establishing free trade with the EU, in the framework of the 'Stability and Association Agreements' (SAAs) being prepared for west Balkan countries, is already under way. A renewed effort to achieve CEFTA accession has also been evident during various bilateral meetings with members of the organisation. In June 2000, for instance, it was reported that 'Strengthening Czech-Croatian economic and political cooperation and Croatia's admission to CEFTA will be the main topics for Croatian premier Ivica Racan's forthcoming two-day visit to Prague' (Czech News Agency (CTK), 8 June 2000).
16. To illustrate, in April 1998, Nenad Porges, Croatian Minister of Economic Affairs, said that it had become 'clear that there will be plenty of difficulties in negotiations with CEFTA countries which have practically one foot in the European Union already. There is some hesitation on the part of the Czech Republic and the latest CEFTA newcomer, Romania. They put the beginning of free trade negotiations into a package regulating our relations with the European Union' (Kiseljak and Ivankovic, 1998:1).
17. This terminology refers to the countries that received invitations to open EU accession talks at the EU Luxembourg (December 1997) and Helsinki (December 1999) Summits, respectively.

REFERENCES

Bailes, A. (1997), 'Subregional Organisations: The Cinderellas of European security', *NATO Review*, **45** (2), pp. 27–31, available at www.mfa.ee/nato/docu/review/articles/9702-8.htm.

Brabant, J. van (1991), 'Renewal of Cooperation and Economic Transition in Eastern Europe', *Studies in Comparative Communism*, **XXIV** (2), 151–72.

CEFTA (1992), *Central European Free Trade Agreement*, Kraków, 21 December 1992 (abbreviated to CEFTA in the text for referencing purposes).

CESTAT Statistical Bulletin, Prague: Czech Statistical Office, various issues.

Cottey, A., (1996), 'Multi-Layered Integration: The Subregional Dimension', Summary of an Inter-Governmental Conference, Bucharest 7–8 October 1996, Warsaw, Institute for East West Studies.

Cottey, Andrew (ed.) (1999), *Subregional Cooperation in the New Europe. Building Security, Prosperity and Solidarity from the Barents to the Black Sea,* Basingstoke: Macmillan.

Czechtrade (1998), *The Czech Republic in the International Economy,* **5** (2), Prague: Czechtrade.

Dangerfield, M. (2000a), 'Subregional Cooperation in CEFTA: Issues and Controversies', paper presented at Rethinking Europe: UACES 30th Anniversary Conference and Fifth Research Conference, Budapest, 6–8 April 2000.

Dangerfield, Martin (2000b), *Subregional Economic Cooperation in Central and Eastern Europe. The Political Economy of CEFTA*, Cheltenham, UK and Northampton MA, USA: Edward Elgar.

Dwan, Renata (ed.) (1999), *Building Security in Europe's New Borderlands*, New York: M.E. Sharpe.

Elteto, A. and M. Sass, (1998), 'Motivations and Behaviour By Hungary's Foreign Investors in Relation to Exports', Working Paper of the Institute for World Economics, Budapest, Hungarian Academy of Sciences, No. 88, January.

Grela, Marek (1997), 'CEFTA and Pan-European Political and Economic Cooperation', in Heinrich Machowski (ed.), pp. 139–42.

Handl, V. (2000), 'Visegrad – Chances for Recovery?', paper presented at Subregional Dimensions of the European Union Enlargement Process, University of Wolverhampton, 23 June.

Inotai, A. (1997), 'Correlations Between European Integration and Subregional Cooperation. Theoretical Background, Experience and Policy Impacts', Working Paper No. 87 of the Institute for World Economics, Budapest, Hungarian Academy of Sciences, September.

Kaczurba, Janusz (1997), 'The Impact of CEFTA', in Heinrich Machowski (ed.), pp. 11–15.

Kiseljak F.and Ivankovic Z. (1998),'Joining the Queue' (Interview with Nenad Porges), *Banka International*, 30 April, available at www.banka-mzb.tel.hr/.banka-mzb/98-01/4queue.html.

Kiss, J. (1997), 'Agricultural Trade Within CEFTA (A Substitute or Supplement to EU Accession?)', Working Paper of the Institute for World Economics, Budapest, Hungarian Academy of Sciences, December.

Köves, András (1992), *Central and East European Economies in Transition: The International Dimension,* Boulder, Colorado: Westview Press.

Lavigne, Marie. (1995), *The Economics of Transition,* London: Macmillan.

Machowski, Heinrich (ed.) (1997), *The Further Development of CEFTA: Institutionalisation, Deepening, Widening?*, Warsaw: Friedrich Ebert Foundation.

Paleckis, Justas (1997), 'The Lithuanian Road Through CEFTA Into the EU?', in Heinrich Machowski (ed.), pp. 121–29.

Okolicsanyi, K. (1993) 'The Visegrad Triangle's Free Trade Zone', *RFE/RL Research Report*, **2** (3), 19–22.

Perczyński, Maciej (1996), 'Poland in the Central European Free Trade Area', in Marek Lubiński (ed.) *Poland: International Economic Report 1995/96*, Warsaw: Warsaw School of Economics, pp. 186–93.

Phinnemore, David (1999), *Association: Stepping-Stone or Alternative to EU Membership?*, Sheffield: UACES/Sheffield Academic Press.

Preston, Christopher (1997), *Enlargement and Integration in the European Union*, London: Routledge.

Richter, S. (1997), *European Integration: The CEFTA and the Europe Agreements*, Research Report No. 237, Vienna Institute for Comparative Economic Studies, Vienna, May.

Rudka, A. and Mizsei, K. (1995), 'East Central Europe Between Disintegration and Reintegration. Is CEFTA the Solution?', *The Rose Occasional Paper Series*, **1** (1), USA and Poland: Institute for East-West Studies.

Toth, L. (1994), 'Trade Among the CEFTA Countries in the Mid 1990s: How to Promote the Expansion of Intra-Regional Trade Flows in Central Europe', Kopint Datorg Discussion Paper No. 27, Budapest, November.

5. Storming the Fortress: The External Border Regime in an Enlarged Europe

David Brown

INTRODUCTION

Two decisions were taken by the then European Community in 1989 that were to have far reaching consequences for its future. The first, which refers to what civil liberties groups have labelled the development of a 'Fortress Europe' mentality, began with the publication of the Palma Document (EC, 1989) and is a prime example of the deepening of integration. The second relates to the somewhat ad hoc response to developments in Central and Eastern Europe (CEE), although this would eventually build into the current enlargement process. It emphasises the widening of membership, with all of its potential consequences in terms of the creation of voting coalitions (including blocking minorities), bargaining between greater numbers of interests, and the amendment of the institutional structure of the European Union (EU). Those contributions to the current enlargement literature that see all previous enlargements as having been accompanied by the deepening of European cooperation and the extension of the competencies of the central institutions argue that the Union can both deepen and widen simultaneously (see Nugent, 1992; Ersboll, 1994). This argument, however, fails to deal with the unique characteristics of the current enlargement process, which suggest that comparisons with previous and more limited extensions of membership may be less than helpful.

The somewhat over-confident fusion of two potentially contradictory forces is challenged by the case study that will form the main part of this chapter, namely the attempts to strengthen the external frontier of the EU, as envisaged in the Palma Document of 1989. In fact, the current moves towards the enlargement of the Union, in which the states least capable of taking on the day-to-day duty of maintaining and securing the external border will perversely be expected to do just that (O'Keefe, 1992:8), will leave the civil libertarians with few concerns. In a wider Union, the likelihood of a 'ring of steel' being established is diminished, as 'recent events in Central and Eastern Europe might ... undermine the overall accomplishments of the Third Pillar' (Vega, 1998:27). Those who have posited the opposing argument, such as the authors of the Palma Document, that external border controls are a vital instrument in tackling the various threats to the internal safety of the EU and are necessary to compensate for the appearance of a 'security gap' have greater cause for concern.

HISTORY OF THE EXTERNAL FRONTIER CONVENTION

The Palma Document, which listed the key compensatory measures to be implemented prior to the completion of the single market, highlighted the need to strengthen controls at the external frontier. This was to ensure that a 'security gap' would not arise from the planned removal of internal frontiers before a suitable alternative was put into place. Supporters of the removal of all internal frontier controls argued that it was an action necessary to complete the 'Four Freedoms' (free movement of capital, services, goods and people). These principles were enshrined in the Treaty of Rome, and given full force by the Single European Act (SEA) and the legislation needed to implement it. However, in proposing this course of action, they underestimated the political and emotional attachment that certain member states had to organising their own border controls. For example, rather than implement swiftly the measures contained within the Palma Document, the United Kingdom refused to accept that Article 7a of the SEA provided a legal basis for the removal of all internal checks.[1] It believed that the Article referred only to European citizens and did not prevent the maintenance of internal border controls for third country nationals. This has remained the official position of all subsequent British administrations, with the current Prime Minister, Tony Blair, reiterating that 'we shall not agree to any lifting of the veto in areas ... such as our border controls' (House of Commons, 1999) after the 1999 Tampere European Council on Justice and Home Affairs. It is important that this attachment is not dismissed merely as a further symptom of the UK's historic antipathy to the 'European project'.

Other member states, including those that founded the European Coal and Steel Community, have felt it necessary to restore their internal controls when their national interest dictated it. For example, Belgium and Luxembourg reintroduced them in 2000 to ensure that people from neighbouring countries did not abuse a governmental amnesty for those illegal immigrants already resident within the state (Castle, 2000). Austria also took the decision to leave the Schengen arrangements temporarily in June 2001 to avoid a repeat of the rioting and demonstrations that marred the 2001 Gothenburg European Council. External frontier problems have also coloured British attitudes to the developments within the Schengen area. It initially refused to join any element of the Schengen *acquis* that would, by implication, involve the removal of its right to exercise frontier controls at its internal borders and this has not changed, even though Britain made an ultimately successful application in May 1999 to participate in the police cooperation elements of Schengen.[2] Britain has also been locked in a diplomatic stalemate with Spain since the Palma Document was produced over the territorial application of the Convention to Gibraltar. An agreement was finally reached between the two sides in April 2000, which allowed Gibraltar to participate in the same Schengen package as had been agreed by the UK (House of Commons, 2000). However, the main victim of the disagreement was the original draft Convention, which has yet to be ratified after almost a decade of discussion. The Convention, which had to be in place before the member states could move onto other compensatory measures, such as the proposed European Information System, was eventually superseded by the incorporation of the aforementioned Schengen *acquis* within the EU as part of the Treaty of Amsterdam. One Commission official later summed up the position thus: 'the External Frontiers Convention is "dead", while a separate Schengen system no longer exists either' (unattributable interview with author, 1999).

Before entering into a deeper discussion of the practical and theoretical problems related to a strategy of framing an external frontier control within an enlarged EU, a brief discussion of the Schengen system is necessary.[3] The Schengen Agreement, signed on 14 June 1985 by the Benelux states, the Federal Republic of Germany and France, and the subsequent Convention of 1990, was seen as a laboratory for the measures that would eventually be necessary to complete an area without internal frontier controls. Originally agreed outwith the auspices of the European Community institutions, the second Chapter of the Convention deals with the crossing of the external frontier of what became known as 'Schengenland'.[4] Following the absorption of the Schengen *acquis* within the Treaty of Amsterdam, this Chapter now forms the benchmark by which the applicant states will be judged, as the *acquis* will have to be implemented in full prior to membership. These Articles (see the Schengen Convention, 1990: Articles 3–8), and others containing more detailed provisions on the various visa and residence permit arrangements required, established the standards by which a functioning external border regime will operate. For example, Article 6 (2b) states that 'all persons must be subject to at least one check making it possible to establish their identities', while a later clause calls for 'an equivalent level of control ... (to) be exercised at external frontiers'. The problem with the latter clause is that it does not remove the possibility of a more pessimistic interpretation, namely an agreement to operate at the lowest common denominator of control. When this Article is placed within the context of the current enlargement negotiations, in which serious concerns about the border policies of all the applicant states have been raised, most notably by the Commission, the pessimistic interpretation may be that which is put into practice.

THEORETICAL CONCERNS

Before entering into a detailed assessment of the capabilities of the states that will be asked to operate such an 'effective surveillance' system, a number of points need to be made concerning the nature of the strategy. The desire to concentrate the majority of surveillance and enforcement measures at the external border is predicated on the assumption that most threats to the internal security of the Union emanate from outside its territory and that they can therefore be held at bay by a strong defensive 'fortification'. Clearly, this is questionable, as France's somewhat erratic relationship with the Schengen Convention, which offers yet another example of the attachment certain states feel towards internal frontier controls, has demonstrated. When the French government insisted in July 1995 on the retention of the internal frontier controls, the reasoning behind its change of stance was based on the threat of a concerted terrorist campaign within the country, rather than a threat originating outside the Schengen territory (Statewatch, 1997). Similarly, when the French government refused to remove its frontier controls with Belgium and Luxembourg – leading one Belgian MP to argue that 'France appears to be an unreliable partner' (ibid.) – the justification rested on the belief that both states were used as transit routes for drugs leaving the Netherlands. These examples reflect the position of the British government towards a strategy predicated on the maintenance of controls solely at the external frontiers of the Union – 'much of the problem with drugs and terrorism is home grown; it is a disease already grown inside the 'soft centre' and the hardening of the shell will do nothing to arrest the disease within' (Statewatch, 1992). With the burden of responsibility placed upon the shoulders of the applicant states from CEE, at present through a series of readmission agreements and, after full membership, through the acceptance of the *acquis communautaire*, it is difficult to sustain the idea that a 'hardening of the shell' will take place either.

DRAWING THE BOUNDARY

The first problem to be considered when imagining some form of 'Fortress Europe' within an enlarged EU is that of where precisely to draw such boundaries – 'if there is to be a "fortress Europe", its Eastern line has yet to be settled' (O'Dowd, 1996:13). Anderson (1996:62) has stated that, over time, all frontiers will, theoretically, be legitimised, regardless of how they were decided upon. However, in the case of certain Baltic States, how long will this process take in practice? Disputes, mainly between Russia, on one hand, and both Latvia and Estonia, on the other, have threatened to stall indefinitely a final agreement on the demarcation of their mutual borders. In the case of Estonia, while agreement was finally reached on the position of the border in 1998, there has still not been a final ratification process, allowing the Russian President Vladimir Putin greater room for manoeuvre (see Brown, 2000). It took over two years for the Estonian and Russian negotiating teams to move from the decision to de-politicise the negotiations, by concentrating on the technical aspects of border management, to the initialling of an agreed document. Therefore, it should not be taken for granted that final agreement will be forthcoming from the Russian side in the immediate future, especially as the issue is loaded with historical significance. The EU is then faced with the dilemma of permitting a state that has not fully agreed its mutual borders to become a member, or of allowing Russia a virtual veto on the matter of who can and cannot qualify for membership. Significantly, the formal position of the Union in this dispute has been to argue that the differences in opinion over the exact positioning of the inter-state border will not prevent Estonia from acceding to membership (unattributable interview with author, 2000).

The position is even less positive in the case of Latvia, with the Russian government continuing to link the issue of border demarcation to the treatment of the Russian diaspora within the country (unattributable interview with author, 2000). While the Russian government's appointment of a co-chairman for the stalled Latvian–Russian Inter-governmental Conference was a step in the right direction, there has been little indication whether this will lead to the signing of papers, already drafted, on the mutual border (Current Latvia, 2000). In fact, Latvia has been taking measures thought necessary to bring about a unilateral demarcation of the mutual border since 1998 in the hope that this will put sufficient pressure on Russia to accept a *fait accompli* (Latvian Ministry of Foreign Affairs, 1998). However, as the situation had still not been agreed at the last meeting of the two sides in November 2000, it seems that the Latvian declaration has not affected the Russian negotiating position significantly (Latvian Ministry of Foreign Affairs, 2000). Without a clear and legally accepted indication of where the external border is situated, it is unclear how the Commission – which has been given the task of assessing the applicants' efforts to meet the *acquis* – is supposed to make a judgement.

TRANS-BORDER CONCERNS

Part of the problem of enforcing a rigorous external border regime is its potentially negative effects on certain trans-national concerns, related to the functioning of inter-state trade and the position of national minorities within a state, as demonstrated by the Latvian example. The Polish minority in the Ukraine and the confused situation regarding national minorities in Romania and Hungary are other examples worthy of consideration. It is estimated that the Hungarian minority in Romania constitutes approximately 7 per cent of the total population (Ciasu, 1999), while the total ethnic Hungarian population outwith Hungary is thought to be approximately three million people (Grabbe, 2000:15). With significant minorities displaced in both states, the tightening of their mutual border and the possible application of visa requirements raises difficult political issues. It would involve the Hungarian government, likely to achieve full membership before Romania, having to insist on ethnic Hungarians possessing full travel documentation to cross the border into what would then be EU territory. This would be an unpopular decision with the Hungarian prime minister and his Romanian counterpart insistent that Hungary should simply not apply the Schengen visa requirements for Romanian citizens (EP, 1999). Senior Polish politicians, including the former foreign minister, Gemerek, have, in the past, made similar promises to their Ukrainian counterparts, despite the fact that the Ukraine is not even a part of the current enlargement process (Grabbe, op. cit.:15). However, pressure from the EU finally forced the Polish government to open discussions with the Ukraine, Russia and Belarus on ending visa-free travel (CEC, 2000:72), but, given the long-standing Polish attitude to such matters, the pressure may yet come to nothing. Dilemmas also exist for the Czech Republic and Slovakia, which operate a visa-free arrangement as one of the terms of the so-called 'Velvet Divorce'. This may be why the Commissioner with responsibility for Enlargement, Günther Verheugen, seemed to suggest that certain groups of states, perhaps the Czech Republic and Slovakia, would accede together: 'I would not rule out the possibility of more than one country joining at the same time on the basis of purely practical considerations' (CEC, 1999). Whether this means that the pace of enlargement will actually be dictated by the fastest state, given that it would be politically difficult to justify holding back the front-runner in order that they join together, has yet to be seen.

Verheugen, in his appointment hearing before the European Parliament, also seemed to contradict himself on the question of inter-state trade, a concern that is high on the agendas of the applicant states. They fear that, by creating new barriers between them and their immediate neighbours, such as the Ukraine and Belarus, the impact on trade will be deleterious.[5] Leaving the advantages and disadvantages of this argument aside (they are considered in detail in Grabbe, op. cit.), Verheugen's response seemed to be contradictory. At first, he appeared to be the champion of economic concerns, stating boldly that 'the European Union's borders cannot be allowed to become a border between rich and poor' and calling for 'an open border that does not prevent trade in goods and services' (EP, 1999a). He then failed to answer a direct question from one MEP on whether he preferred to 'keep to more restricted frontiers' (ibid.). However, later in the discussion he intimated that 'whether that is politically correct or not', the applicant states will have to apply the Schengen criteria fully, regardless of the potential consequences (ibid.). As with the earlier example of the Latvian border discussions, the position of the Commission seems to be one of trying to be all things to all men.

THE 1997 ASSESSMENTS

The 1997 surveys carried out by the Commission highlighted a series of trends that produce cause for concern in relation to the eventual move towards an external border managed and maintained by the applicant states of CEE. Most prominent amongst these was the significant lack of the equipment necessary to carry out such a task in the first place, with the Commission regularly highlighting 'institutional resource constraints and lack of new expertise' (CEC, 1997b). This is hardly surprising considering the low base from which most states started to operate. For example, at the start of 1990, the then Deputy Chief of Police in Romania estimated that his force had 'hardly any cars and only about one police officer per 2,000 of the population' (Gregory, 1994:88). On taking office, his counterpart within the Polish Ministry of the Interior found that the department was not even equipped with a fax machine, a necessity within a European system based on swift information transfer (ibid.:89). This situation is repeated across the region and makes the task of providing 'an equivalent level of control' (Schengen, 1990, Article 6(5)) more difficult. Given that the applicant states have had innumerable other financial commitments to meet in order to satisfy the accession criteria, achieving parity of border control with the existing member states may be beyond their limited resources. While the EU has made funding available through the Phare programme and twinning projects, it has not been of a volume sufficient to assist the applicants effectively in satisfying all elements of the *acquis*, as will be discussed more fully in the final section of the chapter.

Another key deficiency highlighted consistently in the 1997 Opinions concerns the porous nature of CEE borders. To place the matter into context, it should be noted that the potential impact on levels of immigration of relying on an external border operated by states such as Poland and Estonia is disputed, with the somewhat ambiguous statistics encouraging a polarised debate between two starkly different positions. On one side, there is what will be termed the minimalist position, which believes that, as 'the anticipated queues of economic migrants at the EU's gates have failed to materialise' in the past, such concerns are unfounded in the course of the current enlargement process (Wallace and Smith, 1994:440). Taking an opposing view, and occasionally utilising the same statistical predictions to bolster the case, the negative position maintains that it would be complacent to base the current assessment on previous enlargements: an argument with some truth, given the unique scale of the current enlargement process. Rather than believe that the 'worst is over', writers in this school warn that it would be exceptionally risky for the EU to underestimate the levels of illegal migration that may yet become apparent (Kolankiewicz, 1994:490).

Nevertheless, the belief that the level of border management offered by the applicant states will be below that expected of most of the existing members is a great concern in the Commission's Opinions. However, before undertaking a more detailed examination of two of the most prominent applicants, Poland and the Czech Republic, it should be remembered that similar criticism has been aimed at some of the existing member states, most notably those in the south. For example, Italy was criticised by the former German Minister of the Interior, Manfred Kanther, for breaking the 'spirit of Schengen' by allowing hundreds of illegal immigrants into Union territory (Statewatch, op. cit.). At least in the case of the applicant states from CEE, some degree of funding has been made available to assist in the task of managing the external border, with several projects authorised through Phare related to border management (see Phare, 1999). There is no question of the EU extending such funding to its southern states, or of broadening the concept of 'burden-sharing', which is currently reserved for instances of temporary protection of refugees (see Justice and Home Affairs, 1995), to the management of any part of its present external border (unattributable interview with author, 1999). Rather than consider co-financing, certain states, such as Germany and France, seem to be advocating an EU border police force. Such a commitment appears in the SPD's 2001 draft programme (see SPD, 2001) and was also raised in a speech by Lionel Jospin (2001). Such matters are viewed with scepticism by the UK and Barbara Roche, a former Home Office minister, warned that, before such a decision could be taken, 'the Government would want to examine the implications for ... its own frontier controls as well as any precedents for other areas of European Union competence' (cited in Wallace (2001)).

The Czech Republic, as well as demonstrating some of the general concerns raised about all of the applicant states, deserves more specific attention, most notably because of its close relationship with its former 'partner', Slovakia. As the Czech Republic guaranteed freedom of movement to all Slovaks as part of the 'Velvet Divorce', the assessment of its capabilities must also include some reference to the abilities of Slovakia, which was the only applicant to be rejected initially by the Commission for failing to meet the first section of the Copenhagen Criteria. However, there are a number of specific issues concerning the Czech application to be considered first. One initial assessment of the situation in the Czech Republic was of high crime rates and low morale amongst the police and security services (Gregory, op. cit.:90), although the former criticism fails to take into account the significant increase in the police clear-up rate by the time of the Commission's first review. In fact, with the exception of Prague, which saw a 15 per cent rise in its crime rate, the rest of the country experienced substantial increases in the success rates of police organisations, with 41 per cent of crimes solved in 1996 (Ministry of the Interior, 1997). On the other hand, the Commission did concur with Gregory's second point regarding staffing problems, reaching the conclusion that 'the main institutional problems lie in the field of resource constraints ... the lack of expertise with new legislation' (CEC, 1997). The Commission also reported that the Czech Republic was 'hampered by the lack of technical equipment to check machine-readable documents and the fact that its internal communication system is not compatible with international norms' (ibid.).

The Commission was not the only organisation carrying out an assessment of the situation within the Republic, as the Czech government organised its own 'Report on the Security Situation in the Czech Republic'. It boasted of the fact that 'the security situation was stabilised, the number of crimes stagnated' (Ministry of the Interior, op. cit.). However, this in itself is a negative and slightly defeatist claim that fails to realise that success in this area should be predicated on a fall in the crime figures, rather than maintenance of the status quo. In the case of migration flows and the permeability of the Czech border, there is not even that brief crumb of comfort to be found. While the crime figures across the country as a whole may have stabilised, in the area of migration the Report recorded 'a constant increase' (ibid.), with the number of detected illegal border crossings rising significantly. This has left the Czech Republic with the unwanted, and slightly alarming, reputation of a transit state, where 60 per cent of the migrants that enter the country leave again, illegally, within three days (ibid.). This seems to be a more extensive and critical self-assessment of the problems facing the Republic than the Commission's conclusion that the Czech Republic was handling the problems of border management in 'a structured manner' and that it should meet the Justice and Home Affairs *acquis* within a couple of years (CEC, 1997). Concerns over the issue of border control are even more serious when Slovakia is taken into account.

As was noted earlier, the Czech Republic guaranteed freedom of movement with its neighbour, as part of their separation agreement. If this political promise is honoured, it would mean that Slovakia, rather than the Czech Republic, will form part of the border management group to which the rest of the EU has, to some extent, delegated responsibility. Slovakia was the only state to receive a negative response from the Commission in the 1997 Opinions, which should have given some cause for concern. It was noted, for example, that 'the Migration office lack knowledge and experience' (CEC, 1997a:64) and that 2,000 illegal border crossings were registered in 1995. The Commission also raised a question mark over the reliability and honesty of certain judicial and police institutions, while the 'migration and border control systems will require considerable strengthening to cope with continuing pressure' (ibid.:65). Although these are not comments aimed exclusively at Slovakia, it must be remembered that, at the time, the EU was implicitly placing its trust in a state that it had just rejected for membership. However, it is worth noting that the specific reason for the rejection had little to do with border management and that Slovakia was subsequently brought into the enlargement negotiations, when the Union committed itself to full negotiations with all potential candidates (see EC, 1999 for details). By this stage, all political concerns over the role of the Slovakian secret services and the lack of respect for human rights within Slovakia (ibid.) seemed to have been resolved. However, the problem could re-emerge if the Czech Republic and Slovakia do not accede together. While there remains the alternative of making it a condition of membership that the Czech Republic revokes parts of its agreement with Slovakia, this would be likely to have serious political repercussions within the country.

Helmut Kohl, the former Chancellor of Germany, argued that it would be 'unacceptable to Germans if, in the long term, the Western frontier of Poland or of the Czech Republic were to become the Eastern frontier of the European Union' (Pfleuger, 1995:225). Understandably, it was in Germany's interests to ensure the accession of both Poland and the Czech Republic. Not only would they act as a buffer against the combined threats of economic migration and illegal immigration, but there were also, arguably, geopolitical reasons for supporting their candidature; for example, the shift of influence within the EU towards a 'Mittel Europa', with Germany at its axis. This helps to explain the financial commitment made at the time of the signing of a Re-

Admission Agreement with Poland in 1993, by which Poland received DM 120 million as compensation for agreeing to accept any illegal immigrants and asylum seekers that have entered German territory via Poland (Kolankiewicz, op. cit.:490). However, it does not of itself provide a satisfactory reason for including Poland within the membership of the EU, especially as the Schröder administration seems to have cooled its interest in enlargement in recent years. Nor does the initial enthusiasm expressed, most notably by the Kohl administration, give an accurate illustration of the progress that Poland was making. In fact, it is clear from the European Commission's Opinion on the country's application, which does not devote a great deal of time to matters relating to Justice and Home Affairs, that Poland is not the prime candidate that it was originally assumed to be.

In the brief summary of the Polish efforts within the field of Justice and Home Affairs, the Commission managed to highlight a number of practical problems that the Polish administration had, by 1997, failed to tackle. These included poor coordination between various police forces and the need for further steps to be taken to combat corruption. Most alarming, considering the priority given to the maintenance of the external border, was the assessment that 'border management is weak in some areas, principally due to poor facilities and lack of competent administrative structures' (CEC, 1997b:77). The Commission also highlighted a problem common to all of the applicants, namely the ability to maintain and defend the external border. In the case of Poland, considered to be more advanced in their preparations than some of the other applicants, the Commission was still forced to conclude that 'at present, the Polish government does not have effective control on the residence of migrants' (ibid.:67). While attempting to strike a positive note by flagging up a series of measures that were to be placed before the Polish Parliament, including a new aliens law, the Commission still asserted that 'parts of Poland's borders are vulnerable to exploitation by criminal gangs seeking to bring illegal immigrants to the West' (ibid.). Even the promise of 'good things to come' is hardly reassuring and the Commission was sceptical about the suggestion that future legislation would provide the panacea to all of Poland's internal security problems, thereby removing all doubts concerning its eventual accession. In fact, much of the Opinion reserved judgement on the actual working of such legislation until it has been put into practice: 'The capacity to handle asylum and migration questions is not yet assured since the implementing legislation is not yet fully in place' (ibid.:76).

All of this leaves open the question of whether the final element of the Copenhagen criteria – 'the ability to take on the obligations of membership' (EC, 1993) – involves simply ratification of the various measures prior to enlargement, or whether the existing member states will require some demonstration of their capacity to implement them in practice. Brief mention of the relevant debate is required before moving on to assess the progress made in the three years since the initial Opinions were published. Ambiguous comments, such as that from the Commission President: 'It will require a huge effort to ensure that the whole corpus of EU law … is adopted before accession and that it is implemented in practice' (Prodi, 1999) fail to answer the question conclusively. While Prodi states boldly that 'adoption' must take place prior to accession, he seems to imply that the issue of implementation could be postponed until after the benefits of membership have been conveyed. This would seem to be in line with the position taken in the Pre-Accession Pact on Organised Crime, signed in 1998 by the member states of the EU and all applicants, including Cyprus (Justice and Home Affairs Council, 1998). It suggested that, in order to complete the process and satisfy existing members, all the applicant countries had to do was ratify the list of documents provided, thereby reducing the Commission's supervisory role to that of a paper-chase. There was no indication given in the Pre-Accession Pact that the contents of the ratified text had to be seen to operate effectively in practice: all that is contained within Principle Two of the Pact is a list of Conventions that have to be ratified, including the European Convention on the Suppression of Terrorism (1977) and the European Convention on Extradition (1957). In contrast, the official position of the European Commission is that implementation must take place prior to accession. However, this would seem to be an impractical stance, with one official claiming that it would be 'unreasonable' to wait and see how things operated in practice before allowing accession to take place (unattributable interview with author, 1999).

PROGRESS: THE 1999 AND 2000 REPORTS AND BEYOND

The problem, noted in the 1997 Opinion on Poland, in which the Commission found itself unable to make any conclusive judgement on how certain measures would operate in practice, has continued to haunt them up to the present day. Both the 1999 and 2000 Reports lamented the lack of available information from the Polish government, with the preparations for the strengthening of the external border being a case in point. While the Commission accepted that increased resources had been made available, with a 24 per cent increase in the overall budget (CEC, 1999a:51), it was unable to reach a conclusion as to when the Polish border regime would meet the Schengen standards required. Leaving aside the question of targeting resources, to be covered in the final section of the chapter, it is alarming that, three years on, the Polish administration was still unable to provide the Commission with the necessary information. Inevitably, the Commission concluded that 'It is of concern that no overall plan exists which can quantify either the budget required and the number of years needed for achieving even the minimum standards currently expected of an external EU border' (ibid.). This pointed criticism has provoked a much-needed reaction within Poland, which finally produced an overall border strategy in June 2000 (CEC, 2000:72). As yet, the details of this strategy have not been placed in the public domain, nor has the Commission drawn any conclusions from it. While the mere existence of such a programme is a major step forward, Poland has yet to reach the stage that certain other applicants have attained.

As one example of Poland's lack of progress, the Commission was able to state that, in the case of Estonia, the border regime would meet the required standards by 2008, assuming that current progress was continued at the same rate (CEC, 1999b). Further, the 2000 Report offers a number of examples of actions taken in this area, such as the introduction of joint border patrols with Latvia and the abolition of visa-free travel for Russian citizens and does not attempt to alter the 1999 conclusion concerning the 2008 deadline (CEC, 2000a:73). As it stands, this would take Estonia considerably further than the political target that all of the 'first wave' applicants had set themselves of accession by 2003 at the latest. However, Poland was unable initially to attract even that commitment.[6] Significantly, the Commission, while unprepared to provide a timetable for the Czech Republic, as it did for Estonia, was able to state precisely how much more funding is required to bring their border control standards up to the level of the Schengen states. In the 1999 Report, the Commission concluded that this cost would be 68.6 million euro, although there was no accompanying evidence that such funding will be made available (CEC, 1999c:54). That no headline figure was suggested for Poland indicates that it is behind not only Estonia but also the Czech Republic in the process of equalling the Schengen standard.

The Commission also expressed concern that 'a high level of penetration into Poland continues' (CEC, 1999a:51), despite the significant reforms that had been carried out since 1997. In contrast, the Polish Ambassador to the EU argued that, over the same period, the number of illegal crossings from all neighbouring states had declined, with the exception of the Ukraine, for which a 38 per cent increase had been recorded (Truszcynski, 2000). There are two points of note arising from these differing interpretations. First, given that the Poland–Ukraine border is the only area where the Polish Border Guard seems not to have the problem under control, it is unlikely that the EU will agree to Polish insistence that some form of visa arrangement for Ukrainians be waived after accession. Nevertheless, the Polish administration became even more determined not to disrupt relations with the Ukraine after witnessing the problems caused by the imposition of new visa requirements for Russian and Belarusian citizens in 1998 (Oljasz, 1998). However, the failure to regulate its Ukrainian border efficiently over the last three years means that the EU is unlikely to compromise on this issue, as can be seen by the acceptance on the part of Poland to at least discuss the end of visa-free travel with the Ukraine. Second, while the Polish administration is keen to emphasise the positive nature of the figures, the Commission remains unconvinced that Poland has gained any form of control over migration flows within its territory. For example, in the 2000 Report, the Commission noted that 'external pressure on Poland's borders continues to increase' (CEC, 2000:72).

A similar criticism has been levelled at the Czech Republic, which has not managed to tackle its reputation as a 'state of transit' effectively. The Czech government's own figures confirm that, in 1998, 31.5 per cent of foreigners attempted an illegal crossing out of the Czech Republic on the same day that they arrived, while another quarter attempted to leave within five days (Ministry of the Interior, 1999). Unlike Poland, which claimed a drop in all figures relating to illegal border crossings – with the significant exception of that between Poland and Ukraine – the Czech Republic seems to be moving in the other direction. Thus, the number of illegal crossings rose from 26,339 to 44,672 between 1997 and 1998, while the shared border with Slovakia experienced a six-fold increase (CEC, 1999c:52). In fact, the 1999 Report mirrors its predecessor in a number of respects. The 'aliens legislation', which was under consideration in 1997, had still to be adopted by the time the Commission published its second Report in 1999 (ibid.:54). This suggested that such concerns were not high on the list of Czech legislative priorities. As a result, the Commission was unable to come to any conclusion on the detailed elements of visa policy. The issue of funding was also highlighted again, with the Commission demanding that 'words must be followed by deeds' (ibid.). This matter has been partially resolved by the introduction of the Act on the Residence of Aliens, which came into force in January 2000 and aligns the Czech Republic with EU legislation in this area. However, on the more general issue of border management, the 2000 Report continues the negative trend of its predecessors, stating that 'little actual progress has been registered in alignment and ... implementation (CEC, 2000b: 87).

A related concern arises from the procedures adopted by both states after they have successfully rejected an illegal immigrant at their borders. Readmission agreements are in place between both Poland and the Czech Republic, on the one hand, and the Schengen states, on the other, which involve the applicant states 'readmitting' any immigrant reaching Schengen territory via their state. However, the process has not been fully replicated to the east of the applicant states and Poland had, as of the 1999 Report, still not signed a readmission agreement with Russia (CEC, 1999a:51): furthermore, the situation had still not improved by the time of the 2000 Report. While an agreement had finally been made with the Ukraine, it remains to be seen whether this will hold in the face of the political reaction by the Ukrainian authorities to the imposition of a visa requirement. Therefore, while Poland has agreed to take all those 'readmitted' from the Schengen states, there is no process in place to move them on beyond its own borders. While this strategy is effective as far as the interests of the current member states are concerned, it will prove to be counter-productive after accession, when all those currently 'trapped' within the Polish buffer zone will be incorporated within the EU. In the case of the Czech Republic, while the only significant exceptions regarding readmission agreements are with Slovenia and France, there remains a problem of internal control. The Commission concluded that 'most third-country nationals "readmitted" by the Czech Republic at the request of member states are not deported from Czech territory under escort, but simply ordered to leave the country. As a result, most try to re-enter the Union illegally' (CEC, 1999c:51). Given that the Czech Republic actually seems to have the procedures in place to move the 'readmitted' to another destination, their failure to do so is all the more significant.

THE ROLE OF FINANCIAL ASSISTANCE TO CEE

The lack of progress made by the applicant states is important when it is recognised that the last three years' developments have taken place against a backdrop of increased financial support from the EU. Both through the Phare programme and Twinning projects (established in 1997), Justice and Home Affairs have finally been established as priority areas for pre-accession aid.[7] In the case of the latter, the promotion of internal security concerns is one of four major concerns, along with agriculture, structural funding and environmental protection. However, there remains a need for even greater effort from the existing member states. Although the Horizontal Programme on Justice and Home Affairs has been a welcome addition, total spending on Horizontal Programmes comes to less than 5 per cent of the overall Phare budget (EP, 1999b:10). While there is still a need to narrow the resource gap that exists in CEE, this does not necessarily have to be done by increasing the budgetary contribution of the member states constantly. The financial demands already placed on the existing member states are considerable: it is estimated that it would require a 60 per cent rise in the EU's budget to meet the cost of the eastern enlargement (Kolankiewicz, op. cit.:477). The political context makes such increases unlikely, particularly as the British, German and Dutch Governments are all determined to see their budgetary contributions cut, rather than raised further. It should also be remembered that 'throughout Phare's nine year existence, none of the participating countries have used one hundred per cent of their allotted sum' (Oljasz, 1998a:3). Arguably, the need to produce projects to absorb the financial support on offer was a contributory factor in Poland's failure to meet the requirements on fourteen separate undertakings in 1998: rather than utilise the available money better, ill-conceived projects were brought forward, with the end result that the country actually forfeited 34 million euro of its Phare allocation. None of this, however, disputes the calculation that the total Phare funding available only comes to 1.4 per cent of the total EU budget (Mayhew, 1998:140) and 'the conclusion must be that assistance has been marginal to the transition process' (ibid.: 132). Rather than call for ever larger sums to be spent, the European institutions and the applicant states should consider how to spend existing sums better.

The application of the 'burden sharing' concept to the management of the external border, which was accepted as an area of 'common interest' in Article K: 1(2) of the Treaty on European Union, would be in the logical interest of all member states in the long term. However, a senior Commission official declared that it was unlikely to be extended, given the deadlock that had developed around its application in the area of 'temporary protection' of refugees (unattributable interview with author, 1999). Another avenue worthy of further exploration would be the use of the Structural Funds for political, rather than economic concerns, as was suggested in a Home Office High Level Group Report on Organised Crime in 1998 (see Home Office, 1998). The current efforts of the EU to assist the Peace Process in Northern Ireland are a good example of this. In the wake of the 'Good Friday Peace Agreement', Irish government sources were able to claim that their ten border areas would continue to receive the maximum structural funding, despite no longer meeting the Objective 1 criteria (McManus and Kearney, 1998). This has been offered in addition to the Peace and Reconciliation Fund established by the EU in 1994 after the paramilitary ceasefire, which is worth approximately 300,000,000 ECU and sets the precedent of targeting structural finance for political, rather than economic, purposes (Murray Brown, 1998). At the Berlin European Council, a political decision was taken to extend such funding – officially entitled 'transitional support' – until 2006 (EC, 1999a). If such 'peace funding', with its strong cross-border element, was made more widely available, it would allow the existing member states to alleviate some of the problems that are likely to be faced by the new applicants. Although not related directly to border management, embryonic schemes such as this could provide a basis for the future. However, existing member states, such as Spain, with problems similar to those faced in Northern Ireland, might wish to receive some level of funding before it is offered as pre-accession aid to the candidate countries.

Training is another area where greater help could be offered in an attempt to redress one of the most obvious chinks in the armour of the applicant states, the lack of experienced personnel. This has been organised both at a regional level, through relevant programmes in the field of Justice and Home Affairs, such as Odysseus and Grotius, and also bilaterally. Principle Eleven of the Pre-Accession Pact states that 'training should be stimulated, with a view to obtaining a full understanding of organised crime' (Justice and Home Affairs, 1998). Baldwin (1995:479) accepts that there is a positive role for such programmes to play, although he warns that there is no 'substitute for experience'. However those that are most likely to need experience were not included in the training programmes, with senior management being the group targeted, rather than the ordinary policemen who have to put theory into practice. It should also be noted that the 1990 TREVI Programme of Action rejected the proposal, put forward by the then Director of the Netherlands Police Academy, Piet Van Reemen, for a European Police Academy, arguing that 'a simple coming together of curriculae or programmes would not be easy' (Hebenton, 1995:120). That may well be the case, but it would be of great help to the applicant states. The rejection of such an idea does not indicate the level of commitment that will be necessary to ensure that the accession countries are competent enough to provide 'efficient surveillance' of the external border of the EU.

CONCLUSION

Initially, and partially in response to the clear political pressure that was exerted by Helmut Kohl, Poland and the Czech Republic were considered the front-runners for accession. Unrealistic rhetorical flourishes suggested that membership could be on offer as early as the year 2000 (Oljasz, 1998b:1). While this is no longer the case, the insistence by both President Chirac, during a visit to Poland in May 2000 (Jelonkiewicz, 2000:1) and Günther Verheugen (Oljasz, 1999) that Poland should be ready to accede by 2003 still seems to fly in the face of the facts. It is clear that none of the present applicants, even those considered to be prime candidates, will by then be able to provide the 'effective surveillance' necessary to operate the external border of the Union. While the situation prior to the involvement of the applicant states from CEE, including the diplomatic stalemate between Spain and the United Kingdom, could hardly be described as encouraging, the transfer of such an important task to states that are ill-equipped to carry it out will only succeed in making a bad situation worse. The Commission's summary of the current situation in the Czech Republic has a resonance for all of the applicants in relation to the external border regime: 'legislative progress, the reinforcement of administrative capacities and border controls remain inadequate' (CEC, 1999c:51). Indeed, other applicants only bring further complications to the negotiating table, including a lack of resources and experienced personnel, and even lack of agreement as to where, precisely, the 'fortress' should be situated. Although the existing member states could adopt a more pro-active role, both in financing and training, they are unlikely to have the necessary political will to do so. Jacques Santer, the former Commission President, claimed that 'the Commission will not support any dilution of the *acquis communautaire* brought about in the name of enlargement' (Vega, op. cit.:27). However, by planning to build their 'fortress' on such weak foundations, that is exactly what the EU is doing.

NOTES

1. Article 7a is now Article 14 of the Consolidated Version of the Treaty that established the European Community.
2. Given the Common Travel Area, the same statements also apply to Irish policy.
3. Despite the legalities of the changes made at Amsterdam, the system is commonly still referred to by its original title.
4. This now covers all EU member states with the exception of the UK, Ireland and Denmark, which all have special protocols, attached to the Treaty of Amsterdam, that govern their relationship with the Schengen *acquis*.
5. In this context, the President of the Ukraine, Kuchma, spoke of the 'paper curtain' (Grabbe, 2000:17).
6. For more details on both Poland and Estonia's preparations for enlargement, see Brown (2000).
7. The Phare programme established a separate programme for Justice and Home Affairs in 1996 and renewed it again four years later.

REFERENCES

Anderson, Malcolm (1996), *Frontiers, Territory and State Formation in the Modern World*, Cambridge: Polity Press.

Baldwin, R. (1995), 'The Eastern Enlargement of the European Union', *European Economic Review*, **39** (3/4), 475–80.

Brown, D. (2000), 'The New Hurdle: The Prospects for Polish and Estonian Accession to Pillar III in a Post-Tampere European Union', *Perspectives in European Politics and Society*, **1** (1), available at http://raimro.catchword.com/vl=5466922/cl=27/nw=1/rpsv/cw/brill/15680258/v1n1/contp1-1.htm.

Castle, S. (2000), 'Belgium Offers Brief Amnesty for Immigrants', *The Independent*, 11 January.

Ciasu, Dumitru (1999), *Stabilising the Balkans Through European Union Enlargement: A Romanian View*, Paris: The Cicero Foundation.

CEC (Commission of the European Communities) (2000), *Commission Opinion on Poland's Application for Membership of the European Union*, Luxembourg: Office for Official Publications of the European Communities.

CEC (Commission of the European Communities) (2000a), *Commission Opinion on Estonia's Application for Membership of the European Union*, Luxembourg: Office for Official Publications of the European Communities.

CEC (Commission of the European Communities) (2000b), *Commission Opinion on the Czech Republic's Application for Membership of the European Union*, Luxembourg: Office for Official Publications of the European Communities.

CEC (Commission for the European Communities) (1999), 'Questionnaire of Gunther Verheugen, Commissioner Designate for Enlargement', Luxembourg: Office for Official Publications of the European Communities.

CEC (Commission for the European Communities) (1999a), *Regular Report from the Commission on the Poland's Progress Towards Accession*, Luxembourg: Office for Official Publications of the European Communities.

CEC (Commission for the European Communities) (1999b), *Regular Report from the Commission on Estonia's Progress Towards Accession*, Luxembourg: Office for Official Publications of the European Communities.

CEC (Commission for the European Communities) (1999c), *Regular Report from the Commission on Czech Republic's Progress Towards Accession*, Luxembourg: Office for Official Publications of the European Communities.

CEC (Commission of the European Communities) (1997), *Commission Opinion on the Czech Republic's Application for Membership of the European Union*, Luxembourg: Office for Official Publications of the European Communities.

CEC (Commission of the European Communities) (1997a), *Commission Opinion on Slovakia's Application for Membership of the European Union*, Luxembourg: Office for Official Publications of the European Communities.

CEC (Commission of the European Communities) (1997b), *Commission Opinion on Poland's Application for Membership of the European Union*, Luxembourg: Office for Official Publications of the European Communities.

Current Latvia (2000), 'Russia Appoints its Co-chairman to the Latvian–Russian Intergovernmental Commission', available at http://www.mfa.gov.lv/ENG/NEWS/CURRENT/Focus/F-9.htm.

Ersboll, N. (1994), 'The European Union – The Immediate Priorities', *International Affairs*, **70** (3), 413–9.

EC (European Council) (1999), 'Presidency Conclusions of the Helsinki European Council 10–11 December 1999', Luxembourg: Office for Official Publications of the European Communities.

EC (European Council) (1999a), 'Presidency Conclusions of the Berlin European Council 24-25 March 1999', Luxembourg: Office for Official Publications of the European Communities.

EC (European Council) (1993), 'Presidency Conclusions of the Copenhagen European Council', Luxembourg: Office for Official Publications of the European Communities.

EC (European Council) (1989), 'The Palma Document: Free Movement of Persons: A Report to the European Council by the Co-ordinators Group', Luxembourg: Office for the Official Publications of the European Communities.

EP (European Parliament) (1999), 'Romania and the Enlargement of the European Union', Luxembourg: Office for Official Publications of the European Communities.

EP (European Parliament) (1999a), 'Transcript of the Hearing of Gunther Verheugen, Commissioner Designate for Enlargement, before the Foreign Affairs Committee of the European Parliament', Luxembourg: Office for Official Publications of the European Communities.

EP (European Parliament) (1999b), 'Briefing on the Phare Programme and the Enlargement of the European Union', Luxembourg: Office for Official Publications of the European Communities.

Grabbe, H. (2000), 'The Sharp Edges of Europe: Security Implications of Extending European Union Border Policies Eastwards', Paris: Institute for Security Studies of the Western European Union.

Gregory, Frank (1994), 'Unprecedented Partnerships in Crime Control: Law Enforcement Issues and Linkages Between Eastern and Western Europe since 1989', in Malcolm Anderson (ed.), *Policing Across National Boundaries*, London: Pinter Publishing, pp. 85–102.

Hebenton, Bill (1995), *Policing Europe: Co-operation, Conflict and Control*, Basingstoke: St.Martin's Press.

Home Office (1998), 'High Level Group's Report on Organised Crime', London: HMSO.

House of Commons (2000), 'Parliamentary Written Answer by the Foreign Secretary, Robin Cook MP, Regarding the Agreement Between the United Kingdom and Spain Over the Nature of Gibraltar, on April 19th 2000', London: Hansard.

House of Commons (1999), 'Statement by the Prime Minister, Tony Blair MP, on the Outcome of the European Council at Tampere on 19th October 1999', London: Hansard.

House of Commons Select Committee on Foreign Affairs (2000), 'Third Report on Relations with the Russian Federation', London: Hansard.

Jelonkiewicz, W. (2000), 'Conflicting Signals', *Warsaw Voice*, 22 May.

Jospin, L. (2001), 'On the Future of an Enlarged Europe', speech by the Frech Prime Minister. available at http://www.premier-ministre-gouv.fr/en/p.cfm?ref=24924.

Justice and Home Affairs Council (1998), 'Pre-Accession Pact on Organised Crime Between the Member States of the European Union and the Applicant Countries of Central and Eastern Europe and Cyprus', Luxembourg: Office for Official Publications of the European Communities.

Justice and Home Affairs Council (1995), 'Council Resolution of the 25th September 1995 on Burden Sharing with Regard to the Admission and Residence of Displaced Persons on a Temporary Basis', Luxembourg: Office for Official Publications of the European Communities.

Kolankiewicz, G. (1994), 'Consensus and Competition in the Eastern Enlargement', *International Affairs*, **70** (3), 477-93.

Latvian Ministry of Foreign Affairs (2000), 'The State Secretary of the Ministry of Foreign Affairs Discusses the Issues of Russian-Latvian Relations with the Deputy Foreign Minister of Russia on the 16th November.2000', press release, available at http://www.mfa.gov.lv/esearch.htm.

Latvian Ministry of Foreign Affairs (1998), 'Latvia Continues Preparations for Unilateral Demarcation of Border with Russia', available at http://www.mfa.gov.lv/eng/news/current/cur260.htm.

McManus, J. and V. Kearney (1998), 'EU and Clinton Offer Cash Aid', *The Sunday Times*, 12 April.

Mayhew, Alan (1998), *Recreating Europe: The European Union's Policy Towards Central and Eastern Europe*, Cambridge: Cambridge University Press.

Ministry of the Interior (1999), 'Report on the Security Situation in the Czech Republic in 1998', available at http://www.mcvr.cz/dokumenty/bezp_si98/angl/1.

Ministry of the Interior (1997), 'Report on the Security Situation in the Czech Republic in 1996', available at http://www.mvcr.cz/bez_si96/anglicti/A_obash.htm.

Murray Brown, J. (1998), 'Brussels is Pressed for Peace Cash', *The Financial Times*, 17 September.

Nugent, N. (1992), 'The Deepening and Widening of the European Community: Recent Evolution, Maastricht and Beyond', *Journal of Common Market Studies*, **30** (3), 311–28.

O'Dowd, Liam (1996), 'Frontiers of Sovereignty in the New Europe' in Liam O'Dowd (ed.) *Borders, Nations and States*, Aldershot: Avebury Press, pp. 1–14.

O'Keefe, D. (1992), 'The Free Movement of Persons and the Single Market', *European Law Review*, **17**, 4–19.

Oljasz, T. (1999), 'All Dressed Up and No Place To Go', *Warsaw Voice*, 10 October.

Oljasz, T. (1998), 'Uproar at the Border', *Warsaw Voice*, 25 January .

Oljasz, T. (1998a), 'PHARE Fallout', *Warsaw Voice*, 7 June.

Oljasz, T. (1998b) 'Fischer Catches the Mood', *Warsaw Voice*, 8 November.

Pfleuger, F. (1995) 'Poland and the European Union', *Aussenpolitik*, **3**, pp. 225–31.

Phare, (1999), 'The Phare Justice and Home Affairs Programme: 1999', available at http://www.multi-benefit.org/program.

Prodi, R. (1999), 'Speech by the President of the European Commission at a dinner for the Presidents of the Parliaments of the Candidate Countries on November 30th 1999', Luxembourg: Office for Official Publications of the European Communities.

Schengen Convention (1990), Convention Applying the Schengen Agreement of 14th June 1985 between the Governments of the States of the Benelux Economic Union, the Federal Republic of Germany and the French Republic, on the Gradual Abolition of Checks at their Common Borders.

SDP (Social Democratic Party of Germany) (2001), 'Responsibility for Europe', Draft Keynote Proposal for the National Conference of the SDP, available at http://www.spd.de/english/.

Statewatch (1997), 'Schengen: Teething Problems and First Report', available at http://www.poptel.org.uk/cgi-bin/...ode=records&start=13783&lines=242.

Statewatch (1992), 'The UK and the Schengen Accord', available at http://www.poptel.org.uk/cgi-bin/...m&mode=records&start=94&lines=192.

Truszcynski, Jan (2000), 'Problems Concerning the Implementation of the Justice and Home Affairs Acquis by the Candidate Countries: A Polish View', Paris: The Cicero Foundation.

Vega, P. (1998), 'The Impact of the Third Pillar Acquis to the Future Accession Negotiations', Collegium, **11** (2–5), 27–32.

Wallace, H. and A. Smith (1994), 'The European Union: Towards A Policy for Europe', *International Affairs*, **70** (3), 429–43.

Wallace, Lord (2001), 'Speech by Lord Wallace of Saltaire, asking the House of Lords to take note of the report by the European Union Committee on Enlargement and European Union External frontier Controls', *Hansard*, **623**, cols 482–7.

6. EU Expansion to the East: The Problem of Agriculture

Hilary Ingham and Mike Ingham

INTRODUCTION

Agriculture was prominent on the European agenda when the Treaty of Rome (ToR) was signed and it has remained so ever since. In part this was assured by the fact that de Gaulle regarded the Common Agricultural Policy (CAP) as the instrument that would compensate France for any industrial trade losses that French membership of the Community might bring about. However, the agriculture question has always been fraught with difficulties. Thus, the aims of the CAP laid down in the ToR in 1957 (Articles 34–87) were contradictory and there were alternative methods of satisfying them; although this is unsurprising insofar as the new member states had previously operated very different farm policies. In consequence, the details of the CAP were not completed for over a decade, being agreed finally in 1970. On some measures the importance of agriculture has declined since the birth of the Community and there were only seven million farmers in the fifteen member states in 1998, accounting for less than 5 per cent of the Union's workforce (Eurostat, 1999).[1] Nonetheless, the sector received 40,944 million euro from the European Union (EU) budget in 2000, amounting to almost 44 per cent of the total (CEC, 2000), and 40 per cent of all European regulations still relate to the CAP (BCE, 2000). Such figures suggest that the farming lobby has gained a political weight within Europe that is far heavier than the absolute size of its constituency would merit, although the envisaged eastward expansion complicates this calculation considerably.

In this light, it is unsurprising that, more than forty years since the ToR, pressure is mounting for CAP reform. Internally, the Union faces unprecedented challenges if the eastern enlargement finally begins and the agricultural problem will again be central. Externally, the EU's stance towards agriculture is viewed as protectionist and against the spirit of the dynamic that has emerged towards the liberalisation of international trade. The USA, in particular, is keen for the EU to operate a more open access policy to its markets, including agriculture, and future World Trade Organization (WTO) meetings are unlikely to find the status quo in agricultural trade acceptable, despite the failure of the Seattle Round.[2]

Unreformed, the CAP is not viable in an enlarged Union and the EU began to map the future route its agricultural support mechanisms would take in Agenda 2000. However, the reforms enacted to date have been piecemeal and current support mechanisms would certainly not be sustainable in a Union of twenty five.[3] Likewise, while it is recognised within Central and Eastern Europe (CEE) that agricultural restructuring is likely to be necessary before any new members are admitted, the necessary reforms will not be popular in those applicant countries where farmers represent a powerful political lobby. Confronting the agricultural problems that both the Union and its aspirant members face can no longer be delayed. Notwithstanding the generally positive findings in the recent Regular Reports regarding overall progress towards accession (CEC, 2000a), the agriculture Chapters are contentious and remain open. This contribution focuses upon the problems that are likely to arise in the course of the discussions.

The evolution of agricultural support within the Union is examined first, with attention directed towards the main arguments for the initial establishment of a support system for agriculture and the changes in the CAP introduced by both the MacSharry reforms and Agenda 2000. This is followed by a review of the institutional framework that governed agricultural production under state socialism and the differences that existed between various countries in CEE. The historic contrasts in ownership and production patterns are important insofar as 'starting structures' have influenced the pace and nature of agricultural reform in the post-communist era. Following this retrospective analysis, the section also examines the extent to which the CEE countries have implemented successful agricultural reform programmes, with land reform and changes in agricultural employment being taken as the summary indicators. The section concludes with an evaluation of what remains to be achieved. There then follows an analysis of the extent and nature of the support that the EU has already made available to the post-communist applicants in order to aid agricultural reform and rural development. At the time of writing, all of the CEE-10 have won approval for their SAPARD (Special Accession Programme for Agriculture and Rural Development) proposals and the distribution of their planned expenditures provides a useful indication of the paths that their development programmes will follow in the medium term. The chapter concludes with a discussion of the options available to the EU in the face of the problems highlighted in the preceding discussion.

EUROPEAN AGRICULTURE AND THE CAP

Foundations of the CAP

The CAP was established in 1957 and has been one of the most contentious issues within Europe ever since. Its aims were to increase productivity, to provide a fair standard of living for the agricultural community, to assure the availability of supplies, to stabilise markets and to supply consumers at reasonable prices (Hill, 1984). The apparatus designed to achieve these objectives is composed of a complex mixture of instruments and regulations that cover *inter alia* trade controls, price support mechanisms, income transfers, production subsidies, health and environmental regulations and labelling standards. In addition, agriculture has its own unit of currency, the green ECU. The fundamental weakness with the system introduced initially was that the guarantee prices were set well above world levels, resulting in the then European Community having to purchase and store costly stocks. At its height in 1978, the CAP consumed 78.4 per cent of the Community's budget (Williams, 1994:82). While it is indisputable that the policy achieved security of food supplies for its members, the cost was borne by the consumer in terms of higher prices.[4] Furthermore, the CAP was formulated by the original six and favoured temperate climate, northern products. The accession of Spain, Portugal and Greece meant that the CAP was no longer an all-embracing set of measures and much Mediterranean produce either received only limited support or was excluded altogether.

Pressure for Change

Pressure for reform did not just emanate from within the Union. The subsidies to farmers, coupled with the high tariffs confronting potential exporters to the single market, were viewed by many, in particular the USA, to be overly protectionist and anti-competitive. Indeed, WTO deliberations regarding the liberalisation of trade in fifteen commodity groups, including agricultural produce, commenced in Uruguay in November 1982. However, the subject matter proved sufficiently contentious that the Round was not launched formally until September 1986, when ministers accepted an agenda covering the entire 1947 General Agreement on Tariffs and Trade founding articles, making it the biggest trade discussion ever. The Round was scheduled to end in December 1990, but there was no consensus on how to reform agricultural trade, particularly between the Community and the USA, with the latter refusing to sign any agreement that did not cover the sector and the talks had to be extended.

At the outset of the deliberations, the USA demanded the elimination of all subsidies that distorted agricultural trade within ten years. This covered not only the elimination of all import barriers, monetary or other, but also changes in policies for individual commodities to permit the agreed phasing-out of government aid and the use of an aggregate measure that would both establish initial levels of support and permit the monitoring of progress towards their eventual elimination. In November 1992, Europe and the USA struck an informal deal on agriculture that became known as the 'Blair House Accord', which contained four critical elements that were to be incorporated into the CAP during the period 1993 to 1999. First, there was a commitment to tariffy all existing border measures and to reduce tariff levels by 36 per cent.[5] Second, there was an agreement to reduce internal protection measures by one-fifth. Third, there was a commitment to reduce export subsidies and subsidised export volumes by 36 and 21 per cent, respectively. Finally, the so-called 'Peace Agreement' debarred both the EU and the USA from taking unilateral trade action over each other's farm policies. The Round finally ended in April 1994 and the concessions made by the EU led to the MacSharry Reforms.

The MacSharry Reforms

While the MacSharry reforms reduced, but did not eliminate, basic price support mechanisms, the measures adopted introduced inconsistencies into the system.[6] For example, cereal and oilseed guarantee prices were reduced substantially whereas those for milk and sugar remain very high. The policy change benefited consumers (assuming that price cuts were passed on), lowered the costs to the EU of the disposal of excess production, but reduced the producer surpluses enjoyed by European farmers. To compensate for the latter welfare losses, the EU proposed direct income support for farmers, provided that they adhered to certain restrictions regarding input use.[7] The MacSharry reforms mean that support for agriculture within the EU has become more 'de-coupled' from production levels and that the incentive for farmers to over-produce has diminished.[8] Also, there were additional measures that related to the retirement of farmers and to forestry and agro-environmental issues, all areas in which there had been little enthusiasm for reform previously.

Agenda 2000

Notwithstanding the realignment of CAP payments away from production-based indicators brought about by the MacSharry reforms, many felt that they had still not gone far enough. In particular, concerns were expressed about quality, both of the agricultural products themselves and of the environments in which they were produced. The common opinion was that farmers should be regarded as the guardians of the land they utilised and that agriculture should be integrated more closely with the rural economies in which it is practised. Simultaneously, negotiations with CEE applicant countries were proceeding and the Commission produced a strategy paper in 1995 outlining how EU agriculture should develop in the face of eastward enlargement, as it was abundantly clear that the CAP would then be inoperable if unreformed (CEC, 1995).

Given the issues left open by MacSharry, the true foundations of Agenda 2000 were laid in the Buckwell Report (CEC, 1996). This noted that 'Society can therefore afford to become more concerned with the way its food is produced, the quality and variety of that food, the environmental effects of food production systems and the balanced development of rural areas' (ibid.). On the issue of enlargement, the report noted that there would be a strong incentive for CEE farmers to boost their production levels under the current schedule of CAP payments.[9] If this were to happen, it would simply increase EU surpluses, given the global trend towards the abolition of export subsidies. Furthermore, such a move would inflate land values and exacerbate the problems associated with the rationalisation of farm holdings. One way to avoid this outcome would be to apply strict supply controls in the CEE countries, although these would serve merely as an incentive for their farmers to increase production as soon as possible in order to be able to lay claim to larger quotas at the initial bargaining table (ibid.).

Buckwell recommended a Common Agricultural and Rural Policy for Europe, the objective of which would be 'to ensure an economically efficient and environmentally sustainable agriculture and to stimulate the integrated development of the Union's rural areas' (ibid.). The proposed strategy consisted of four main elements: market stabilisation measures to protect those commodities at risk from uncontrollable market fluctuations; environmental and landscape payments to guard against damage and the depletion of rural areas and to foster their cultural and social fabric; rural development incentives to promote agriculture and stimulate non-agricultural opportunities; and transition adjustment assistance that would cushion the move from a purely agricultural policy (CAP) towards a rural one. There is, however, one omission from this list: the report did not recommend any extension of direct income support for farmers. What it did do was champion diversification into areas such as processing, the use of farm equipment for non-agricultural activities (agri-tourism), off-farm usage of farm equipment and non-farm enterprise. For the CEE countries, the report noted that it was not feasible to shield the farming sector behind a wall of price support while out-migration from the rural areas occurred.[10] Instead, it recommended that farmers in the region be assisted to promote local development via infrastructure and human capital improvements and small and medium sized enterprise growth. Village renewal schemes and the development of marketing systems were also viewed as important elements of rural development.

In its final form, Agenda 2000 did promote rural as opposed to purely agricultural development: 'the reformed CAP is a step towards supporting the broader rural economy rather than agricultural production, and ensures that farmers are rewarded not only for what they produce but also for their general contribution to society' (CEC, 1999). The programme included further moves away from price support towards direct payments to farmers and, in this respect, it can be regarded as an extension of the MacSharry reforms.[11] The cuts in support prices varied in timing and magnitude; for example, those for cereals and beef commenced in 2000, while those for dairy products were not scheduled to be introduced until 2005 (OECD, 2000). The impact of the reforms depends on two factors: the way in which they are implemented (this is the prerogative of the Commission and the European Council) and how they affect the decision-making of the various agents involved, particularly the producers. The OECD (ibid.:32–3) provided an analysis of projected outcomes under Agenda 2000 vis-à-vis those that would have occurred had the CAP continued along the lines of the 1992 reforms. Its calculations reveal that the former yield smaller short-term excess production of cereals and beef and, from 2005, smaller surpluses for dairy products. This means that there is less reliance on subsidised exports and public stocks for most commodities than was the case prior to 1995.[12]

Two other facets of Agenda 2000 merit attention. First, it recognised explicitly that although consumers within the Union wish to have agricultural produce that is competitively priced, they are increasingly concerned with the issue of food safety. In particular, it noted the public's increasing awareness of environmental issues and the fact that, historically, the CAPs system of price supports encouraged extensive farming methods that cause environmental degradation. Second, Agenda 2000 introduced two new financial instruments into the EU budget, earmarked to help the pre-accession countries prepare for membership, and these will be discussed in more detail below.

The Future

Despite the failure of the WTO Seattle Round at the end of 1999, discussions are proceeding regarding further liberalisation of agricultural trade. At present, the 'blue box' clause allows countries to exempt domestic support payments from reduction commitments if they are linked to programmes that limited production. This is likely to become contentious in the near future as the US, following the passage of the FAIR (Federal Agriculture Improvement and Reform) Act in 1996, has placed its payments in the 'green box' – minimal distortions of production and trade – leaving the EU member states, along with Iceland, Norway and Slovakia, as the only countries using such exemptions (Tangermann, 1999). Two solutions to this looming problem are possible. One would require the EU to implement a phased reduction in its compensation payments, although the reaction of farmers to any such move would undoubtedly be hostile, particularly if this were forced upon Europe by the WTO (ibid.). Alternatively, the EU could de-couple its payments from production. While this would be relatively painless for crop production, major changes would be required with respect to livestock payments. Nevertheless, in an October 1999 speech regarding the Millennium Round, the Commissioner for Agriculture stated that 'the Agenda 2000 reforms will form the basis of our negotiating position' and that 'the continuation ... of the blue and green boxes is very important for the Community' (Fischler, 1999). At the same time, the Commission also regards it as important that non-trade issues, such as the multi-functional role of agriculture, food safety and quality and animal welfare, be addressed.

AGRICULTURE IN CEE

The Historical Perspective

Under state socialism, agricultural production took place in three distinctly different types of enterprises. The collective was the dominant organisational form in numerical terms throughout much of the region, with Poland and Slovenia being the only countries where such farms were of little or no importance. These enterprises were formed when individual farmers 'pooled' their assets – land and non-land – ostensibly in order to gain economies of scale, increase agricultural productivity and reduce inequalities in rural incomes (Meurs, 1999:4). The nature of state control over the collectivised farms varied enormously; in some cases they were exploited ruthlessly to provide a surplus for the purposes of central government whereas, in others, more decision-making autonomy was left in the hands of the farm management (ibid.).[13] Notwithstanding the numerical importance of the collectives, the vast majority of agricultural output in most CEE countries was produced on state farms. These tended to be larger than the collectives and were granted privileged access to agricultural vehicles and other inputs, such as fertiliser.[14] Within these enterprises, production took place on state-owned land with state-owned assets. Finally, in Poland and Slovenia the authorities failed to implement a collectivisation policy successfully and a significant private farm sector operated throughout the communist period. However, while numerous, these farms tended to be very small, often resembling little more than a household plot.

Agricultural production within CEE was characterised by an excessive use of all factors of production, with the result that both labour and capital productivity were low. Furthermore, part-time farming and off-farm activities were important phenomena. Workers from the large state farms were allowed to earn extra income from their domestic plots and, in addition, many of the large farms were engaged in non-farm activities. This strategy provided employment for workers during seasons with low agricultural labour needs and also allowed the farm to fulfil its role as an economic, social and political organisation. The economic activities undertaken ranged from food processing to construction, while their social role included functions such as the maintenance of schools and medical centres.

The Impacts of Transformation

Price and trade liberalisation, coupled with cuts in subsidies to agriculture, caused a decline in the demand for agricultural labour. However, agricultural wages fell considerably more than the price of other inputs, which provided a counter-incentive for the adoption of more labour-intensive farming practices (Macours and Swinnen, 1998).[15] On the other hand, an inverse relationship between growth and the share of agriculture in total employment is a stylised fact of economic development. Part of the decline in farm employment as growth proceeds derives from a change in comparative advantage towards other sectors of activity and part from the introduction of labour-saving technology in agriculture.

In the event, adjustments in agricultural labour markets have been far from uniform across CEE countries. While the Czech Republic, Estonia, Hungary and Slovenia witnessed employment declines of at least 30 per cent over the period 1990 to 1997, the size of the agricultural workforces in Bulgaria, Lithuania and Romania increased, as shown in Table 6.1. Thus, despite the fact that most economies within the region exhibited impressive growth rates in the second half of the 1990s, the evidence suggests that it did not draw on labour from the agricultural sector. Therefore, for some countries within CEE, agriculture has become a buffer zone. On the positive side, the sector has provided some income and food and has absorbed workers made redundant in other sectors, but it has led to a subsistence farming culture that is impeding further adjustment. Nonetheless, for many farmers in CEE, non-farm sources of support (both earned and transfer payments) remain important, particularly in Poland and Slovenia where family farms predominate.

Table 6.1 Trends in CEE agricultural employment

	1980	1990	1997	% change 1980–90	% change 1990–97
Bulgaria					
N ('000)	1 039	735	745	-29.2	1.3
Share (%)	23.8	17.9	23.3	-24.8	30.2
Czech Republic					
N ('000)	517	514	201	-0.6	-60.9
Share (%)	10.2	9.6	4.3	-5.0	-55.2
Estonia					
N ('000)	143	100	51	-30.1	-49.5
Share (%)	16.3	12.0	8.0	-26.4	-33.3
Hungary					
N ('000)	-	906	295	-	-68.2
Share (%)	-	17.9	8.5	-	-54.7
Latvia					
N ('000)	-	-	183	-	-
Share (%)	-	15.5	16.6	-	7.1
Lithuania					
N ('000)	394	344	348	-12.7	1.2
Share (%)	22.2	17.8	20.8	-19.6	16.9
Poland					
N ('000)	5 304	4 330	3 983	-18.4	-8.0
Share (%)	30.6	26.6	25.8	-13.1	-3.0
Romania					
N ('000)	3 023	3 055	3 322	1.1	8.7
Share (%)	28.6	28.2	39.7	-1.3	40.9
Slovakia					
N ('000)	331	294	143	-11.1	-51.4
Share (%)	14.6	12.0	8.9	-17.8	-25.8
Slovenia					
N ('000)	87	72	54	-17.4	-24.7
Share (%)	-9.7	8.4	5.6	-13.4	-33.3

Source: Adapted from OECD (1999:44).

Considerable differences also exist in the sources of farm labour. In Poland and Slovenia, the family accounts for over 80 per cent of total labour input whereas the figure for Slovakia is less than 15 per cent (OECD, 1999:43). Also, while it is sometimes noted that young people have left the rural areas during the transition era, the available data do not suggest that a dramatic ageing of the agricultural workforce has occurred (ibid.). Employment on large-scale farms has declined more rapidly than on family farms. In most countries, the former state farms have either been liquidated or have shed labour, whereas little adjustment has taken place on the family enterprises, which rely heavily on unpaid labour. This has given rise to considerable regional variations within countries: in Poland, for example, the reductions in labour input in the northern and western parts of the country, where the large state farms were located, far exceed those witnessed in the east, where most small-scale family farms are to be found.[16]

The history of land ownership represents a key determinant of the path that reform has taken (Swinnen, 1999), with the organisational form of the farming sector differing significantly across countries at the start of the transition process, as shown in Table 6.2.[17] In the main, collective and cooperative farms dominated, although their share of total farmland varied from 80 per cent in Hungary to only 4 per cent in Poland. Likewise, more than 40 per cent of farms in Latvia were classified as state-owned, whereas the corresponding figure in Slovenia was only 8 per cent. Major changes have taken place since 1989 and the state farms have collapsed in all countries, except Romania and Slovakia, while all countries have witnessed declines in their collective and cooperative sectors. With the exception of the Czech Republic and Slovakia, individual farms now dominate agricultural landholdings. While new corporate farms have begun to appear, they still only account for one-third of farmland in the Czech Republic, Estonia and Lithuania, where they are most significant.

Reference to Table 6.3 indicates that the chosen path towards land reform has also differed, both by country and by organisational form, although the desire to move agricultural assets – both land and non-land – from public to private ownership has been central everywhere. In essence this means that land reform in CEE is rightly to be regarded as part of the overall privatisation process and, as such, it has raised important issues regarding the resultant distribution of property rights: only when individuals possess full rights to land can they be regarded as true owners. Swinnen and Mathijs (1997) note that property rights can be characterised by ownership, use, usufruct (the right to income) and alienation (the right to transact, i.e. to sell). Considering first the collective farms, the individual farmers retained their ownership rights (i.e. a formal title to their land) throughout the communist

Table 6.2 Distribution of farmland by organisational form in CEE (%)

	Collective/ Cooperative 1998 (pre-1990)	State 1998 (pre-1990)	Individual 1998 (pre-1990)	New Corporate 1998
Bulgaria	42	6	52	-
	(58)	(29)	(13)	
Czech Republic	43	2	23	32
	(61)	(38)	(-)	
Estonia	-	-	63	37
	(57)	(37)	(6)	
Hungary	28	4	54	14
	(80)	(14)	(6)	
Latvia	-	1	95	5
	(54)	(41)	(5)	
Lithuania	-	-	67	33
	(61)	(30)	(9)	
Poland	3	7	82	8
	(4)	(19)	(77)	
Romania	12	21	67	-
	(59)	(29)	(12)	
Slovakia	60	15	5	20
	(69)	(26)	(5)	
Slovenia	-	4	96	-
	(-)	(8)	(92)	

Source: Adapted from OECD (1999:67).

period; what they did not have was the right to sell; although they sometimes enjoyed the right to the income from the land.[18] As individuals retained ownership, restitution was the only politically acceptable solution, even though it has been shown that it is not the most efficient means of privatisation (ibid.).[19] The same argument does not hold for the other assets of the collective farms, as those that the original members brought with them were replaced by newer equipment through time and this collective property has been sold in the majority of cases.

Nevertheless, land restitution raises some interesting issues. First, physical reclamation of the same plot of land was sometimes impossible; for example,

Table 6.3 Average farm sizes by organisational form in CEE (hectares)

	Collective/ Cooperative 1998 (pre-1990)	State 1998 (pre-1990)	Individual 1998 (pre-1990)	New Corporate 1998
Bulgaria	637	735	1.4	-
	(4 000)	(1 615)	(0.4)	
Czech Republic	1 447	521	34.0	690
	(2 578)	(9 443)	(5.0)	
Estonia	-	-	19.8	449
	(4 060)	(4 206)	(0.2)	
Hungary	833	7 779	3.0	204
	(4 179)	(7 138)	(2.0)	
Latvia	-	340	23.6	309
	(5 980)	(6 532)	(0.4)	
Lithuania	-	-	7.6	310
	(2 380)	(1 880)	(0.5)	
Poland	222	620	7.0	333
	(335)	(3 140)	(6.6)	
Romania	451	3 657	2.7	-
	(2 374)	(5 001)	(0.5)	
Slovakia	1 509	3 056	7.7	1 191
	(2 667)	(5 186)	(0.3)	
Slovenia	-	371	4.8	-
	(-)	(470)	(3.2)	

Source: Adapted from OECD (1999:67).

when a factory or a road had been built on the site and, in such cases, individuals were offered an 'equivalent' plot. However, when this occurred, the individual retained the legal title to the original holding and the use and usufruct rights of the substitute; that is, incomplete rights over two parcels of land. Second, CEE countries have been unwilling, in general, to restitute to foreigners, despite the fact that the pursuit of such a strategy might bring an inflow of cash and expertise into their farming sectors.[20] Finally, Romania's adopted policy was driven more by distributional (i.e. equity) than efficiency concerns and a maximum of 10 hectares was restituted, with the remainder being allocated to farm workers.

An alternative policy stance has been adopted for the state farms because of the different ownership structure of the land prior to the communist era. State farmland throughout the region was owned previously by 'foreigners, religious institutions, and large (feudal) landowners, state-owned or [was] unusable' (Swinnen, op. cit.:653). In view of this, there has been little political pressure for restitution and the land has tended to be leased prior to sale. For example, the state farms in Poland were located in the north and the west of the country on land that was part of Germany prior to 1945. Restitution would have involved giving land to foreigners, so selling the land was more expedient politically. In contrast, nationals formerly owned state farmland in Slovenia, so this was one country that did embark upon a policy of restitution.[21]

While a detailed evaluation of each country's land reform policy is beyond the scope of this contribution, note can be made of certain general implementation problems that have arisen.[22] De Janvry (1981) and Hayami (1991) both argue that the ruling class hinder land reform because they are resistant to change, but are prepared to tolerate limited restructuring if it is consistent with their retention of political dominance. From this perspective, land reforms can be expected to be sufficient only to achieve the political objectives of the ruling authorities (Swinnen, op. cit.). Under this scenario, reform packages will typically be characterised by a complex set of rules and insufficient means of execution. Although it may seem paradoxical to apply such Marxist analysis to the countries in transition, examples abound of land reform programmes that are both complex and uncertain, insofar as there are few details on how to implement the relevant laws. Also, much discretion has been granted to local governments and farm managements under the policies that have been adopted (ibid.:656). Furthermore, the return of post-communist governments in many countries has resulted in new laws and regulations that, in general, have reduced the impact of de-collectivisation and no CEE country can yet be regarded as having a fully functioning market in land.

Outstanding problems

The above discussion makes clear that land reform procedures throughout CEE are far from complete and that, as a result, the farm structure remains sub-optimal. Quite simply, there are too many farmers operating on plots that are too small. As Figure 6.1 indicates, there are over 18.5 million farmers in the region, compared with just over 7 million in the EU (Eurostat, op. cit.). Figure 6.2 puts these statistics into perspective and confirms that agriculture's share of total employment in CEE is radically different from that in the EU.[23] Only the Czech Republic, Hungary and Slovakia have less than 10 per cent of their workforces employed in the sector, while in Romania the figure is in excess of 40 per cent.[24] Predictably, much of this labour is unproductive, with BCE (op. cit.) citing a 1998 EU report on the ten front-running applicant countries that found that, if productivity were raised to only half of that prevailing in the EU, four in ten farmers would be redundant. Ideally, structural adjustment should see labour move from agriculture to more productive activities, but this has not been happening. The impediments to mobility include poor educational achievements, lack of transport infrastructure, poorly developed housing markets and a marked lack of desire on the part of rural residents to move to urban areas.

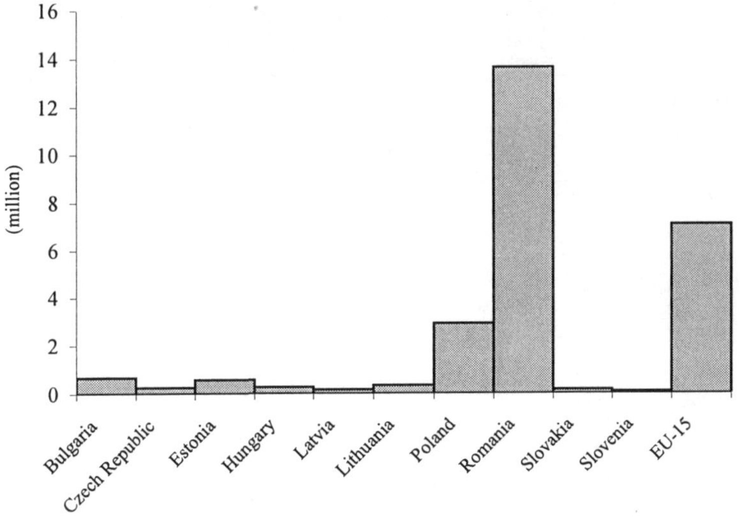

Source: EU data from Eurostat (1999), CEE data supplied by the OECD.

Figure 6.1 Agricultural employment in CEE and the EU-15

Severe as the labour surplus may be, CEE agriculture also faces other hurdles in its fight to become more competitive. First, it has a highly underdeveloped agri-business sector that is likely to be hit hard by accession; not only will it have to cope with EU legislation, higher guaranteed farm prices will increase its input costs. Second, farmers will have to change their underdeveloped agri-business sector that is likely to be hard hit by accession; not only will it have to cope with EU legislation, higher guaranteed farm prices will increase its input costs. Second, farmers will have to change their farming practices to satisfy health and safety legislation within a Union that is increasingly concerned with food safety. In addition, poor sanitary

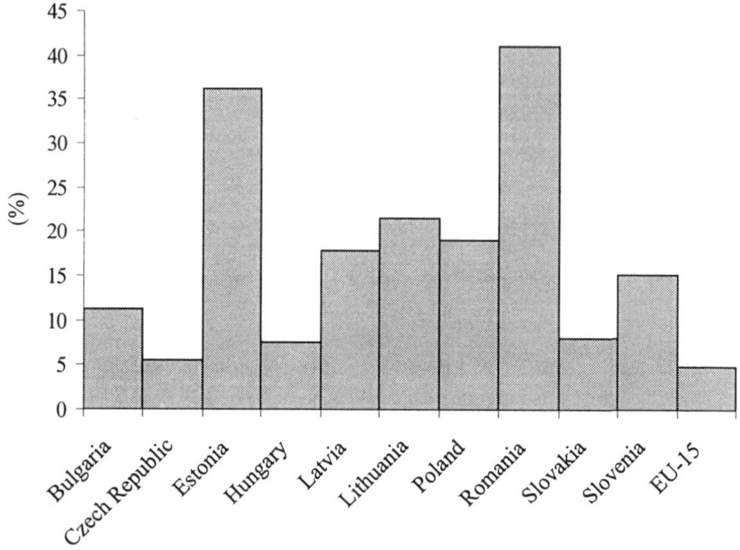

Source: As for Figure 6.1.

Figure 6.2 Employment in agriculture (% of total) in CEE and the EU-15

standards within the rural regions act as a brake on development and diversification: for example, in a recent Commission report on Polish agriculture, it was noted that half of the rural population have their drinking water supplied by wells, two-thirds of which do not meet required standards due to nitrate and bacterial contamination. Also, few villages have sewage systems and 74 per cent of total waste from farm holdings, both human and animal, remains entirely untreated and goes directly onto the land (CEC, 1998).

EU POLICY STANCE

Pre-Accession

Since the start of the transition process, the EU, in common with other major agencies, has been advancing funds to CEE to aid restructuring, primarily, although not exclusively, through the Phare programme.[25] The clearest statement of the EU's position on assistance to the pre-accession states was laid down in Agenda 2000. Between 2000 and 2006, the EU budget contains 21.8 billion euro earmarked for pre-accession aid, a fund that is available to all applicant countries until they accede to full membership. This will be delivered under three programmes, of which the long-running Phare is one, although it has now been more narrowly focused towards two specific priorities. First, 30 per cent of its monies are to be directed to institution building, including the adaptation and strengthening of democratic institutions, public administration and organisations that have the responsibility for implementing and enforcing Community legislation. The remainder of Phare finance will be channelled towards investment support. In addition, two new instruments have been introduced.[26] The Instrument for Structural Policies for Pre-Accession (ISPA) finances major environmental and transport infrastructure developments from its annual budget of 1,058 million euro. It is designed to operate in a manner akin to the Structural Funds, insofar as national governments must provide one-quarter of the funds for a project although, in exceptional circumstances, ISPA will fund up to a maximum of 85 per cent of the cost. However, for agriculture, the most important of the new instruments is the Special Accession Programme for Agriculture and Rural Development (SAPARD), which provides 520 million euro per year to aid the implementation of the *acquis communautaire* in the sector and to promote the sustainable development of rural areas.[27]

SAPARD represents a radical new approach to pre-accession aid since the candidate countries themselves are responsible for the management of the projects, from selection through to final payment (CEC, 2000b). However, the SAPARD agencies in each of the pre-accession states are charged with putting three priorities above all else: improving market efficiency, quality and health standards; maintaining and creating jobs; and the furtherance of environmental protection. The Commission envisages that the programme will generate a large number of relatively small-scale investment projects, each tailored to the specific needs of a particular rural locality. As with ISPA, SAPARD operates on a co-financing basis, with the proportion of EU funding capped at a maximum of 75 per cent for any one undertaking. The scheme encourages private sector participation although such partners must contribute at least half of the required total funding.

With one exception, all candidate countries had their initial SAPARD plans endorsed by the STAR committee at its meeting in September–October 2000, with approval for Romania's proposals being delayed until November of the same year.[28] Proposed expenditure by the candidate countries falls under three heads: 'efficiency of the agri-business sector', 'rural conditions' and 'human capital/technical assistance', with the allocations to them within each country being presented in Table 6.4. Without exception, the candidate

Table 6.4 SAPARD allocations 2000–06

	Efficiency of agri-food sector (%)	Rural conditions (%)	Human capital/ technical assistance (%)	Total (million euro per annum, constant 2000 prices)
Bulgaria	70.4	19.5	10.1	53 026
Czech Republic	60.5	34.3	3.1	22 444
Estonia	60.1	36.0	3.9	12 347
Hungary	56.2	40.7	2.8	38 173
Latvia	54.0	40.0	6.0	22 226
Lithuania	68.0	29.0	4.0	30 345
Poland	54.6	40.5	4.8	171 603
Romania	19.0	68.9	10.1	153 243*
Slovakia	57.5	35.5	5.0	18 606
Slovenia	75.0	24.0	1.0	6 447

Notes: * 2% of Romania's funds are not allocated to any of the three heads detailed above.

Source: Derived from CEC (2000c, d, e, f).

countries have targeted the agri-business sector as their priority area and it is scheduled to receive more than half of the total funding in each. Indeed, Slovenia has allocated three-quarters of the total monies available to it. Nevertheless, the allocation to rural areas varies considerably: Hungary, Latvia and Poland have all devoted more than 40 per cent of their funds to this purpose, whereas the corresponding figure for Bulgaria is less than one-fifth.

All of the pre-accession states plan to devote very little of their available aid to human capital/technical assistance; only Bulgaria and Romania have allocated more than 10 per cent of their total funding to this head, while the figure is as low as 1 per cent in Slovenia. This distribution of funds is puzzling, as rural inhabitants in the region tend to be among the most poorly educated sections of the population. In Poland, for example, only 2 per cent of students in institutions of higher education come from the rural areas and 58 per cent of farmers have no secondary-level education at all, nor any formal agricultural training (CEC, 1998:61). It is hard to see how rural economic diversification can be promoted if the countries are unwilling to channel funds towards the enhancement of human capital, particularly as the evidence suggests that this is complementary to physical capital investment (Kilkenny, 1998).

Post Accession

Before any CEE countries accede to the EU, serious consideration will have to be given to their eligibility for funding under the mainstream programmes, in particular the CAP. The EU calculated that the cost of admitting the ten front running countries to the CAP would be 12 billion ECU (CEC, 1996).[29] However, the CAP is changing and by the time of the first eastwards expansion, price supports will have fallen further and direct income payments will have become a more important element of farmers' remuneration packages. Thus, direct payments constituted 60 per cent of the agricultural budget in 1997 and this is projected to rise to 67 per cent by 2006. As such, access to direct payments represent the major issue of contention for CEE farmers (Buckwell and Tangermann, 1999).

The position of the EU vis-à-vis direct income payments to CEE farmers is quite clear: they will not be eligible, since the monies represent compensation to EU farmers for the injury caused by the reduction in price support levels and, as CEE farmers never enjoyed these guaranteed minimum prices, there is nothing to compensate them for. This line of argument can be challenged on two grounds. First, the EU's system of payments does not conform to theoretical models of compensation, since it does not relate payment to the severity of the injury suffered. Furthermore, there are no plans to phase out the payments. Second, it could be argued that Austria, Finland and Sweden, all of which entered the EU after 1992, when the reduction in price support began, should also be excluded. It also needs to be recognised that the extension of direct payments to CEE farmers would have distributional effects. In particular, relative land values would change, depending upon the nature of production, as some farmers would receive large payments while others would receive very little.[30] At the same time, the landless and the rural poor would get nothing (ibid.).

On the other hand, refusal to extend direct payments to CEE countries would provide their governments with an incentive to raise their level of support to agriculture prior to membership.[31] Upon accession, farmers in these countries would find that their guaranteed minimum prices decline and they could then argue that they had been injured by membership and required compensation. If any CEE country were to adopt this strategy, however, it could have severe inflationary implications (ibid.). Nevertheless, there is no suggestion that the EU is faltering in its stance towards the extension of the direct payments scheme to any new entrants from the east: 'There is little doubt that the post-Agenda 2000 budget for EU agriculture would not stand the inclusion of CEECs in the current schemes for direct payments' (ibid.:248).[32]

PROGNOSIS FOR THE FUTURE

Agriculture is at the fore of the current CEE accession negotiations. The candidate countries have prepared their position papers and negotiations with the Union on the agriculture Chapter are underway. There are indications, however, that these might not run smoothly. For example, the EU is adamant that CEE farmers will not be eligible for direct payments, but this is in sharp contrast to Poland's position, as outlined in a recent newspaper interview with the Deputy Minister of Agriculture, who is Poland's main negotiator for the agriculture Chapter: 'The Polish position was prepared on the basis of several assumptions. One of the most important was that when Poland becomes a member of the EU, Polish farmers will be subject to the same agricultural policies, including direct payments' (Warsaw Voice, 2000).

The existence of such chasms leads naturally to the analysis of the options available to the EU and CEE governments. The most generous offer that the EU could make to the candidate countries would be to leave the CAP unreformed, admit the CEE-10 and grant them immediate access to the funds. However, the budgetary cost of this strategy would be unsupportable without increasing the contributions from existing members, which would not meet with approval. At the opposite end of the spectrum, the status quo could be maintained and the Union would remain a club of fifteen. In the early post-communist years, this possibility was viewed as untenable because the prospect of membership locked in the reforms in CEE that were in progress and countered any possible resurgence of Russia (Lavigne, 1999). Although the same arguments do not hold true today, permanent exclusion of the CEE countries is not an option that the EU is considering, as is clear from the proceedings in Nice (CEC, 2001), where the necessary institutional reforms for enlargement were agreed.

An intermediate position would be to admit some, although not all, of the candidate countries, but impose a transitional period before they could receive any agricultural payments. The Mediterranean enlargement provides a precedent for such a move, but it would be politically unpopular in the CEE countries and they will almost certainly argue that they have waited too long already. It is also unclear how long any such transitional period would be. If the EU argued that CEE agriculture would be excluded until restructuring was complete, then it could well last for decades. A rather harsher variant of this scheme would be to grant some, or even all, of the CEE-10 membership, but to permanently restrict CAP payments to the EU-15. Obviously, this would also be unpopular in CEE, where governments would claim that the new entrants were being treated as second-class citizens. However, a two-tier Europe already exists in effect, with an inner-core in the eurozone, while the UK, Sweden and Denmark retain their own currencies. It is not envisaged that any CEE country would adopt the common currency immediately upon accession and, if they were also to be barred from certain budgetary funds, they would form a de facto third-tier. Such an outcome would render the EU a much looser structure than those who champion greater integration would like.

With the applicant countries themselves having requested 340 transitional arrangements for agriculture alone, twice as many as the sum total requested for all other areas (CEC, 2000a), the agricultural questions to be resolved for there to be an orderly and mutually acceptable enlargement of the Union appear to be intractable and threaten to expose the inclusion agenda of the past decade as little more than rhetoric. Indeed, the latest Regular Reports on the candidate countries (CEC, 2001a) still find deficiencies in agricultural restructuring and progress towards implementation of the *acquis* within the sector and the Commission's stated aim of concluding negotiations on the agriculture Chapter by the middle of 2002 appears to be ambitious. The EU is no stranger to both internal and external discord over agricultural policy, but the forthcoming months will provide it with some of the strongest challenges with which it has yet been confronted.

NOTES

1. In 1957 agriculture accounted for 35 per cent of total employment in Italy and 25 per cent in France (Williams, 1994: 46).
2. The following CEE countries are already members of the WTO: Czech Republic (acceded 1 January 1995), Hungary (1 January 1995), Latvia (10 February 1999), Poland (1 July 1995) and Slovakia (1 January 1995). Furthermore Lithuania is an observer, which commits it to starting accession negotiations.
3. This chapter will only consider the accession of those CEE countries which have already opened negotiations with the EU; that is, Bulgaria, Czech Republic, Estonia, Hungary, Latvia, Lithuania, Poland, Romania, Slovakia and Slovenia (the CEE-10).
4. By 1980, the self-sufficiency quotient for wheat, for example, had risen to 114 per cent (Williams, 1994:49).

5. Tariffication involved expressing non-tariff barriers as tariff equivalents and combining these with specific import duties to create a single tax. This increased transparency for potential importers into the EU.
6. The scale and timing of the reductions in support varied by commodity. A comprehensive list of the revised support measures can be found in Colman and Roberts (1997:107).
7. For livestock, the restrictions refer to historic herd sizes and a maximum stocking density, while for arable crops, the farmer has to agree to 'set aside' land in order to receive such payments.
8. Strictly speaking, the EU payments are not pure direct income support since the monies received are linked to past production levels; as such, they are more correctly referred to as compensation payments (OECD, 1994). However, as the direct income payments terminology is employed within Brussels, the convention is followed here.
9. The ability of farmers to increase production is of course limited by their assets. This issue is addressed more fully below.
10. It is not at all clear that the expected out-migration would actually occur (Ingham et al., 1998).
11. Although the final reform package was known as Agenda 2000 there also existed several prior proposals, of the same name, to which member states did not agree. To avoid confusion, the OECD refers to the final, accepted measures as The Berlin Agreement (OECD, 2000).
12. The actual success of the programme depends upon world prices (in euro) and the manner in which the reforms are implemented (OECD, 2000).
13. Meurs (1999) cites Hungary as an example of a country where the collective farms were granted significant local control and Bulgaria as an example of one where state control dominated. However, the Bulgarian government eliminated the collective farms in the 1970s by merging them into the state farms to form agro-industrial complexes (ibid.).
14. Thorough accounts of agriculture under state socialism can be found in OECD (1999) and Swinnen et al. (1997).
15. Agricultural wages fell by 82 per cent in Romania, 60 per cent in Poland, but only 18 per cent in Hungary (OECD, 1999).
16. In certain eastern regions, agricultural employment actually increased during the 1990s (Ingham and Ingham, 2001).
17. Swinnen (1999) points to the length of communist rule, the ethnicity of pre-collectivisation owners and the pre-collectivization concentration of land ownership as factors underlying reform trajectories.
18. In Russia, collective farmers had only the right of use.
19. Hungary is a partial exception in that some collective farmland was sold and some was given away to those with no former title (Swinnen, op. cit.).
20. The Czech Republic and Slovenia represent two notable cases where foreign restitution was resisted: they would have had to return land to Germans and Italians, respectively.
21. The other countries that restituted state farmland were Latvia and Lithuania. Restitution also remains a possibility in Romania although the government remains undecided about which privatisation policy to adopt (Swinnen, op. cit.).
22. The various contributions to Swinnen et al. (1997) provide excellent country studies.
23. The data are taken from Labour Force Surveys. In the case of Poland, for example, the official employment count registers over 4 million farmers, representing 27.5 per cent of all in work (GUS, 1999).
24. In the EU-15, the comparable figure is less than 5 per cent, a figure that includes Greece and Portugal, where 18 per cent and 13 per cent of the workforces are employed in agriculture, respectively (Eurostat, 1999).
25. While all CEE countries can now benefit from Phare (Poland, Hungary Assistance to the Restructuring of the Economy), the name of the programme has remained unchanged.
26. Once a country joins the EU it will no longer be eligible for pre-accession funding.
27. Full details of these programmes can be found at http://europa.eu.int/.
28. STAR is the EU's Committee on Agricultural Structures and Rural Development.

29. There exist different cost estimates depending upon the assumed scenario; a summary is given in Senior Nello and Smith (1997).
30. A counter-argument is that land prices in CEE will be distorted if these payments are not received.
31. At present, support to agriculture, measured as Producer Subsidy Equivalent, is lower in CEE than it is in the EU (BCE, 2000).
32. Buckwell and Tangerman (1999) discuss the possibility that the CEE countries might have sufficient voting strength within the Union to guarantee themselves access to direct payments. However, the text of the Nice Treaty (CEC, 2001) provides the 10 CEE countries with only 101 votes out of the 258 required to succeed under the qualified majority-voting scheme.

REFERENCES

BCE (Business Central Europe) (2000), 'Off to Market', *Business Central Europe*, July/August, pp. 45–52.

Buckwell, A. and S. Tangermann (1999), 'Agricultural Policy Issues of European Integration: The Future of Direct Payments in the Context of Eastern Enlargement', *Moct-Most*, **9**, (3), 229–53.

CEC (Commission of the European Communities) (2001) *Treaty of Nice*, Official Journal of the European Communities, C80/1, Brussels: CEC.

CEC (Commission of the European Communities) (2001a), *Regular Reports from the Commission on Progress towards Accession by each of the Candidate Countries*, available at http://europa.eu.int/comm/enlargement/report2001/index.htm.

CEC (Commission of the European Communities) (2000), *General Budget of the European Union for the Financial Year 2000*, Brussels and Luxembourg: CEC.

CEC (Commission of the European Communities) (2000a), *Regular Reports from the Commission on Progress towards Accession by each of the Candidate Countries*, available at http://europa.eu.int/comm/enlargement/report_11_00/index.htm.

CEC (Commission of the European Communities) (2000b), *SAPARD: Special Pre-Accession Assistance for Agriculture and Rural Development*, Agriculture Directorate General, Brussels: CEC.

CEC (Commission of the European Communities) (2000c), *Rural Development Programmes for Poland, Hungary, Bulgaria, the Czech Republic, Latvia and Slovenia Endorsed*, IP/00/1009, Brussels: CEC.

CEC (Commission of the European Communities) (2000d), *Rural Development Programmes for Estonia, Lithuania and Slovakia Endorsed*, IP/00/1211, Brussels: CEC.

CEC (Commission of the European Communities) (2000e), *Euro 150 Million Rural Development Programme for Romania Endorsed*, IP/00/1343, Brussels: CEC.

CEC (Commission of the European Communities) (2000f), *SAPARD:How the Multi-Annual Financing Agreement Works*, DN: MEMO/01/106, Brussels: CEC.

CEC (Commission of the European Communities) (1999), *Europe's Agenda 2000: Strengthening and Widening the European Union*, Brussels: CEC.

CEC (Commission of the European Communities) (1998), *Agricultural Situation and Prospects in the Central and Eastern European Countries: Poland*, Directorate General for Agriculture (DG VI), Brussels: CEC.

CEC (Commission of the European Communities) (1996), *Towards a Common Agricultural and Rural Policy for Europe*, Brussels: DG V1, available at: http://europa.eu.int/comm/dg06/publi/buck_en.

CEC (Commission of the European Communities) (1995), *Study on Alternative Strategies for the Development of Relations in the Field of Agriculture Between the EU and the Associated Countries With a View to Future Accession of These Countries*, Agricultural Strategy Paper, CSE(95) 607, DGVI and DGI: Brussels.

Colman, David and Deborah. Roberts (1997), 'Economics of the CAP in Transition', in: Michael J. Artis and Norman Lee (eds), *The Economics of the European Union*, 2nd ed., Oxford: Oxford University Press, pp. 89–117.

Eurostat (1999), *Labour Force Survey: Results 1998*, Luxembourg: Office for Official Publications of the European Communities.

Fischler, F. (1999), 'WTO Negotiations - Agricultural Aspects', available at: http://europa.eu.int/comm/trade/2000_round/civagr02.htm.

GUS (Główny Urząd Statystyczny) (1999), *Employment in National Economy 1999*, Warsaw: GUS.

Hayami, Yujiro. (1991), 'Land Reform', in: Gerald Meir (ed.), *Politics and Policymaking in Developing Countries. Perspectives on the New Political Economy*, ICS Press: San Francisco, pp. 155–71.

Hill, Brian. E. (1984), *The Common Agricultural Policy: Past, Present and Future*, London: Methuen.

Ingham, H. and M. Ingham (2001), 'Who Are Poland's Farmers and What Do They Do?', paper delivered to British Association of Slavonic and East European Studies Conference, Fitzwilliam College, Cambridge, 8 April.

Ingham, H., M. Ingham, and G. Węcławowicz, (1998), 'Agricultural Reform in Post-Transition Poland', *Tidjschrift voor Economische en Sociale Geographie*, **89** (2), 150–60.

Janvry, A. de (1981), 'The Role of Land Reform in Economic Development: Policies and Politics', *American Journal of Agricultural Economics*, **63** (2), 384–92.

Kilkenny, M. (1998), 'Transport Costs and Rural Development', *Journal of Regional Science*, **38** (2), 293–312.

Lavigne, Marie (1999), *The Economics of Transition*, 2nd edition, Basingstoke: Macmillan.

Macours, K. and J. Swinnen (1998), 'Agricultural Labour Adjustment during Transition in Central and Eastern Europe', Policy Group Working Paper, No. 16, Department of Agricultural Economics, Katholiecke Universteit, Leuven.

Meurs, Mieke (1999), 'The Continuing Importance of Collectivization', in: Mieke Meurs (ed.), *Many Shades of Red: State Policy and Collective Agriculture*, Oxford: Rowman and Littlefield Publishers Incorporated, pp. 1–33.

OECD (Organisation for Economic Co-operation and Development) (2000), *OECD Agricultural Outlook 2000–2005*, OECD: Paris.

OECD (Organisation for Economic Co-operation and Development) (1999), *Agricultural Policies in Emerging and Transition Economies*, OECD: Paris.

OECD (Organisation for Economic Co-operation and Development) (1994), *Agricultural Policy Reform: New Approaches. The Role of Direct Payments*, OECD: Paris.

Senior Nello, S. and K.E. Smith (1997), 'The Consequences of Eastern Enlargement of the European Union in Stages', EUI Working Paper RSC No. 97/51, Robert Schuman Centre, European University Institute.

Swinnen, J.F.M. (1999), 'Land Reform Choices in Central and Eastern Europe', *The Economics of Transition*, **7** (3), 637–64.

Swinnen, Johan F.M and Erik. Mathijs (1997), 'Agricultural Privatisation, Land Reform and Farm Restructuring in Central and Eastern Europe: A Comparative Analysis', in: Johan F.M. Swinnen, Allan Buckwell and Erik Mathijs (eds), pp. 333–73.

Swinnen, Johan F.M., Allan Buckwell and Erik Mathijs (eds) (1997), *Agricultural Privatisation, Land Reform and Farm Restructuring in Central and Eastern Europe*, Aldershot: Ashgate.

Tangermann, S. (1999), 'Europe's Agricultural Policies and the Millenium Round', *World Development*, **22** (9), 1155–78.

Warsaw Voice (2000), 'En Route to the EU', **44** (62), available at http://www.warsawvoice.com.pl/v627/PV13.html.

Williams, Allan M. (1994), *The European Community*, 2nd ed., Oxford: Blackwell Publishers.

7. Social Europe East and West

Gillian Pascall and Nick Manning[1]

INTRODUCTION

It is important to consider the nature and importance of the social dimension of the European Union (EU) at the beginning of the third millennium and how this will affect and be affected by the further widening of membership to the countries of Central and Eastern Europe (CEE). There is broad agreement that the concern of EU social policy with workers and labour mobility renders it an adjunct of economic policy, although the current importance and future potential of social Europe are much disputed. Streeck (1995:407) argues trenchantly for 'the insignificance of Community social policy in the integration process', while Walby (1999:118) proposes that 'the social powers of the EU are underestimated and under evaluated in current social theory'. Some assessment of the significance of the social dimension is a prerequisite for understanding what the affect of eastward expansion is likely to be. It is also necessary to consider the impact of widening on social policy making in the EU and whether social powers at the supranational level will be strengthened or whether greater diversity will mean increased pressure for national level decision-making.

Analysis of these issues will proceed through the use of contrasting examples that are of particular interest in the context of enlargement. Provisions for equal opportunities between men and women were written into the Treaty of Rome (ToR) and are agreed widely to be the most successful part of social policy making and its implementation at the European level. The effectiveness of policies against poverty, on the other hand, is questioned equally widely. In CEE countries, gender relations are challenged and changing in the early post-communist period, but how will these be affected by EU membership and what will be the consequent role of women? The spread of poverty in CEE has affected children especially and the prospects for the poor of the region in an enlarged Europe represent a critical concern. Will the extended Union be an engine of social development or will the convergence criteria bring new economic shocks and new inequalities? If the EU is constructed as a labour market, with social policy targeted at workers, this has significant implications for women and children. They are less likely to have paid employment and the relations of unpaid work are especially important for them, in both west and east. These issues will be explored mainly with reference to the Czech Republic, Poland, Hungary, Estonia and Slovenia.

THE SOCIAL DIMENSION

It is important first to consider how the EU might be characteried as a social power. Clearly, there is no one single social policy or welfare regime of Europe to compare with the single market. Nevertheless, the welfare regimes of member states are constrained by the powers of the EU and it is impossible to analyse the former without reference to the latter and to the way that they have been exercised. There is a lot of room between a characterisation of Europe as a welfare regime in itself and Europe as no player at all and an attempt to locate social policy making more precisely in this very large space is necessary

The EU in 2000: Social Power or Economic Cypher?

Any empirical picture of Europe's decision-making structures in the area of social policy would have to show the existence of supranational powers in its institutions and their vigorous expression throughout the history of the European Court of Justice (ECJ) to which nation states are subject. The effectiveness of these bodies in delivering social policy is open to question, but there can be no argument that they make it: 'the EU possesses characteristics of a supranational entity, including extensive bureaucratic competencies, unified judicial control, and significant capacities to develop or modify policies' (Pierson and Leibfried, 1995:1). The present structure falls short of the traditional federal model, but it is one in which 'national welfare state regimes are now part of a larger, multi-tiered system of social policy. ... the governance of social policy occurs at multiple levels. Member states profoundly influence this structure, but they no longer control it' (ibid.:77).

European social power is exercised mainly through regulation rather than through taxation and public expenditure. While the constitutional authority vested in the EU through treaties and directives gives it some control over national governments, taxation and social expenditure still remain largely devolved. The EU has been characterised as a 'regulatory state'; that is, as 'a new type of state' in which 'powers are primarily articulated through its legal powers to regulate markets, rather than through the power to tax and spend on welfare, or through the monopoly over the legitimate use of violence' (Walby, op. cit.:124). Europe contains the powers of member states and gives rights that individuals can claim over their governments. Walby (ibid.) further argues that its power is becoming a more significant welfare tool as the forces of global markets weaken the traditional spending and taxing supports of social welfare. However, while the account of the EU's regulatory powers is unimpeachable, her argument for their greater significance is debatable.

The notion and practice of Europe as a single market clearly precedes Europe as a power in social policy. The EU began as a coal and steel community: only 12 of the 248 articles of the original European Economic Community Treaty were devoted explicitly to social policy (Hantrais, 2000:2). But the implications of these beginnings for the nature, significance and momentum of social Europe are open to discussion. Some argue that the dream to integrate social Europe is history: national welfare states were built on the struggle between labour and capital. Now, in the context of a weakening of labour power in relation to increasingly mobile capital, there is no force for social policy. The battle for social Europe has been fought and lost (Streeck, 1995; Bornscheir and Ziltener, 1999). Others, however, view the EU as having been vigorous and proactive in developing strategies against the global market:

> The EU is a polity which has responded aggressively to the perceived threat of globalization. It is no passive victim in the manner often postulated as the role for nation-states within globalization theory. During this process the strength of this polity has grown considerably, becoming a fully fledged supra-state, developing new policy capabilities, sometimes at the expense of the sovereignty and capacity for action of its member states. The EU has demonstrated a response to globalization in which a polity has been significantly reconfigured and aggrandized. (Walby, op. cit:134)

Nevertheless, social policy has not flowed freely in the wake of economic policy and its development has been slow and contested:

> Despite the predictions of the early theorists of the European Community that the integration of the European market would lead to the integration of social security and labour market organisation, social integration has proven to be anything but spontaneous. Nor has there ever been consensus even on the desirability of social integration ... advances in social and labour market policy at the European level have been gradual and

> piecemeal – and mostly unsatisfactory, for their supporters as much as for their opponents. (Rhodes, 1998:80)

If there is no clear trajectory of social policy following in the wake of economic union, then the future of social Europe is open to question, to political action and to change in the context of expansion eastward. This raises questions about the politics of an expanded Europe and about the bargain that the countries of CEE will be able to strike.

Enlargement: Implications for the EU as a Social Power

Support for integration within Europe is widespread in CEE, particularly among elites, although not unquestioning (Kolankiewicz, 1994; Freudenstein, 1998; Neumayer, 1999). More opinion poll respondents see their countries' futures in the EU rather than in any alternative: 45 per cent in Poland; 42 per cent in Hungary and 38 per cent in the Czech Republic (ibid: 144). There is then a widespread hope that the EU will be a positive force for development. However, perceptions of the difficulties of joining the EU have grown, with people beginning to see themselves as 'running in order to leap aboard an already speeding train' (Kolankiewicz, op. cit.:480). Also, it might be difficult politically for the countries of CEE to accept supranational power:

> As the full scale of what is required dawns on their citizens, applicant governments are finding the popularity of their great project is in decline. For peoples who have got rid of communism, set up their own institutions and currencies, launched market economies and started to create free societies all within the past 10 years, new and onerous reforms ordered by their governments at the EU's behest are becoming hard to bear. Opposition to the whole EU project is growing in places such as Slovenia. Yet it's surprising there has not been more. (Bates, 1999)

In social policy terms, diversity within the EU has already increased with the accession of Sweden and Finland, on the one hand, and Spain, Portugal and Greece, on the other. The former increased the representation of welfare regimes based on social citizenship, while the southern European countries have a distinctive character, with weak welfare states and strong expectations of family based welfare. The history of Soviet domination has given the countries of CEE a different profile again and, while they may be moving towards western systems, institutional change in the field of social policy has been much less than politicians at first promised. The EU's expansion to the east will reduce the dominance of corporatist models of welfare and incorporate a wider range of regime types, hence giving Europe an even more 'variable geometry' (Rose and Haerpfer, 1995). Such institutional diversity may hinder the development of social policy, but there are pressures in the opposite direction. The countries of CEE will find nothing new in having a social agenda driven by economic requirements, although it may become increasingly difficult for people to accept. This might therefore lead to pressures from the citizens of the accession countries for Europe to play a more active social role.

GENDER AND EQUAL OPPORTUNITIES

Even the most sceptical commentators on Europe's social powers concede some significance and effectiveness to its equal opportunity policies. For example, one author, in a generally critical review of the development and exercise of social power at the European level, described the 'inequality of men and women in the labour market' as one of two successful areas of action (Streeck, op. cit.:400). 'Superstate feminism' may be evident exaggeration (Hoskyns, 1992; Duncan, 1996a:400), but the success of EU driven policies for equal opportunity between men and women is a main plank of the argument that social Europe should be taken seriously (Walby, op. cit.).

The EU in 2000: Superstate Feminism or Grand Fiction?

Member states are committed under Article 119 of the ToR to the principle 'that men and women should receive equal pay for equal work'. If EU treaties are regarded as 'a de facto constitution of the EU' (ibid.:121) then this aspect of gender equality was part of its founding constitution, giving rights to which individuals can lay direct claim over the heads of governments. Market logic has encouraged gender equality as stronger EU members, with women more highly integrated in employment and education, have defended their economies against competition from lower wages. After a dull start, the second wave of the women's movement in the 1970s provided a stimulus to both legal testing and to the Council Directives on Equal Pay (1975), Equal Treatment at Work (1976) and Equal Treatment in Social Security (1978). In 1986 there followed Directives on Self-Employment and Occupational Pensions, while a Directive establishing 14 weeks maternity leave – with 80 per cent pay conditional on employment – was agreed as a health issue in 1992. The Social Charter (1989) and the Social Chapter of the Maastricht Treaty 'were further developments of the core idea of Article 119' (Walby, op. cit.: 131). The Amsterdam Treaty (1997) empowers the Council of Ministers, acting unanimously, to take 'appropriate action' to combat discrimination based on sex, racial or ethnic origin, religion or belief, disability, age or sexual orientation. The 1990s also saw Directives on Working Time, Parental Leave, Burden of Proof in Sex Discrimination and Part-time Work. The ECJ has played a key role in interpreting the equal pay principle expansively (Neilson, 1998; Walby, op. cit.). All of this provides legislation of considerable scope that forces policy change on national governments (Mazey, 1998) and provides individuals with redress against them. It also created a political forum in which interpretations of gender equality issues can be challenged and changed (Meehan, 1993) and from which policy networks can emerge (Hoskyns, 1996). Even critical commentators acknowledge that in this area EU intervention has been 'amazingly rich and innovative' (Rossilli, 1997:64).

However, while the legal framework of rights has tended to expand to produce a body of some scope – at least in relation to gender equalities in paid employment – implementation is another question. Problems at national level make it hard for women to claim their rights: 'The fragmented policy process, arduous legal procedures, and scarce resources of equal-opportunity agencies (leading to insufficient financing and support of individual claimants) have hindered successful legal representation' (Ostner and Lewis, 1995:173). Such criticism of legally regulated rights is not confined to the EU. Most accounts of national UK policy implementation of equal opportunities legislation tell the same story (Morris and Nott, 1991). Neither have national governments always hastened to meet their legal obligations and, even when they have, it has sometimes been in terms of levelling down. Furthermore, some states have opt-outs from EU legislation.

Despite rights to gender equality being built into the constitution and legal practice of the EU, women in Europe earn less than men, have less secure work, receive fewer benefits from work and lower pensions in old age (Hantrais, op. cit.:113; Arber, 1999). Innovative legislation has not so far succeeded in containing gender inequalities, even in the rewards from paid employment. As such, whether the EU as a single market is a powerful underlying force to polarise incomes, security and the advantages from work – between men and women, and between women, as well as between other groups of socially included and excluded – is a key issue (Borchorst, 1994; Duncan, op. cit.:401). In the 1990s, the EU's pre-occupation with deregulating the labour market may have had more real impact on women than the extension of legislation to protect them (Rossilli, 1999).

Paid employment has been central to European legislation and action for gender equality. Most hard law – the treaties and directives – has concerned rights attaching to paid work. Unpaid work is not covered by this approach:

> Students of gender issues have repeatedly stressed the problems of treating labour-market issues in isolation from the broader environment that encompasses gender relationships. The EU builds on a narrow notion of equality that implies treating working women like working men. EU law applies only to the working population or to people 'actively seeking employment'. Only the family concerns of continuously employed wage earners attract political attention. (Ostner and Lewis, op. cit.: 159)

The ECJ has been a force for wide interpretation of equal pay, but it has drawn the line to exclude unpaid work, arguing that 'it was not the job of the Court to settle questions concerned with the organisation of the family or to alter the division of responsibility between the parents' (ibid.:165). The maternity leave directive was enacted finally on health grounds rather than as an issue of gender equality. The Social Charter is about workers not citizens.

Features of patriarchal systems other than the household division of labour are also neglected: male violence, sexuality and culture, and the interactions between these. Thus the roots of women's unequal position are ignored (Duncan, 1996a:412). While the concerns of European social policy have widened from paid employment to working motherhood, child care and parental leave (Hantrais, op. cit.:112), mainstreaming gender policy in education and training (Rees, 1998) and even to some of the wider structures of power (Rossilli, 1997:65), these areas tend to have been covered by soft law – such as recommendations – rather than by legally binding directives and treaties.

When EU policy filters through national governments, its implementation results in variety. European gender policy affects women's entitlements, but it does not eradicate differences of cultural, social and economic practice in the way that work and care are managed. The social policy paradigm of the six founder members was dominated by a Christian Democratic tradition in which policies were built around a male breadwinner and women's citizenship was mediated through men (Duncan, 1996; 1996a:408–9). It is important to consider whether the historical dominance of this model survives in EU policy making and the extent to which the accessions from Scandinavia and from the southern rim countries weakened the early outlook.

While equal opportunities policies present the EU as a modernising and liberalising force in terms of gender, other tendencies may be found in the political, economic and social principles of the Union that owe more to its historic core than to its current diverse membership. The male breadwinner model flourishes and is embedded in the citizenship rules (Ackers, 1994). The free movement of labour is central to EU policy making and has resulted in rights for migrant workers, as well as their families, to the benefits and entitlements of their country of residence, but the breadwinner is typically male. There are thereby two levels of rights, as all other migrants have to bring their own entitlements with them, and this may have serious implications for partners – particularly women divorcing, separating, cohabiting – whose rights hang on their relationships. Cohabitees may have fewer rights than married women and partners are likely to lose their residence entitlement on the breakdown of the relationship. The narrow interpretation of work in the EU to exclude that which is unpaid creates a category of people with roles and duties, but without recognition. Work has already been interpreted to include part-time music teaching too poorly rewarded to provide subsistence and also occupation as a member of a religious community, but not voluntary or unpaid care work. Ackers proposes that people who have entitlements as carers – through schemes such as paid volunteering, social assistance or Invalid Care Allowance – could become entitled to citizenship (ibid.:394–6). This would resolve serious problems, given that carers are at present derivative citizens.

If EU systems are seen as a gender regime in themselves, they appear deeply contradictory. Original provisions for the equal treatment of men and women are contained within the core of the European constitution and law, while there has been an innovative and developmental tendency to stretch the definition of work and thereby the application of the principle of equal treatment in both statute and practice. However, traditional assumptions about gender roles are also rooted in EU institutions. Furthermore, the EU is really a set of gender regimes into which have been incorporated the diversified and diversifying tendencies of the Scandinavian regimes, on the one hand, and the southern rim regimes, on the other, which multiplies the contradictions.

The Extended EU: Implications for Gender Equality

Social policy in the EU is constituted as legal regulation rather than as social provision through taxation, benefits and social services, although there is some redistribution through regional policy and the social funds. The gender regimes of the countries of CEE have been regulated through constitutional entitlements to equality in both paid employment and the family, but without the legal apparatus to enforce them, and these entitlements have changed little in the transition period. To this extent, the history of gender equality in the EU and its eastern neighbours is similar. In general, the provisions had a broader base in CEE than in Western Europe, with equality extending beyond paid employment to equality in marriage and divorce, taxation and benefits and was more deeply rooted historically (UNICEF, 1999:vii–viii; Pascall and Manning, 2000). The applicant countries will have little difficulty in meeting the standards for gender equality in the EU, with levels of gender development being high in relation to their stage of social and economic development (see Figure 7.1). The desire to accede will sustain these regulatory frameworks and offer some protection to women's interests.

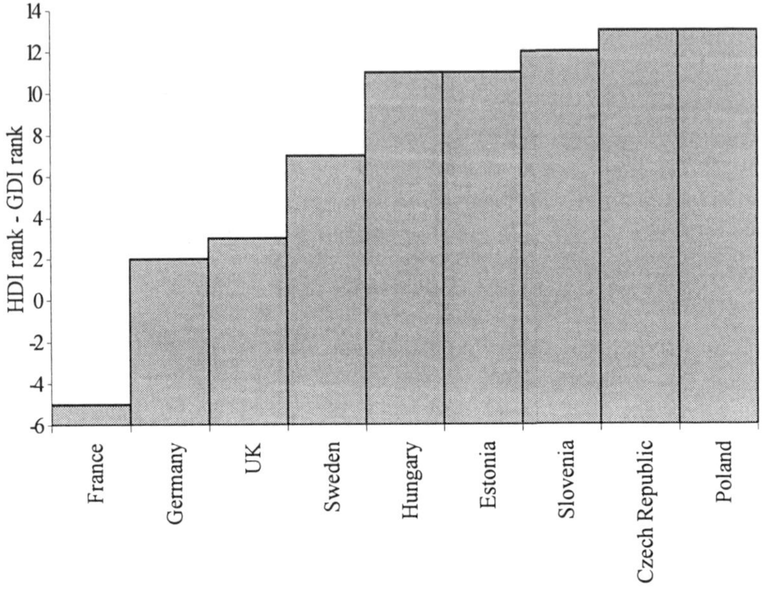

Source: http://www.undp.org/hdro/98gdi.htm.

Figure 7.1 Gender development (GDI) v. human development (HDI): 1995

Legal regulation is not the only strategy for gender equality in CEE. Women's position as paid workers in the communist era was also supported by social provisions that drew upon a range of strategies, such as kindergarten, paid parental leave, rights to leave to care for children with disabilities and family allowances that involved high levels of spending. In principle, many such supports remain, but their value has been eroded as the capacity to fund them through taxation has been reduced and as liberal ideology undermined their political support. The tendency has been for a decline in nursery provision – virtually to zero in the Czech Republic – while kindergarten enrolments have been sustained at a level close to that in the communist era (Figure 7.2). At the same time, parental leave entitlements have tended to increase, allowing parents to care for their own children.

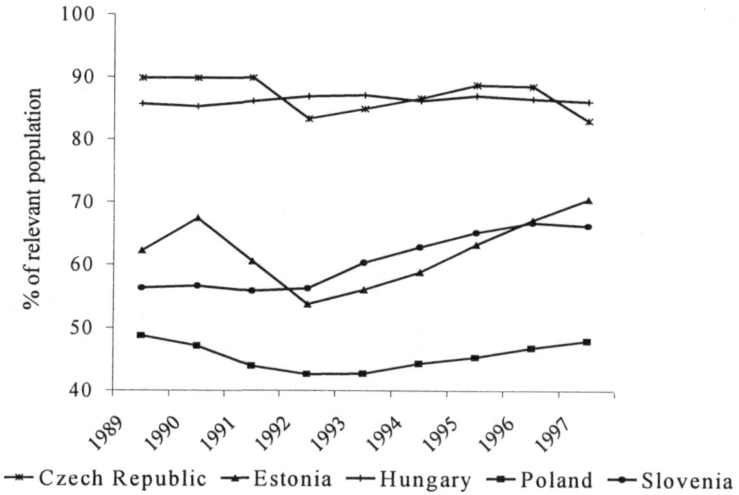

Source: UNICEF (1999), Statistical Annex, Table 7.1.

Figure 7.2 Kindergarten enrolment rates

These trends have implications for gender equality in paid employment. There are widespread fears that women's position at work is damaged if they avail themselves of parental leave; not to mention the difficulty of affording it as the support for associated benefits has fallen (Fajth, 1996; Firlit-Fesnak, 1997; UNICEF, op. cit.:41–57; Pascall and Manning, op. cit.). Women's need for paid employment and the social supports for them to pursue it in the post-communist era are not diminished: indeed, participation rates remain high (Figure 7.3) and recognition of the costs of unpaid care work remains widespread (Figure 7.4). But there is little in the EU's current constitution or political imagination to lead to the expectation that strategies involving social spending will gain support and even current spending levels may well come under pressure as the economies of CEE are brought into line with those in the west.

Making legal regulation work in practice is a serious problem. The processes of law are cumbersome and expensive and individuals tend to become locked in unequal struggles with employers or government departments. Legal institutions themselves tend to be male dominated and while no one seeking greater equality between men and women would dispense with equality legislation, neither should they place too much faith in the ability of the law to bring it about. Such difficulties can be expected to be more exaggerated in CEE, with its brief history of access to the law in

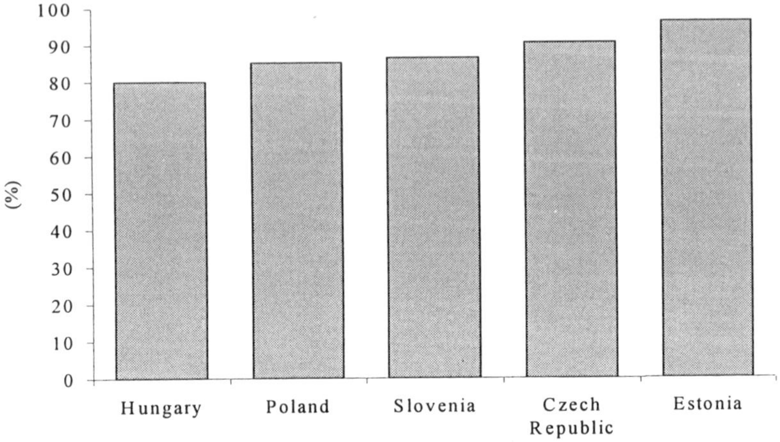

Source: http://www.undp.org/hdro/iwompart.htm.

Figure 7.3 Female participation rate as percentage of male rate, 1995

defence of individual freedoms, extreme constraints of economy and minimal infrastructure in the form of equal opportunity commissions and legal aid. All 27 countries of CEE and the former Soviet Union have signed and ratified the 1979 United Nations Convention on the Elimination of All Forms of Discrimination against Women, but the development of machinery to implement it has been slow and 'there are few mechanisms to strengthen the prosecution of discriminatory actions against women' (UNICEF, op. cit.:17). New means by which central governments can monitor women's issues (for example, equal opportunities secretariats) are beginning to be put into place, but they have to work against a historic deficit of civil society institutions and social action to implement broad claims as rights for individuals (ibid.: 106; Pascall and Manning, op. cit.).

Despite an apparent ideology of equality from the top, the experience of women at work and in families in countries of CEE during the Soviet era was not of liberation. High participation in paid employment has changed little in the transition period and women's work is usually full-time (UNICEF, op. cit.:24), with the gender pay gap being narrow by western standards (Figure

7.5). But the restrictions of the communist period hindered the development of women's political consciousness and there was no women's movement to compare with feminism's second wave in the west. There was therefore little basis for challenge to a traditional division of domestic labour, with women's total workload (both paid and unpaid) averaging 70 hours per week, about 15 hours more than women in Western Europe (Figure 7.6).

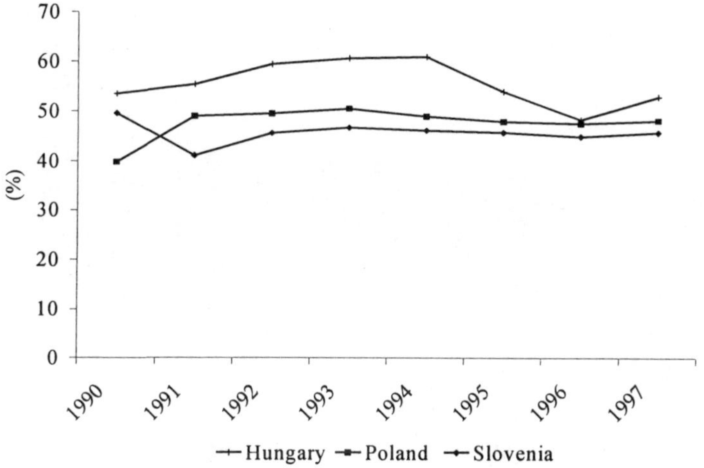

Source: UNICEF (1999), Statistical Annex, Table 10.6.

Figure 7.4 General government expenditure to GDP ratios

Gender equality is constituted presently around paid employment in the EU and is weak in exactly the areas that women in CEE countries most lack. They have had the support to undertake paid work and have higher levels of participation and more equal earnings than their counterparts in many western countries. Also, they have had legal frameworks offering equality. Any challenge to other aspects of gender inequality is at present, however, tentative. Reaction against Soviet ideology is giving support to traditional patriarchal ideologies, which encourage traditional family roles or, in the case of Poland, restrict abortion. Men's violence has begun to be acknowledged, and there is the beginning of crisis support for women, but it is far from what is needed for women's protection. In particular, the unpaid work of care in families has fallen to women – as in most western countries – and is undermining their position in employment and increasing their economic dependence. Sociàl supports were always too small to avoid the double burden, but they were a significant element in supporting women's employment. The increasing fragility of these measures in the transition economies exposes women to more unpaid work at home and to more inequality at work.

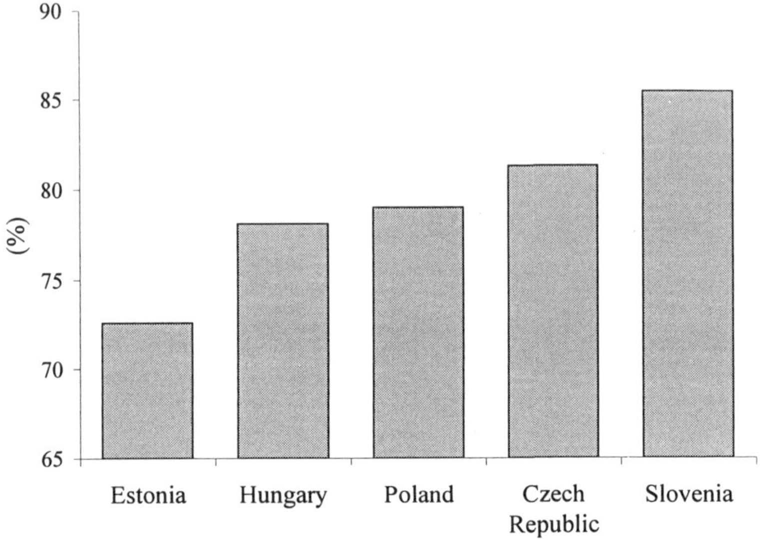

Source: UNICEF (1999), Table 2.2.

Figure 7.5 The gender pay gap: female to male monthly wages, 1996–99

EU social policy has so far co-existed with a diversity of gendered welfare regimes and filters through national legislatures and cultural spectacles to produce very different policies in practice and the admission of countries from CEE will only add to the diversity. Regimes within the current EU may be conceptualised in terms of male breadwinner/female carer (Germany, Ireland), on the one hand, and dual earner (Sweden, Finland, Denmark), on the other. The southern European countries introduced a further distinction, with weak state provision and stronger expectations of families and of women's unpaid contribution. Gender relations in CEE are based on two earners, but differ from the Scandinavian model in their more extreme expectations of women as unpaid workers. The dominance of the breadwinner model – already lessened by the accession of Sweden and

Finland – will be further reduced as transition countries with a longer history of high female participation in paid employment join.

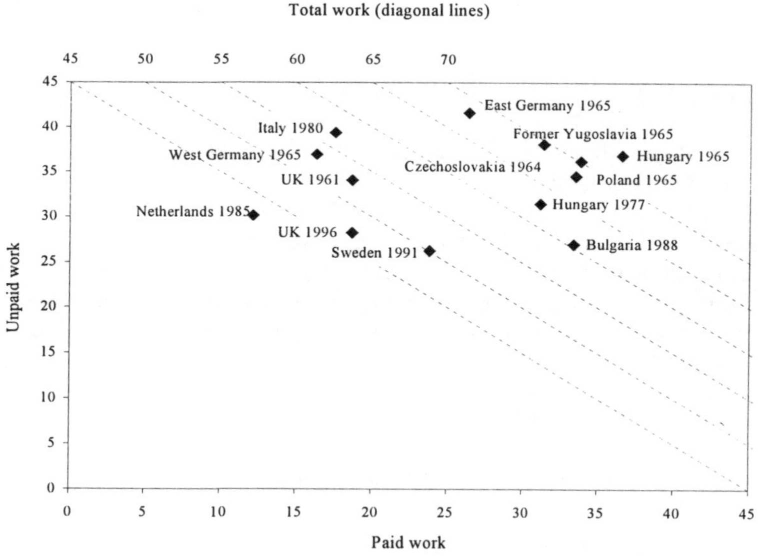

Source: UNICEF (1999), p. 25; Bittman and Gooding, 1998.

Figure 7.6 Average weekly hours paid/ unpaid work: women 20–59

The relationship of women in CEE to their families will raise many important issues if their countries join the EU. The Soviet gender system enabled – indeed forced – women's labour market participation and enhanced their access to independent incomes and presumably their independence within families. Divorce was – in theory – easy. But poverty and housing shortage constituted severe deterrents to living outside traditional family forms. The transition has probably already increased women's dependence on families as other social supports have diminished: and, with the male breadwinner model underpinning welfare provision and increasing women's dependence in and on the family, joining the EU might do more of the same. The indications from Sweden are that women feel that their position has been weakened since accession (Gould, 1999) and, as families have been a key source of support during the transition period for women in CEE, the traditions and structures of Western Europe and the EU seem more likely to support this trend than to interrupt it. So any advantage they may gain from access to individual rights through EU equality legislation may be counteracted by increased family dependence as social supports to motherhood are challenged in a single market economy ever less tolerant of public spending.

CHILD POVERTY AND SOCIAL EXCLUSION

As children attract little comment within the politics and economics of European Monetary Union (EMU) or debates about accession, it is timely to ask 'how the interests of those not in the labour market, such as children, are represented in the social dialogue' (Atkinson, 1998:16). Recent publications have challenged this omission and provided some material evidence connecting the wide issues of European economic and social policy to children's experience of poverty and exclusion (ibid.; Micklewright and Stewart, 2000; UNICEF, 2000). But any effort to understand the likely impact of accession on child poverty and exclusion has to acknowledge the limitations of the available data and debate.

The EU in 2000: Policies for Social Exclusion

A wide range of policies, from the macroeconomics of employment and interest rates, wage levels, unemployment and its distribution among households to social policies focusing on spending on benefits, education and health affect child poverty and exclusion. The United Nations Children's Fund's (UNICEF) cross-national analysis concluded that:

> it is progress on all fronts - reducing poverty among lone-parent families, reducing the proportion of children in workless households, reducing severe wage inequalities at the bottom end of the income scale, and preventing too wide a gap from opening up between state benefit payments and average wages - that will most effectively lower child poverty rates. (ibid.:16–17)

Therefore it is important to consider social policies that are intended to reduce child poverty and exclusion within the context of economic policies that may well be doing the opposite: 'As a general pattern, ministries of finance set policies and targets designed to achieve overall economic goals while ministries of social affairs follow behind picking up the pieces' (ibid.:17).

If the range of policies that affect child poverty and exclusion is wide, so also are the ways in which to calibrate it. Household income is clearly central, but is not enough in itself: ideally, we should know something about how income is distributed within households, as well as between them. Recent comparative analysis of child well-being using the Human Development Report's new index of deprivation in industrialised countries identifies four 'domains': material well-being, health and survival, education and personal development and social inclusion/participation (Micklewright and Stewart, 1999a:7). Account would need to be taken of all of these factors in considering the impact of accession on the children of CEE.

In absolute terms, poverty is a serious issue for the children of Eastern Europe, with the US official poverty line showing poverty rates of 83.1, 90.6 and 93.1 per cent in the Czech Republic, Hungary and Poland, respectively (UNICEF, 2000:7). Standards of living closer to current EU norms are something children in joining countries may hope to gain. But poverty relative to national living standards is a serious issue too. In these terms, the children of CEE currently fare rather better, with only 5.9, 10.3 and 15.4 per cent living in relative poverty in the Czech Republic, Hungary and Poland, respectively, although these figures may well rise with marketisation and insertion into the EU. Poverty relative to national living standards is widely argued to be the most important key to the well-being of children – to their participation in social life, their health and their education – and higher living standards for the majority may well be bought at the price of increasing distress among those excluded. There have been widespread expectations that the social market would widen inequalities between those able to use its benefits and others and the extension of social policy has often been justified in terms of redressing the polarisation created by the market forces of unifying economies (Hantrais, op. cit.:146–7). The trend during the 1990s, however, was towards a strengthening neo-liberal perspective – long established in economic policy – which has 'grown more prominent in social policy since the Delors Presidency and the White Paper on Social Policy (1994)' (Duffy, 1998:231).

Policies for further integrating the market have raised concerns about its social impact. Atkinson (op. cit.), for example, has raised the question of the impact of monetary union on children and given the rather alarming answer that, for all the intellectual and policy input to EMU, we do not even have the tools to address the issue. Many of his arguments are pertinent to the impact of EU membership for children from CEE. The consequences of macroeconomic policy for young people might be seen in terms of jobs (of their parents and of their own prospects), pay, the effects of taxes and transfers (including child benefits and education grants), interest rate effects on borrowing and saving, housekeeping costs, level and quality of provision of education, health and health charges. However, much of this data does not exist in a form that allows measurement. For example, information on unemployment in households with children and price indexing that takes account of families with children is available too late for their interests to be taken into account. These issues are especially pertinent because:

> Bringing up children cannot be postponed: The child during whose early years hospitals have long waiting lists may have permanently reduced health status; children whose new school is postponed as a result of public expenditure cuts cannot relive their formative years; young people entering the labour market in a recession may suffer an enduring disadvantage relative to those cohorts who entered at a time of expansion. In the macroeconomic trade-off between output and inflation variability, the temporal vulnerability of children should be a particular concern. (ibid.:17)

Poverty was not a political priority for the founder Community members. The European Social Fund was instigated to 'improve employment opportunities for workers and to contribute to the raising of their standard of living'. Its task was that of 'rendering the employment of workers easier and of increasing their geographical and occupational mobility within the Community' (Hantrais, op. cit.:148). The emphasis on markets and workers squeezed out concerns about the marginalisation and exclusion of others. However, the Fund has operated programmes against social exclusion since the mid-1970s and their targets and extent have increased through time. In particular, the Single European Act introduced more funds, priority areas and socially defined groups: the long-term unemployed, women migrants and people with disabilities. But the scale of the social funds has always been small and, by the mid-1990s, despite increases in the size and diversity of the Community and a broadening of policy objectives and increases in the budget, they only stood at around 0.3 per cent of the Union's GDP (ibid.:149).

The Structural Funds have more to do with integrating the territory than with integrating the least advantaged in the territories (Duffy, op. cit.: 237). But the scale of such integration itself is very limited, leaving great economic and social diversity within Europe. Disparities in GDP per head have been reduced since the early 1980s, while incomes have on average been rising (Micklewright and Stewart, 1999a:28); but 'Territorial differences in per capita income between the Union territories are twice those between regions of the United States' (Duffy, op. cit.:234). Also, other measures of economic exclusion – child poverty, worklessness among households with children and unemployment among young people – all point to increasing disparities between countries in relative terms (Micklewright and Stewart, 1999a:28; 1999b).

Policies to combat social exclusion have been constrained within narrow limits, with labour market policies prioritised throughout the Amsterdam Treaty, which had little to offer on aspects of social exclusion, such as housing, that go beyond its confines. Liberal economics and the principle of subsidiarity serve to inhibit wider social powers (Duffy, op. cit.:231). In March 2000, the Lisbon meeting of the European Council called for decisive steps to eradicate poverty, noting specifically a concern for Europe's children (UNICEF, 2000:19). There have been some pressures towards miminum standards of social assistance but, as yet, there have been no EU policies to legislate for minimum income or to integrate or harmonise the varied social security systems of the member states (except for adherence to equal opportunity principles). Indeed, harmonisation of policies is explicitly excluded in Title VIII (employment) and Title XI (social policy, education, vocational training and youth) (Duffy, op. cit.:239). UK experience illustrates the very small impact – even irrelevance – of the EU to children in low income households in the recent past: child poverty tripled in the 1980s and 1990s, bringing a fifth of the country's children into poverty. National government policies are now prioritising social expenditure on children, using a wide range of policies relating to employment, educational under-achievement, rates of teenage pregnancy and a national childcare strategy (UNICEF, 2000:8).

There is then only very limited EU social policy on social exclusion and that which exists is supported by limited legislation and financial resources and has minor impacts. While children are benefiting from the generally rising living standards in Europe, the risk of exclusion from the process has increased. A recent study, using a variety of indicators of child welfare – including economic well-being, mortality, education, teenage fertility and life satisfaction – concludes that: 'on average children's quality of life (measured in several dimensions) is on the rise across Europe, but the risks of being excluded from improvements are also on the rise, and these risks are becoming increasingly different across countries' (Micklewright and Stewart, 1999a:72–3).

The Extended EU: Implications of Expansion for Child Poverty in CEE

Positive socio-economic prospects for the integration of Europe and for the one hundred million people in ten applicant countries of CEE are widely predicted by economists. They believe that the latter states will respond to investment in modernising machines and equipment and will grow at rates two or three times those of western members. With average per capita incomes of 30 to 40 per cent of those in the present EU, they will take decades to reach western levels, but the gap will narrow steadily. These processes should be stimulated by EU structural investments, though it may be too much to hope that current rules, developed around a more limited group of nations, will be maintained (Mikelka, 1998).

While absolute standards of living have been much lower than in the west, historically the countries of CEE restrained income inequalities, especially among families with children, and this pattern continued in the early transition period. The evidence of the Luxembourg Income Study, for example, is that more Austrian and German children lived below their national relative poverty thresholds than did Czechs or Slovaks, as also did more UK children with two parents than their Hungarian or Polish equivalents. Children of lone parents in Poland and Hungary were found not to be much more subject to poverty than children of two parent families. Public transfers – especially family allowances – were a critical element in keeping both lone-parent and two-parent families out of poverty (UNICEF, 1999:50). Children in the Czech Republic and Slovakia have been particularly well protected from relative poverty, with their rates of 2 per cent being below those in Finland (3 per cent) and Sweden (4 per cent) (Micklewright and Stewart, 2000:10). Figure 7.7 shows the income levels of the poorest and richest 20 per cent in a number of nations: it indicates the comparative equality in those countries wishing to join the EU as well as the distance the poorest have to travel to reach the levels of most western European countries. The transition has meant widening inequalities of earnings, higher unemployment and falling levels of transfers to families; in particular, the exchange of universal family benefits for targeted transfers. Poland's poorest 20 per cent now have 7 per cent of total income instead of the 9 per cent they had in 1990 and, across the region, 'available evidence suggests families with children have suffered greater income losses than households without children' (UNICEF, op. cit.:10).

There are fears among the people of CEE that these inequalities will increase further if they join the EU. While acceding nations are predicted to gain from joining, it is expected that the benefits will be distributed unevenly and in favour of entrepreneurs and officials, while agricultural workers, the poor, manual workers and employees of state enterprises are seen as likely losers (Juchler, 1999; Neumayer, op. cit.:147). There are particular fears, and public sympathy, for Polish agricultural workers (Juchler, op. cit.). Also, a majority of Poles (51 per cent) believe that integration within Europe will bring a widening of the differences between rich and poor (Neumayer, op. cit.:148) and some expect that an increase in social conflict may follow (Juchler, op. cit.:492).

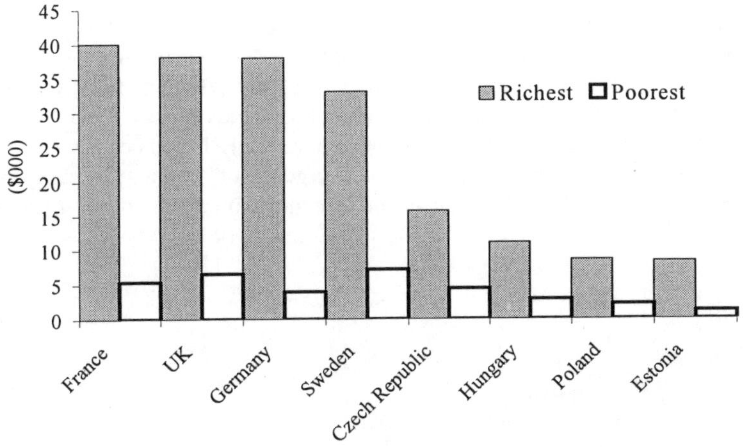

Source: http://www.undp.org/hdro/ihpprof.htm.

Figure 7.7 Real GDP per capita: poorest and richest 20%, 1980–94

The EU has not built a European welfare regime against poverty. There have been projects to combat poverty and to harmonise the measurement and understanding of it, but not a European welfare system to prevent or respond to it. Leibfried (1992) describes four poverty regimes that have co-existed in Europe with little sign of harmonisation from the bottom up – Scandinavian, Bismarck, Anglo-Saxon and Latin Rim – and argues that they are incompatible because they start from different or even contradictory goals. Expansion to the east will add to the diversity as the countries of CEE have had distinctive welfare regimes (which are changing in some respects but not all), based on employment guarantees rather than unemployment insurance, on women's labour market participation, on services and allowances for children and on the provision of public goods and services. The administrative obstacles to integration of strategies against poverty will surely grow as these systems add to the differences that exist already within the Union.

The wide economic disparities between the old and the new Europe will add to the problems of addressing poverty at the European level. The richest applicant, Slovenia, is well behind the poorest current member, Portugal, with the Czech Republic, Hungary, Poland and Estonia lagging by even more (Figure 7.8). Transition brought GDP losses throughout CEE and 1989 levels have been regained, except in Estonia, only recently (EBRD, 1999:73). The welfare systems in these countries have been resistant to structural change, but have been eroded by the reductions in national income, inflation and the difficulty in sustaining public expenditure (Gotting, 1998; UNICEF, op. cit.). Poverty in its wider sense – including access to health and education – has spread as these services have deteriorated. EU membership may well bring further pressures towards the convergence of spending levels in such services, as appears to have happened to education among current members,

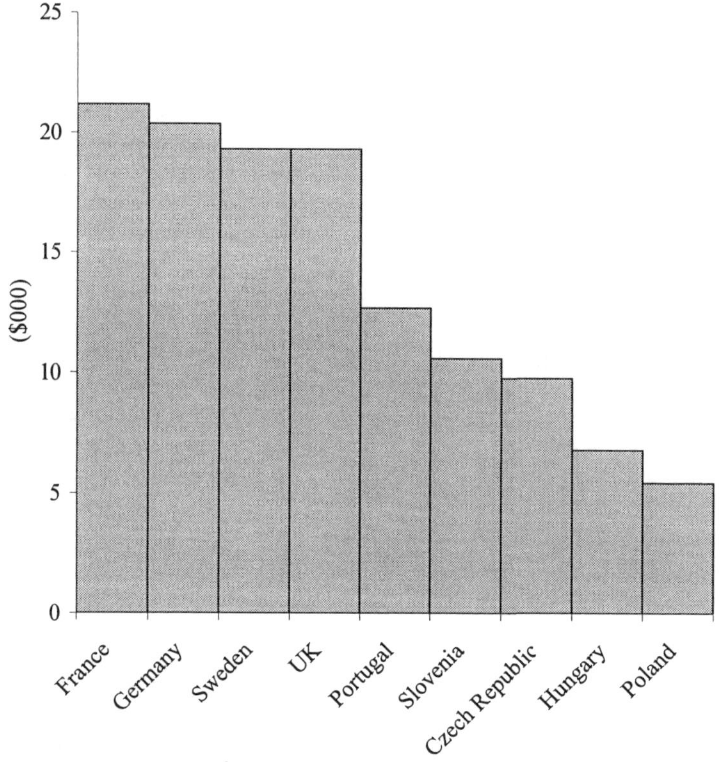

Source: http://www.undp/org/hdro/ihpprof.htm.

Figure 7.8 Real GDP per capita, 1995

with falling shares of expenditure being observed in traditionally high spending countries such as the Netherlands and Sweden (Micklewright and

Stewart, 1999a:47). These pressures may threaten some of the achievements of the Soviet era, especially the high enrolment rates for sixteen-year-olds in the Czech Republic and mathematics scores which are among Europe's best (Micklewright and Stewart, 2000:19). Reducing spending on supporting parents in employment - on nurseries, kindergartens, parental leave and so on - poses further risks of increasing relative poverty. Rising levels of social stress are suggested by declining fertility rates in all applicant countries.

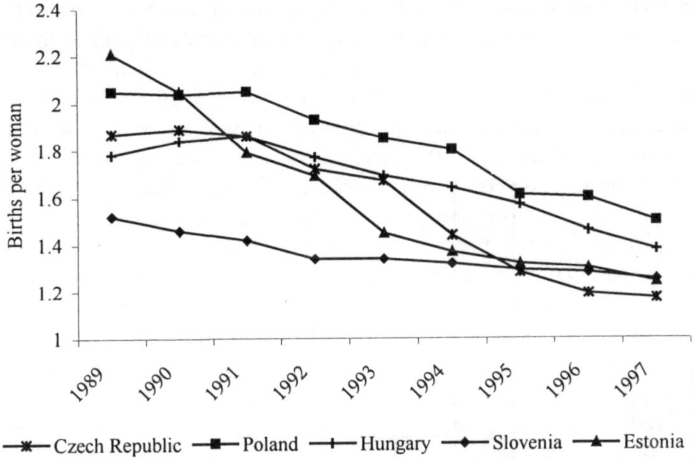

Source: UNICEF (1999), Statistical Annex,Table 2.2.

Figure 7.9 Reproductive behaviour: total fertility rate

Reference to the unification of Germany is pertinent. This brought together two countries as disparate economically as the north and south of Europe, but with wholly different economic systems (Leibfried, op. cit.). The 'massive inflow of capital and technical expertise from West Germany' has brought generally rising living standards and advantages to some groups, for example younger mobile workers. But, five years after reunification, severe social problems were evident: East Germans still felt deprived, comparing themselves with the west rather than with Poland or Russia; and there was an 'unprecedented demographic implosion', with drastic declines in marriage and birth rates. Children were among the losers of these processes: 'Several years after reunification, economic welfare indicators show mixed results, especially for families with children. While all have benefited from increased incomes and improved consumption possibilities, the relative welfare position of women and children has changed dramatically, leaving them increasingly vulnerable' (UNICEF, 1995:86–7). This experience suggests that, even with massive investment, it is possible for national economic inclusion to be accompanied by widening social exclusion.

The historical evidence, the administrative hurdles and the scale of the economic task to be undertaken add up to formidable causes for concern about the welfare of the children of CEE as they join the EU. But, as argued above, their parents and grandparents tend still to hope and to see the EU as an agent of social change. On its own, however, this does not amount to effective political pressure to address poverty. It must be hoped that the growing number of members with lower living standards will weight the bargaining in favour of more serious social action in this field. A precedent for this was set after the last accession of poorer members, with it being possible to see the attendant increases in the Structural Funds and the creation of a Cohesion Fund as part of the bargain over economic and monetary union wrested by the newcomers to compensate for the economic and social risks attached to further market integration. Incomes in the 'Cohesion Four' did indeed grow relative to other member states in the early years following their accessions, especially in Ireland where 'income per head rose from 64 per cent to 83 per cent of the EU average over 1983–93' (Micklewright and Stewart, 1999a:17). It was only in Ireland though that this trend continued into the 1990s, allowing the country to reach the EU average. In achieving this, the country benefited significantly from transfers through the social funds, gaining an average of 10.8 per cent of them over the years from its entry to 1990, while Greece gained 7.1 per cent and Portugal 2.2 per cent (Carrubba, 1997:472). The countries of CEE represent significant markets and investment opportunities and they may be able to claim social investment from the EU in exchange for opening these up, but the scale of the problems they face is very large in comparison with those of previous entrants.

Policies to reduce disparities of income within and between nations, to include the excluded - whether they are lone parents, ethnic minorities, the unemployed or migrant workers - need some political solidarity. What prospects are there for social citizenship on a Europe-wide basis (Rhodes and Meny, 1998)? It has been argued that such a social contract is possible practically, but now politically unlikely, undermined by the economic developments of the Thatcher era:

> The notion of self-regulating markets, promoted within the international sectors of advanced industrialized economies, has a logic of its own that tends towards the creation, not of integrated blocs of welfare states, but of international institutions to uphold private property and contractual exchange. This in turn provokes various divergent movements for social protection, based on nationalistic, ethnic, religious, regional, class or

> sectional principles (all of which tend to fragment the rational-legal order of the welfare state era), and on narrower mutualities of like incomes and tastes, which erode the economic basis of collectivization. (Jordan, 1998:262)

The prospects for the poor of CEE as their countries join the EU seem likely to be mixed. Rising national prosperity will bring more access to international goods and services, though living standards will remain well below those of Western Europe. The nations of CEE will have some leverage to enhance social investments against social exclusion, but there is no evidence at present of a political dynamic towards integrative policies on the scale that would be needed for east to meet west or even to resist the growth of inequalities. National welfare systems are likely to continue to be the main players in combating poverty, with the EU playing a marginal role. Being part of Europe will bring expectations that may well make people feel more disadvantaged, even while living standards are rising. It is also likely that the advantages of joining will be distributed unequally and that women and children will be among the losers.

CONCLUSION

The social powers of Europe emerged from a very small base in a Community led by market forces, but they have been growing and the EU is now a player in social policy that cannot be ignored by national governments. It has also developed politically in the context of globalisation to counter perceived threats to national sovereignties. However, the rhetoric of social Europe is much stronger than the reality. Legislation, especially for gender equality, affects and limits national governments, while social action programmes have played some role in developing strategies against discrimination and exclusion. But social spending at the European level remains small and there is no integration of welfare systems to match the integration of currencies and markets.

Gender policy sees the EU at its most powerful, with a constitutional commitment to equal pay, a Court of Justice willing to place wide interpretations on this and a gradual widening of the coverage of issues related to equality in paid employment through directives, as well as softer law. This will add to the resources of women in CEE as they make claims for equality. The benefit though is small and will help little in defending, within the more liberal economic climate of the EU, the social supports that have made it possible for them to combine paid and unpaid work.

The best news for the children of CEE is that their national living standards should rise: the stimulus to growth should help to narrow the gap between east and west. There should be resources to access consumer goods and services, as well as to sustain the high levels of investment in education, health and parenting which characterise their social polities and are crucial for their futures. The gap in material living standards is very large, however, and narrowing it will take time and material gains may or may not be enough to stop children from feeling worse off as comparisons with the west become more pressing. Also, the benefits from rising national standards of living are likely to be unequally spread. The tendency to increasing inequality started by the transition is likely to be pushed further by EU membership, conforming to its rules and responding to the pressures to reduce social spending. Relative poverty is likely to rise, with all that means for the health and social participation of children from poor households. The powerful educational achievements of, and supports to parents in, the accession countries will need powerful defence.

The history of European intervention is that it is stronger on creating the conditions for social exclusion than on implementing social policies to contain it. Social spending by the EU has been miniscule and there has been no attempt to construct a single welfare regime of Europe to compare with the single currency. In this context, child poverty has flourished wherever national governments have allowed it. While social Europe takes small steps forward, it has far to go before it poses a serious challenge to child poverty and exclusion. If a pessimistic conclusion regarding social exclusion is to be avoided, then:

> The new solidarities needed for a social contract, that could provide the basis for European social citizenship, would require political brokerage at the national and the EU level. Political elites would need to be convinced that they would get good electoral returns on policies for social integration, and new institutions to harmonize the interest of collectivities which are currently antagonistic or divergent in their orientations. (ibid.:257)

The extension of social Europe has been slow and erratic, but is likely to be given some further impetus through the accession of new members from CEE. The greater economic and social diversity this will bring will create some pressures for an extension of the social powers of the EU. The growing inequality within CEE already triggered by the transition and likely to be pushed further by market integration may also create political pressures for policies to combat social exclusion and to engineer a more socially cohesive Europe. The wider politics of the EU do not look friendly to the policies supporting women's employment that have been strengths in CEE or to prioritising the interests of the increasing numbers of socially excluded or, more broadly, to increasing the social impact of the EU through social spending. Much will continue to depend on national policies rather than European ones, although much will also depend on how the incoming governments use their leverage to gain protection for their high levels of social investment in education, health and support for parents and to contain the impetus to greater social inequality.

NOTE

1. We would particularly like to acknowledge the debt we owe to UNICEF colleagues at ICDC, Florence, for access to their data and to Peter Taylor-Gooby for his helpful comments.

REFERENCES

Ackers, L. (1994), 'Women, Citizenship and European Community Law', *Journal of Social Welfare and Family Law*, **16** (4), 391–406.

Arber, Sara (1999), 'Gender Inequalities in European Societies Today', in Thomas Boje, Bart Van Steenbergen and Sylvia Walby (eds), pp. 66–83.

Atkinson, A.B. (1998), 'EMU, Macroeconomics and Children', Innocenti Occasional Papers, EPS 68.

Bates, S. (1999), 'Clubbed Together', *The Guardian*, 29 June.

Bittman, M. and R.E. Gooding (1998), 'An Equivalence Scale for Time', Discussion Papers, no. 85, Social Policy Research Centre, University of New South Wales, available at http://www.sprc.unsw.edu.au/.

Boje, Thomas, Bart Van Steenbergen and Sylvia Walby (eds) (1999), *European Societies: Fusion or Fission?*, London: Routledge.

Borchorst, Annette (1994), 'Welfare State Regimes, Women's Interests and the EC', in Diane Sainsbury (ed.), *Gendering Welfare States*, London: Sage, pp. 26–44.

Bornschier, Volker, and Patrick Ziltener. (1999), 'The Revitalization of Western Europe and the Politics of the "Social" Dimension', in Thomas Boje, Bart Van Steenbergen and Sylvia Walby (eds), pp. 33–52.

Carrubba, C.J. (1997), 'Net Financial Transfers in the European Union: Who Gets What and Why?', *Journal of Politics*, **59** (2), 469–96.

Duffy, Katherine (1998), 'Combating Social Exclusion and Promoting Integration in the European Union', in Carey Oppenheim (ed.) *An Inclusive Society: Strategies for Tackling Poverty*, London: Institute for Public Policy Research, pp. 227–52.

Duncan, Simon (1996), 'The Diverse Worlds of European Patriarchy', in Maria Garcia-Ramon and Janice Monk (eds) *Women of the European Union: The Politics of Work and Daily Life*, London: Routledge, pp. 74–110.

Duncan, S. (1996a), 'Obstacles to a Successful Equal Opportunities Policy in the European Union', *European Journal of Women's Studies*, **3** (4), 399–422.

EBRD (European Bank for Reconstruction and Development) (1999), *Transition Report 1999 – Ten Years of Transition*, London: EBRD.
Fajth, G. (1996), 'Family Support Policies in Central and Eastern Europe', National Academy of Sciences/National Research Council Task Force on Economies in Transition workshop, Washington D.C.
Firlit-Fesnak, Grazyna (1997), 'Polish Families in the Transformation Period', in Ulla Björnberg and Jürgen Sass (eds), *Families with Small Children in Eastern and Western Europe*, Aldershot: Ashgate, pp. 143–58.
Freudenstein, R. (1998), 'Poland, Germany and the EU', *International Affairs* **74** (1), 41–66.
Gotting, Ulrike. (1998), 'In Defence of Welfare: Social Protection and Social Reform in Central and Eastern Europe', in Martin Rhodes and Yves Meny (eds), pp. 125–54.
Gould, A. (1999) 'The Erosion of the Welfare State: Swedish Social Policy and the EU', *Journal of European Social* Policy, **9** (2), 165–74.
Hantrais, Linda (2000), *Social Policy in the European Union*, 2nd edition, Basingstoke: Macmillan.
Hoskyns, Catherine (1996), *Gender: Women, Law and Politics in the European Union*, London: Verso.
Hoskyns, C. (1992), 'The European Community's Policy on Women in the Context of 1992', *Women's Studies International Forum*, **15** (1), 21–8.
Jordan, Bill (1998), 'European Social Citizenship: Why a New Social Contract (Probably) Will Not Happen', in Martin Rhodes and Yves Meny (eds), pp. 244–65.
Juchler, J. (1999), 'Poland's Attitude Toward the European Union – Progress Despite Tension and Increasing Skepticism', *Osteuropa*, **49** (5), 486–92.
Kolankiewicz, G. (1994), 'Consensus and Competition in the Central and Eastern Enlargement of the European Union', *International Affairs*, **70** (3), 477–95.
Leibfreid, Stephan (1992), 'Towards a European Welfare State? On Integrating Poverty Regimes into the EC', in Zsuzsa Ferge and Jon Kolberg (eds), *Social Policy in a Changing Europe*, Frankfurt: Campus, pp. 245–80.
Liebfried, Stephan and Paul Pierson. (1995), *European Social Policy*, Washington: The Brookings Institution.
Mazey, S. (1998), 'The European Union and Women's Rights: From the Europeanization of National Agendas to the Nationalization of a European Agenda?', *Journal of European Public Policy*, **5** (1), 131–52.
Meehan, Elizabeth (1993), 'Women's Rights in the European Community', in Jane Lewis (ed.), *Women and Social Policies in Europe*, Aldershot, UK and Brookfield, US: Edward Elgar, pp. 194–205.
Micklewright, J. and Stewart, K. (2000), 'Child Well-Being in the EU and Enlargement to the East', UNICEF Florence: Innocenti Research Centre.
Micklewright, J. and Stewart, K. (1999a), 'Is Child Welfare Converging in the European Union?', Innocenti Occasional Papers No. ESP 69, Florence: UNICEF International Child Development Centre.
Micklewright, J. and Stewart, K. (1999b), 'Is the Well-being of Children Converging in the European Union?', *The Economic Journal*, **109** (459), pp. F692–F714.
Mikelka, E. (1998), 'The Extension of the European Union – Costs and Benefits for the Countries of Central and Central and Eastern Europe', *Economicky Casopis*, **46** (2), 159–85.

Morris, Anne and Susan M. Nott. (1991), *Working Women and the Law: Equality and Discrimination in Theory and Practice*, London and New York: Routledge/Sweet and Maxwell.

Neilson, J. (1998), 'Equal Opportunities for Women in the European Union: Success or Failure?', *Journal of European Social Policy*, **8** (1), 64–79.

Neumayer, L. (1999), 'Hungarian, Polish and Czech Public Opinions and Political Parties Facing European Integration', *Revue D'Etudes Comparatives Est–Ouest*, **30** (1), 139–64.

Ostner, Iliona, and Jane Lewis (1995), 'Gender and the Evolution of European Social Policies', in Stephan Leibfried and Paul Pierson (eds), pp. 159–93.

Pascall, G., and N. Manning. (2000), 'Gender and Social Policy: Comparing Welfare States in Central and Central and Eastern Europe and the Former Soviet Union', *Journal of European Social Policy*, **10** (3), 240–66.

Pierson, Paul and Leibfried, Stephan (1995), 'The Dynamics of Social Policy Integration', in Stephan Liebfried and Paul Pierson (eds), pp. 432–66.

Rees, Teresa (1998), *Mainstreaming Equality in the European Union: Education, Training and Labour Market Policies,* London: Routledge.

Rhodes, Martin (1998), *European Social Policy*, London: Longman.

Rhodes, Martin and Yves Meny (eds) (1998), *The Future of European Welfare: A New Social Contract?*, Basingstoke: Macmillan.

Rose, R., and C. Haerpfer. (1995), 'Democracy and Enlarging the European Union Eastwards', *Journal of Common Market Studies*, **33** (3), 427–50.

Rossilli, M. (1999), 'The European Union's Policy on the Equality of Women', *Feminist Studies*, **25** (1), 171–82.

Rossilli, M. (1997), 'The European Community's Policy on the Equality of Women: from the Treaty of Rome to the Present', *The European Journal of Women's Studies*, **4** (1), 63–82.

Streeck, Wolfgang (1995), 'From Market Making to State Building? Reflections on the Political Economy of European Social Policy', in Stephan Liebfried and Paul Pierson (eds), pp. 389–431.

UNICEF (United Nations Children's Fund) (2000), 'A League Table of Child Poverty in Rich Nations', Innocenti Report Card, Issue 1.

UNICEF (United Nations Children's Fund) (1999), *Women in Transition*, Florence: UNICEF.

UNICEF (United Nations Children's Fund) (1995), *Poverty, Children and Policy: Responses for a Brighter Future*, Florence: UNICEF.

Walby, S. (1999), 'The New Regulatory State: the Social Powers of the European Union', *British Journal of Sociology*, **50** (1), 118–37.

8. Regional Development and EU Enlargement

Mike Ingham, Hilary Ingham and Ronald McQuaid[1]

INTRODUCTION

Emphasis on economic and social cohesion to support the process of European integration has led to increasing attention being paid to regional differentiation, particularly following the Maastricht Treaty on European Union. This relates not simply to the divergence in income and unemployment levels, which remains considerable, but also to the technological discrepancies and differential access to the growth and employment opportunities created by the new economy (Guersent, 2001). It is further recognised that the interests of future generations must be given due regard in regional development programmes and this means that environmental concerns weigh heavily in the process of policy formulation at the European level. The ambitions of European Union (EU) level regional policy interventions have therefore evolved considerably from those espoused in the Treaty of Rome. Nevertheless, any expansion of the Union beyond its current eastern borders will introduce spatial inequalities of a totally new order of magnitude to those experienced in the past and render the attainment of the desired cohesion all the more problematic.

Nevertheless, neither grand visions of the continent nor recognition of spatial inequality are of themselves adequate justifications for the operation of a European regional policy. Indeed, beyond ensuring equality of opportunity, some would question the appropriateness of such policies at either supranational or national level (see Chisholm, 1990). Under this view, the role of market forces in promoting trade through the exploitation of comparative advantage and in driving migration and capital flows are central to the process of development, although factor mobility is a highly sensitive issue in the context of enlargement (Blazyca, 2002). In consequence, the case for regional policy is often couched in terms of the slow operation of market forces, the pervasiveness of market failure and the contrast between efficiency and equity (Armstrong, 2001). But this still leaves open the question of why it should be conducted at the European level. One part of the usual justification is that the economies of the member states are increasingly interdependent and that effective supranational coordination can serve to limit the conduct of beggar-my-neighbour regional policies at the national level. European level policies may also be useful as signals to underpin the commitment to cohesion. Furthermore, it might be justified on the grounds that it can help to coordinate different aspects of policy, for example, in the sectoral, social and regional areas.[2]

Before examining the ways in which European regional policy has evolved, it is important to consider how a region is defined for this purpose. As discussed in the next section, the division of Europe's space is not based on exact science and can lead to potentially misleading international comparisons being drawn. Predictably, the countries of Central and Eastern Europe (CEE) did not, in the past, divide their territories in ways that conform to the requirements of European legislation. Nonetheless, given their transparent desire to gain access to regional assistance, and as part of their need to strengthen local democracy under their accession partnerships, they are now well on the road to compliance in this field. However, the European Commission's recent redefinition of its regional classification may mean that Poland will pay a price for having been an early mover in local government reform.

Armed with an appreciation of the delineation of European space, it is then appropriate to describe the ways in which the regionally focused policies of the EU have evolved in line with the drive to deepen the character of the Union at the same time as its boundaries have expanded to encompass an ever more diverse range of countries. The fact that the most disadvantaged regions were to be found in the poorest member states, whose governments are ill equipped to pursue independent policies designed to foster cohesion, merely underlined the case of the advocates of an overarching regional policy. Ultimately, however, the result was an increasingly unwieldy system of support that would be incapable of meeting the challenge of the most ambitious wave of enlargement envisaged to date. Nevertheless, the reforms heralded under Agenda 2000 were accompanied by the introduction of a range of pre-accession instruments for the applicant countries from CEE that are designed to promote some greater degree of convergence before admission is granted.

Given the institutional background, it is important that the details are judged against the scale of the problem that has been confronted to date and, even more telling, that which will be faced in the future. This is the focus of the fourth section, which looks at the magnitude of regional difference within the current 15 members of the EU, how these have evolved over the past decade and how these would be affected by the entry of ten new, low income transition states. While brief, this enquiry provides a summary introduction to the ongoing debate regarding the concept of convergence and its relevance to cohesion within both the current EU and that which might emerge in the future. Certain concluding comments close the work.

THE DIVISION OF EUROPE'S SPACE

Since the early 1970s, the territory of the Community has been divided into a threefold hierarchy of regions known as the Nomenclature of Territorial Units for Statistics and commonly referred to by the acronym of NUTS. These form the basis for the collection, development, harmonisation and dissemination of Community regional statistics and represent the targets of various spatial development policies. When the major revision of the Structural Funds came into force in 1989, the area of the then 12 member states was apportioned between 64 NUTS 1 regions, 167 NUTS 2 basic administrative regions that are sub-divisions of level I regions and 824 NUTS 3 sub-divisions of level 2 regions.[3] No ideal size of region was defined and neither was any objective means of designation prescribed: they were established on the basis of 'gentlemen's agreements' (CEC, 2001:2). In the usual case, this meant that they were identified in terms of national administrative practice, normally being places where certain levels of government exercise their powers in relation to regional policy. This unscientific procedure has prompted the observation that 'The English slang meaning of the French acronym of the territorial divisions of the European Union – "nuts" – today describes quite well, from an economic perspective, the EU regional classification' (Casellas and Galley, 1999:553).[4] Nevertheless, they were viewed as a 'coherent system' for allocating the Structural Funds in a 'rational and consistent way' (CEC, op. cit.:2).[5]

While of itself by no means the greatest problem associated with expansion to the east, the applicant countries did not possess, at least initially, NUTS-comparable regional designations. Without them, their accession would introduce unacceptable complications into the system of administrating regional/structural assistance and this, coupled with internal tensions regarding changes in the delineation of EU space, prompted the Commission to conclude in February 2001 that, for the first time, there needs to be a legal base for the NUTS classification (ibid.).[6] It argued that

Table 8.1 Distribution of NUTS regions in the EU

	Maximum/Minimum Population Size ('000)*		
	NUTS 1 3 000/7 000	NUTS 2 800/3 000	NUTS 3 150/800
Austria	3	9	35
	(3)	(9)	(35)
Belgium	3	11	43
	(3)	(9)	(43)
Denmark	1	1	15
	(1)	(1)	(15)
Finland	2	6	20
	(2)	(6)	(19)
France	9	26	100
	(9)	(26)	(100)
Germany	16	40	442
	(16)	(40)	(543)
Greece	4	13	51
	(4)	(13)	(51)
Ireland	1	2	8
	(1)	(1)	(8)
Italy	11	20	103
	(11)	(20)	(103)
Luxembourg	1	1	1
	(1)	(1)	(1)
Netherlands	4	12	40
	(4)	(12)	(40)
Portugal	3	7	30
	(3)	(7)	(30)
Spain	7	18	52
	(7)	(18)	(52)
Sweden	1	8	21
	(1)	(8)	(24)
UK	12	37	134
	(11)	(35)	(65)

Note: * The old NUTS distribution is in parentheses.

Source: CEC (2001).

'objective criteria' are needed in order to ensure 'impartiality' when regional statistics are compiled for policy purposes and that amendments of the classification's structure should render regions 'more homogeneous in terms of population size' (ibid.:6). The proposed new rules of classification are presented in Table 8.1 and, although they reduce the population disparities within a given level considerably, there remain not only a large range within each but also no necessary economic logic behind them.[7] In the usual case, regional disparities within the EU are measured at the NUTS 2 level of aggregation and corrective measures targeted accordingly.

As of the November 2001 Regular Reports, the majority of applicant states had established at least a preliminary NUTS classification of their territories, as indicated in Table 8.2, and most of these are consistent with the Commission's proposed revisions. In many cases, however, these remain as yet statistical units and do not reflect administrative competencies. The

Table 8.2 Provisional distribution of NUTS regions in CEE

	Maximum/Minimum Population Size ('000)		
	NUTS 1 3 000/7 000	NUTS 2 800/3 000	NUTS 3 150/800
Bulgaria	0	6	under construction
Czech. Republic	0	8	14
Estonia	Provisional NUTS classification still pending		
Hungary	0	7	20
Latvia	0	0	5
Lithuania	0	1	5
Poland	0	16	44
Romania	0	8	42
Slovakia	0	8	4
Slovenia	0	2	12

Source: CEC (2000, 2001a).

exceptions to this are the Czech Republic, Hungary and Poland where local government reforms have accompanied the new classifications. In the latter case, the Commission have praised the political reforms, although they had been the cause of bitter domestic argument throughout the 1990s and had only finally been introduced at the beginning of 1999. In the light of the recommendations of February 2001, however, Poland's actions appear premature. Four of the NUTS 2 regions, which are represented by newly created regional (voivodship) levels of government, exceed the maximum population size established by the Commission (GUS, 2000). As discussed below, with Objective 1 status being conferred at the NUTS 2 level, this introduces major potential problems. Furthermore, several of Poland's NUTS 3 regions exceed the maximum population size specified in the new recommendations and Objective 2 status is normally conferred upon areas on this tier. However, this second problem is not likely to present such severe problems as the first, given that the NUTS 3 regions have been created as amalgamations of the new counties (powiats) and presumably could be re-arranged without undue political upheaval.

REGIONAL DIFFERENTIATION AND EU POLICY

The original Treaty of Rome made reference to the need to consolidate economic unity and reduce disparities between regions in the then European Community, although the means by which it was hoped to achieve this were not explicitly regional policies. Thus the first two Structural Funds to be established one year later in 1958 were the European Social Fund (ESF) and the European Agricultural Guidance and Guarantee Fund (EAGGF). Only the latter could be said to have had an indirect regional focus, although later reforms were to see some ESF funds directed towards priority spatial areas (Croxford and Wise, 1988). In fact, it was not until 1975 that the European Regional Development Fund (ERDF) was established as another Structural Fund.[8] It aimed to assist those regions affected by industrial decline and to counter-balance the significant support given to the agricultural industries of the member states. This introduced for the first time the notion of redistribution between richer and poorer regions of the Community.

However, the character of current EU regional policy owes most to the major reform of the Structural Funds that became effective from January 1989 (Armstrong, 2001; CEC, 1989). The overhaul was prompted by three developments. First, the accession of Portugal and Spain in 1986 had increased regional disparities considerably and doubled the size of the population resident in the least favoured regions. Second, prompted by the major structural implications of the single market, Article 130A of the Single European Act (SEA) of 1987 introduced economic and social cohesion, involving a reduction in the 'disparities between the various regions and the backwardness of the least favoured regions' (see Comfort, 1988:544), as a key objective of the Community. Third, there was a growing recognition that the mechanisms for providing assistance under the Structural Funds had become complex and unwieldy.[9]

The 1989 reforms introduced five key principles for the operation of the Structural Funds. The first was that assistance was to be concentrated on five priority objectives, as described in Table 8.3, which also provides detail on which of the Funds were to be available for each activity.[10] Objective 1 status was conferred upon those regions whose GDP per capita was less than (or close to) 75 per cent of the Community average. Objective 2 covered regions with rates of unemployment above the Community average and an above average share, but declining total, of employment in industry.[11] Areas eligible under Objective 5(b) were designated by a Management Committee composed of representatives from the member states that was charged to take into account aspects of rurality, peripherality and agricultural weakness. The reforms also coordinated the operation of the Commission's grant-awarding instruments (the Structural Funds) with those instruments available to it for advancing loans. The latter comprised most notably the European Investment Bank (EIB) and the European Coal and Steel Community (ECSC), although these bodies had in any case always exhibited a bias towards the more disadvantaged regions.

The second principle was that there should be a close partnership between the Commission and the member states and their competent authorities at the appropriate levels in pursuit of the goal of subsidiarity. Third, the structural actions were to be consistent with the economic strategies adopted in member states at the local, regional and national levels. Fourth, increased efficiency in the administration of the Funds was to be achieved, in part through enforcement of the criterion of additionality. Finally, emphasis was placed on the simplification, monitoring and flexibility of the implementation of structural actions.[12]

It is significant that from 1989 allocations from the Funds were to be determined by the EU's own designation of areas eligible for assistance, rather than by decisions of the member states themselves taken in the course of the conduct of their own regional policies. Within this framework, the Objective 1 regional development plans prepared nationally were normally expected to cover one NUTS 2 level territory.[13] Regional and social conversion plans (Objective 2) and rural development plans (Objective 5(b)), on the other hand, could be conceived at the NUTS 3 level. Measures to combat long-term unemployment and the occupational integration of young people (Objectives 3 and 4) could be drawn up at the national level, although the areas to benefit had to be separated into those already covered under Objectives 1, 2 and 5b and others.[14] However, this distinction was made 'in the interests of clarity' (CEC, 1989:29) and with the disadvantaged regions housing disproportionate numbers of both young and long-term unemployed, they also benefit considerably from actions under the ESF.

Table 8.3 Structural funds 1989–93

Priority Objective	Structural Funds	Share of Budget (%)[a]
(1) Promoting the development and structural adjustment of the less-developed regions	ERDF ESF EAGGF (Guidance Section)	62.2 (80% of ERDF)
(2) Converting the regions, border regions or part regions (including employment areas and urban communities) seriously affected by industrial decline	ERDF ESF	11.1
(3) Combating long-term unemployment	ESF	13.3[b]
(4) Facilitating the occupational integration of young people	ESF	
(5) Envisaging the reform of the CAP		
(5a) adapting production, processing and marketing structures in agriculture and forestry	EAGGF (Guidance Section)	6.7
(5b) promoting the development of the rural areas	ERDF EAGGF (Guidance Section)	3.3

Notes:

a The figures do not sum to 100 as a result of funds being reserved for transitional and innovative measures.

b This allocation is shared between Objectives (3) and (4).

The Maastricht Treaty, which entered into force in 1993, again emphasised the importance of economic and social cohesion, but this time in the light of the potentially destabilising effects of the move towards the adoption of a single currency. In pursuing the latter objective, it was recognised that the cohesion of poorer members would be compromised by the nominal convergence criteria adopted for monetary unification. Indeed, while the 'Delors II' proposals emanating from Maastricht regarding the speed at which Structural Funds expenditure should increase were diluted at the 1992 Edinburgh Summit, those regarding the new Cohesion Fund for less prosperous member states were accepted.[15] However, while cohesion is concerned in some way with the distance between lagging and more prosperous regions, it is not easy to define precisely, except in terms of that degree of disparity that is politically and socially acceptable: furthermore, it is almost certainly a dynamic target (Begg and Mayes, 1993). Nevertheless, it can be assumed that it will come about only if real convergence in the form of greater equality of income per head, unemployment rates etc. can be achieved.

The 1993 agreement adopted six priority Objectives (1–5(b)) for the Structural Funds over the budget period 1994–99, to which was added Objective 6 in 1995 with the accession of Finland and Sweden, as described in Table 8.4. Eligibility for Objective 1 status required that a region's GDP per capita be less than 75 per cent of the EU average and covered one-quarter of the population of the Union.[16] Objective 2 status, covering 16.4 per cent of the EU population, was linked to three criteria: an unemployment rate above the Community average, an above average percentage share of industrial employment and a declining total of industrial employment. While assisted area status in the two preceding categories was conferred for the entire planning period, this was not the case under Objectives 3, 4 and 5(a), although much of the support did in fact go to areas covered under Objectives 1, 2, 5(b) and 6. To qualify under Objective 5(b), a region had to have a low level of socio-economic development – assessed on the basis of GDP per capita – and to satisfy two out of three additional criteria: a high level of agricultural employment, a low level of agricultural incomes, a low population density and/or significant migration trends. This covered 8.8 per cent of the population of the Union. Finally, Objective 6 status was reserved for certain remote areas of Finland and Sweden and covered only 0.4 per cent of the total EU population.[17] The Objectives agreed in 1989 were therefore expanded somewhat in this subsequent period, although the extension of the coverage of the spatially targeted Structural Funds to encompass over half of the population of the Community, including many in richer member states, was criticised as a contradiction of the stated aim of concentrating resources on less prosperous regions (Bachtler and Michie, 1994).

Agenda 2000, which the European Council formally adopted on 21 June 1999, recognised three significant challenges that will confront the EU in future years and that necessitated a redefinition of the implementation methods of its economic and social cohesion policy. First, an anticipated enlargement that will bring into membership 105 million people whose average income is barely one-third of that of the prevailing EU average. Second, the budgetary rigour required to ensure successful implementation of full economic and monetary union. Third, the competitive pressures arising from globalisation, which make it necessary to assist disadvantaged regions and the most vulnerable groups on the labour market in order that they might benefit from new development opportunities. In an attempt to meet these new challenges, the regulatory framework of the Structural Funds was simplified, although the volume of resources allocated to them is projected to decline in both absolute and relative terms over the planning period to 2006 (CEC, 2001b:13; CEC, 2000a:5).

Under the new regulations, the number of Objectives has been reduced from seven to three. Objective 1 covers the promotion of the development and structural adjustment of regions considered to be lagging behind. These are NUTS 2 regions with per capita GDP less than 75 per cent of the EU average or those areas formerly covered under Objective 6. Objective 2 is new and supports the economic and social conversion of areas facing structural difficulties. It brings together the old Objectives 2 and 5(b) while extending them to cover other areas, including those highly dependent on the service sector, urban areas and areas dependent upon the fishing industry. The unifying theme is that support is awarded to regions lacking economic diversity. Objective 3 supports the adaptation and modernisation of policies and systems for education, training and employment. As such, it brings together the old Objectives 3 and 4 and covers areas not designated under Objective 1. It will serve as a reference framework for all human resource actions in the member states and takes into account the Employment Title in the Amsterdam Treaty and the new European employment strategy. Transitional funding arrangements have been established for regions that previously had Objective 1, 2 or 5(b) status, but are no longer eligible under the new Objectives 1 and 2.[18] Table 8.5 provides details of the funding sources available to each Objective and the distribution of the total Structural Funds between them.[19]

Table 8.4 Structural funds 1994–99

Priority Objective	Structural Funds	Share of Budget (%)
(1) Promoting the development and structural adjustment of regions whose development is lagging behind	ERDF, ESF EAGGF (Guidance Section) FIFG*	67.6
(2) Converting regions seriously affected by industrial decline	ERDF ESF	11.1
(3) Combating long-term unemployment and facilitating the integration into working life of young people and those excluded from the labour market	ESF	10.9
(4) Facilitating the adaptation of workers to industrial changes and changes in production systems	ESF	

Table 8.4 Continued

Priority Objective	Structural Funds	Share of Budget (%)
(5a) Speeding up the adjustment in agricultural structures in the framework of the reform of the CAP and facilitating the structural adjustment of the fisheries sector in the framework of the reform of the Common Fisheries Policy	EAGGF (Guidance Section) FIFG	5.0
(5b) Facilitating the development and structural adjustment of the rural areas	ERDF, ESF EAGGF (Guidance Section)	4.9
(6) Promoting the development of regions with an extremely low population density	ERDF ESF EAGGF (Guidance Section), FIFG	0.5

Note: * FIFG (Financial Instrument for Fisheries Guidance) is not a Structural Fund but finances structural actions in the fisheries sector within the framework of the Structural Fund programmes.

Source: CEC (1999).

Table 8.5 Structural funds 2000–06

Priority Objective	Structural Funds	Share of Budget (%)[a]
(1)	ERDF ESF EAGGF (Guidance Section) FIFG[b]	69.7
(2)	ERDF ESF	11.5
(3)	ESF	12.3

Notes:

a The figures do not sum to 100 as a result of funds being reserved for transitional and innovative measures.

b For the 2000–06 budget period, FIFG is a Structural Fund which supports accompanying measures to the Common Fisheries Policy in areas not covered by Objective 1.

Source: CEC (1999).

ASSISTANCE FOR THE TRANSITION ECONOMIES

Western development aid began to flow to the countries of CEE as soon as they rejected their former communist rulers and shattered the unity, however shallow that might previously have been, of the old Soviet bloc. The initial motivation was almost wholly political, with the support meant to ensure that there would no return to the past and to neutralise any attempts by Russia to reassert its control over the region. In the event, the western cause was advanced by the collapse of the Soviet Union in 1991, although democracy and the market economy took root at varying, and not always unidirectional, rates across what quickly became known as the transition states.

Assistance from Europe effectively took two forms: market access and formal aid programmes. The former is discussed in greater detail in Read (2002) so attention here will focus largely upon the latter. The first structured instrument was the aid programme for restructuring the economies of Poland and Hungary (Phare), which was established in 1989 as a vehicle for financial and technical cooperation in support of economic and political transition. However, the country coverage of the programme was widened to cover other transforming states in the following year. Its original budget allocation was 4.2 billion euro for the period 1990–94. Over the years 1993 to 1998, the largest element of the Phare budget was allocated to the STRUDER programme for structural development in selected regions, which were chosen on the basis that they would be most severely affected by economic restructuring, as well as for economically fragile rural areas. The latter also benefited from the RAPID initiative for infrastructure development in rural regions. In addition, 480 million euro of Phare finance was used for agricultural restructuring programmes over the years 1989 to 1998, more than half of which was allocated to Poland and Romania. As discussed in Kennard (2002), the Phare budget was also applied to cross-border regional cooperation agreements. For the period 1995–99, the budget was increased to 6,693 billion euro, although 13 partner countries were eligible for finance by 1996.

Notwithstanding the transition induced recession that swept through the post-communist states, economic relations between the EU and its eastern neighbours strengthened rapidly as the countries of CEE reoriented their trade flows from those that obtained under the Council for Mutual Economic Assistance towards the west. Although the evidence suggests that the benefits of this were captured disproportionately by Western Europe (Read, op. cit.), ten CEE states had applied formally to join the EU by June 1996. The trends to have emerged by 1995 were regarded by incoming President Santer as sufficiently optimistic for him to set the Commission the task of strengthening the Union and preparing for its enlargement (CEC, 1997). This set in train the developments that were to see the heads of member-state governments agree to Agenda 2000 at the Amsterdam Summit in June 1997, which was subsequently ratified by the European Parliament on 16 July of that year. In practice, this document represented the launch of the expansion process proper and introduced two new pre-accession funding instruments. At the same time, it refocused the activities of Phare, which was allocated a budget of 1,587 billion euro per annum for the period 2000–06, with 30 per cent being for institution building in pursuit of compliance with the *acquis* and 70 per cent for infrastructure projects. All countries of CEE are eligible to receive this funding, apart from the Commonwealth of Independent States (CIS), although administration of the programme remains in the hands of the Commission.[20]

The Instrument for Structural Policies for Pre-Accession (ISPA) is the largest of the new initiatives and it was allocated a budget of 1,058 billion euro per annum, which is to be devoted to projects with a minimum size of 5 million euro. As its name implies, the programme is oriented towards the future accession of the ten CEE applicant states. In application, it is targeted at environmental improvements and the upgrading of transport infrastructures, in particular with reference to the extension of the Trans-European Transport Networks (TEN).[21] ISPA currently operates with ex-ante approval of tendering and contracting by the Commission, although it is intended that this transitional arrangement will disappear as aid to the beneficiaries is decentralised. The second new initiative, also directed towards the ten CEE applicant states, is the Special Pre-Accession Programme for Agricultural and Rural Development (SAPARD), which has been allocated a budget of 529 million euro per annum and is managed by the applicants themselves, following acceptance of their overall strategies by the Commission. The scheme is similar in intent, albeit somewhat broader in application, to the old Objectives 5(a) and 5(b). As this programme is examined in detail in Ingham and Ingham (2002), it will not be considered further in this contribution. It is intended that expenditure from the two new funds will be applied to areas of deficiency identified in the relevant Accession Partnership. If any applicant state is admitted into membership before the end of the current budget period, it will cease to be eligible for the pre-accession funds and the agreed budget will thereby be distributed amongst a smaller number of beneficiaries.[22] The schemes represent a substantially increased commitment to the pre-accession states on the part of the EU, although this has been brought about at the expense of reduced allocations to the Structural and Cohesion Funds.

REGIONAL DIFFERENTIATION IN EUROPE

The actions described in the preceding section have been undertaken in the belief that regional disparities within the EU are already too large and will increase further with enlargement to the east. This judgement can be grounded in concerns about both equity and efficiency, although the more oblique notion of economic, political and social cohesion pervades the official documentation. In any event, regional inequality is both universal and persistent. It has also been a characteristic of different economic and political environments, although the communist states may have succeeded in limiting its extent at the cost of lower overall rates of development. Here, some attempt is made to examine the magnitude of the imbalances that EU regional policy has been attempting to correct and those that it will face in the future if enlargement proceeds. This, however, raises at least two questions. First, what are the appropriate measures of inequality? To the extent that it is the individual who is the focus of attention, one might ideally like these to include some indicator of the standard of living or quality of life. In practice, the variables that are normally used represent simple proxies of the ideal and this treatment will, like many others, focus on GDP per capita and rates of unemployment. Second, what is the appropriate spatial unit for the examination of difference? In the context of the EU this is normally undertaken at the level of NUTS 2 regions, although some analysts choose to examine differences at the NUTS 1 level (e.g. Dewhurst and Mutais-Gaitan,

1995). The usual convention is adopted here, notwithstanding the comments made earlier regarding the definition of such areas.

Having determined what to measure and over which spatial unit, there remains the issue of how the resultant inequality should be measured. At least in its narratives, as exemplified by its Second Cohesion Report (CEC, 2001c), the Commission tends to focus upon extreme decile ratios. On this basis, it was led to conclude that some limited reduction in GDP per capita differences across the regions of the Union had occurred between the years 1988 and 1999. It recognised, however, that these will increase markedly in the face of any expansion to the east. As of the time of the Report, in an enlarged Union of 27 – the current EU-15 plus the CEE-10, Cyprus and Malta – the bottom 10 per cent of NUTS 2 regions in terms of GDP per capita would be located exclusively in eastern Poland, Bulgaria and Romania, together with Latvia and Lithuania. These areas have a mean GDP per head, measured in terms of purchasing power parity, which is only 31 per cent of the EU average. This contrasts with the situation at present in which the bottom 10 per cent of regions have a GDP per capita that is 61 per cent of that figure. Currently, Ipeiros in Greece is the only NUTS 2 region with a per capita GDP that is less than half of the mean, but the admission of 12 new members would mean that 79 million people live in regions that are poorer than this. In the Union of 15, the top 10 per cent of regions have an output per head that is 2.4 times that of the bottom decile, while the admission of the 12 new members would more than double this figure to 5.3.

Superficially, at least, labour market performance in the candidate countries is more similar to that in the EU-15 (ibid.). Thus in 1999, the unemployment rate in the 12 applicant states averaged 10.2 per cent compared to 9.3 per cent amongst current members and the former figure increases only slightly if attention is restricted to the CEE-10. Indeed, the disparities across regions within the current Union, where the highest decile averaged rates almost eight times higher than the lowest decile, are actually somewhat greater than those revealed in CEE. However, these figures mask the fact that the transition is still incomplete in all pre-accession countries and there remains a real risk that unemployment may rise in many of their regions in the coming years (ibid.).

As noted at various points in the preceding discussion, the policy concern is with cohesion and the convergence of real magnitudes that is necessary to achieve it. The issue of convergence, both within the EU and in a wider international setting, has inspired a large literature and the emphasis on outlying observations in EU commentaries satisfies few of the desired statistical criteria.[23] Although a number of convergence measures have been defined (Barro and Sala-i-Martin, 1991, 1992; Chatterji, 1993) and notwithstanding the fact that new endogenous growth theory would question the rationale underlying its expected existence (e.g. Romer, 1990), attention here will focus upon simple σ and β convergence.[24] The former compares the cross-section dispersion of the chosen indicator at different points in time while the latter examines the evidence to see if initial poor performers have tended to catch up to the early leaders over some specified period. In neither case, however, is a test of the effectiveness of regional policy possible or implied.

σ Convergence

CEC (2001c) provides detail on GDP per capita, relative to the EU average, for NUTS 2 level EU regions in 1988 and 1998 and for CEE-10 regions for 1998. It also reports unemployment rates for 1989 and 1999 for the EU regions and for the CEE regions for 1999. Thus, while this data set permits comparisons over time for the current members, nothing can be said about evolutions over time in the applicant states and various problems surrounding the availability and consistency of data from other sources render it impossible to provide alternative estimates for all of them. However, data are available for the 49 pre-1999 voivodships of Poland that enable comparisons to be made over certain short periods terminating in 1998. Here estimates of the variability in GDP per capita, relative to the national average, for the years 1988, 1992 and 1997 and of registered unemployment rates for the years 1991, 1994 and 1998 are utilised.

With the possible exception of the reduction of inequality between the extreme outliers in the distribution, Table 8.6 points to only a very modest reduction in the dispersion of per capita GDP across the regions of current member states over the years 1988 to 1998. This finding has some reflection in the findings of Dewhurst and Mutais-Gaitan (op. cit.) for NUTS 1 level regions over the preceding decade. More striking, albeit from only one observation, is the fact that the dispersion in the per capita GDPs of the applicant countries is almost twice that obtaining within the EU itself. When the two data sets are merged, an even more vivid impression of the scale of the regional problem that would exist if a mass enlargement were to take place in the short-term emerges. In particular, it can be noted that, relative to the EU average, there would be a difference of more than 700 per cent between the most and least prosperous regions and that the coefficient of variation would leap to 80 per cent. Nevertheless, the data for Poland place these figures in a slightly more optimistic light insofar as there are clear signs that the internal distribution of per capita output would appear to have converged during the first years of transformation.

The data presented in Table 8.7 draw a somewhat mixed picture of the

Table 8.6 Relative GDP per capita

		Range	(Highest-Lowest)/ Lowest (%)	Standard Deviation	Coefficient of Variation
EU-15					
	1998	143.7	343.78	25.17	0.26
	1988	138.2	373.51	24.93	0.27
CEE-10					
	1998	93.1	431.02	18.23	0.45
EU-15+CEE-10					
	1998	163.9	758.50	32.47	0.80
Poland					
	1997	118.5	192.37	20.75	0.24
	1992	154.4	236.22	27.74	0.30
	1988	142.5	246.63	28.52	0.32

Source: All EU-15 and 1998 CEE-10 data are from CEC (2001c). Data for Poland computed and supplied by Zaklad Badan Statystyczno-Ekonomicznych.

behaviour of rates of unemployment within the EU. Thus, while there was a compression of regional differentials between 1989 and 1999, the overall rate of unemployment within the fifteen increased from 8.4 to 9.4 per cent. The more uniform distribution at the close of the period reflected a situation in which the highest recorded rates had in fact fallen a little at the same time as there had been increases at the lower end of the spectrum. In short, there was a more even sharing of a greater risk. The simple mean of unemployment across the regions of the applicant states was, at 10.6 per cent, not too dissimilar to the position in the EU in 1999, although all measures of dispersion in the former were appreciably lower. This impression is confirmed when the CEE and EU data are combined, which highlights the fact that both the highest (Calabria, Italy) and lowest (Åland, Finland) unemployment regions lie within the boundaries of the current Union and that the addition of the CEE-10 reduces the overall variability in the data somewhat.

With open unemployment not officially enumerated until the beginning of 1990 in Poland, it is not possible to make a direct comparison with the EU statistics and, for comparative purposes, three observations prior to the local government reform of 1999 that ended the initial regional time-series of data have been chosen. The first is for December 1990, by which time the national rate of unemployment had already risen to 6.1 per cent (GUS, 1992). These figures could, of course, be tainted inasmuch as restructuring was proceeding at different speeds across the country and given that registration was not

Table 8.7 Unemployment rates

		Range	(Highest-Lowest)/ Lowest (%)	Standard Deviation	Coefficient of Variation
EU-15					
	1999	26.6	1 266.67	5.13	0.59
	1989	30.7	3 411.11	5.13	0.64
CEE-10					
	1999	18.7	584.38	4.63	0.44
EU-15+CEE-10					
	1999	23.6	1 266.67	5.08	0.56
Poland					
	1998	17.9	688.46	4.15	0.35
	1994	23.0	306.67	5.34	0.30
	1990	9.4	447.62	2.11	0.30

Source: All EU-15 and 1998 CEE-10 data are from CEC (2001c). Data for Poland from GUS (1992, 1995, 1999).

subject initially to qualification criteria (OECD, 1992). The second observation is therefore taken at December 1994, the year in which national unemployment peaked at 16.9 per cent, but by which time the registration criteria had been tightened considerably (GUS, 1995). Finally, use is made of the final observation on the old 49 voivodships at December 1998 when the national unemployment rate stood at 10.4 per cent (GUS, 1999).[25] Unlike the GDP data, the figures do not indicate a clear convergence of unemployment rates across space as the last decade unfolded. Thus, while the standard deviation declined from the peak in 1994, the coefficient of variation indicates that this reduction was less than that observed in the mean unemployment rate. As discussed further below, differences in regional labour market performance represent a worrying portent.

β Convergence

Movements in the degree of σ inequality over time do not indicate necessarily that there have been changes in the position of disadvantaged regions relative to more privileged areas. This issue is more appropriately considered by focusing attention on β convergence, which occurs when the rate of growth of some variable is inversely related to its starting value. Following in the spirit of Barro and Sala-i-Martin (1992; 1991, op. cit.), there is unconditional convergence if β in the following regression equation is positive:

$$(1/T)ln(y_{it}/y_{it-T}) = \alpha - (1/T)(1 - e^{-\beta T})ln(y_{it-T}) + \mu \quad (8.1)$$

i = region
t = time
y = the variable of interest
T = the length of time between observations
μ = a disturbance term.

Given the constraints on data availability, it is not possible to conduct an analysis of this kind for the CEE-10 as a whole, although a comparison of the situation in the EU-15 and in Poland will once again be provided as an example of the trends in the two halves of Europe. The findings from estimating such equations by non-linear least squares are presented in Table 8.8.

Although the equation does not fit the data particularly well, there is significant evidence that some modest convergence between the GDP per capita of EU regions took place between 1988 and 1998. This of course confirms the impression conveyed by CEC (2001c).[26] Although β does not quite achieve desired levels of significance, the data for Poland might be taken to imply divergent regional growth, at least between 1992, when national output began to grow again, and 1997. The unemployment figures tell a similar story in that there appears to have been quite strong regional convergence within the current boundaries of the EU, but equally strong divergence between the voivodships of Poland, once the labour market trough had been passed in 1994.[27] If the Polish situation is a true reflection of that in the other applicant countries, the results of this analysis suggest that cohesion and the convergence necessary to achieve it will remain very much to the fore of concern in an expanded Union.

None of this should be taken to imply that the EU is unaware of the challenges that eastward enlargement will present. In its Second Cohesion Report (ibid.), the Commission classified CEE regions into four broad types. It was most optimistic about the major metropolitan areas, notably capital cities such as Prague, Bratislava and Budapest, which have enjoyed significant increases in service sector employment, have high levels of

Table 8.8 Non-linear least squares convergence regressions

	β^*	R^2	F	N
GDP				
EU-15				
1988–98	0.01535 (5.454)	0.1475	34.7424	196
Poland				
1988–97	-0.08191 (0.777)	-0.0092	0.5609	49
1988–92	0.01507 (0.509)	-0.0153	0.2756	49
1992–97	-0.02532 (1.859)	0.0409	3.0487	49
Unemployment Rates				
EU-15				
1989–99	0.05629 (6.761)	0.2977	82.4008	193
Poland				
1990–98	-0.00692 (0.659)	-0.0124	0.4111	49
1990–94	0.06522 (3.184)	0.2031	13.2305	49
1994–98	-0.05955 (3.819)	0.1801	11.5462	49

Note: * t-statistics are given in parentheses.

investment, skilled labour forces, better infrastructure endowments and favourable geographic locations. They exhibit lower levels of unemployment and higher wage levels than other regions. Western border regions, which have become much less peripheral since the onset of transition, were also cast in a favourable light. They possess skilled workforces with low labour costs and good infrastructure, both of which have stimulated markets, encouraged investment and generated falling levels of unemployment. The majority of the most disadvantaged regions are the rural areas situated on what would be the eastern periphery of an enlarged EU. These are characterised by low levels of investment, poor infrastructure endowments and limited human capital. In addition, they have economic structures dominated by low productivity, often subsistence, agriculture. While this has contained unemployment levels to date, future restructuring will be likely to lead to large-scale job losses. Finally, the Report saw old industrial regions as having been most adversely affected by the transition. They have suffered from a combination of privatisation, enterprise restructuring, trade reorientation and the loss of subsidies, while failing to attract new business or investment. In consequence, they tend to exhibit high levels of unemployment, which are made more troublesome by the low and outdated skill portfolios of their workforces. Furthermore, restructuring is far from complete and could cause serious economic and social problems in the future. The outstanding question is therefore whether the EU has the weapons in its armoury to assist in overcoming these spatial disparities and hence strengthen the cohesion that will be required if further enlargement is to be accomplished successfully.

CONCLUSION

Concern about regional inequality within the EU dates back to the Treaty of Rome and explicit policies aimed at reducing it have operated since 1975. The evidence produced here, in common with most other contributions in the field, suggests that, in terms of per capita output, convergence is indeed occurring, albeit at a slow pace. It is possible that this trend is due to the operation of supranational regional policies, although certain caveats need to be borne in mind. First, the regions at which EU policy has been targeted are extremely heterogeneous and would rarely satisfy the criteria for an economic space. At worst, this could reduce the quest for evidence on convergence to little more than econometric curiosity. Second, the evidence for convergence in Western Europe is strongest for the post-war era predating the inception of the ERDF. Furthermore, the entry into membership of the poorest EU countries followed some time after that. Third, the transfers involved in the quest for regional equalisation have been small. Fourth, not only have there been a continuous series of shocks exerted on the European economy, ongoing globalisation has also undoubtedly affected development trajectories within it. The fact that there is no evidence of convergence in rates of unemployment across the Union must also be added to this list.

Whatever the underlying mechanisms, the cohesion of the EU has not to date been seriously threatened by the regional inequalities that obtain within its territory. Arguably, this might be because it has so far been a relatively modest venture. However, it is now on the verge of embarking upon two undertakings of immense potential significance. The first is monetary unification, a topic covered elsewhere in this volume. The second is expansion to a range of transition economies on the east of the continent with levels of development way below those of even the poorest current member. Often lacking the administrative means of implementing effective regional policies of their own and certainly without the resources, this will provide the sternest test yet of the EU's ability to reduce spatial inequality quickly and to the benefit of its citizens and its own cohesion. If regional policy can be effectively marshalled from above and if current members were willing to pay, the goal might be an achievable one. However, the indications regarding the latter are not optimistic: current net contributors to the EU budget do not wish to pay more and its beneficiaries do not wish to receive less. At the same time, the monetary unification project demands fiscal prudence. In this light, any evidence, however weak, that the applicant countries have embarked on divergent regional development paths, such as that uncovered for Poland, is cause for concern.

NOTES

1. The authors are grateful to Jan Kowalski for comments on an earlier version of this chapter.
2. For a lengthier discussion of these matters, see Armstrong, 2001; Swann, 1995; Williams, 1994.
3. Not all member states conform to the required three-level hierarchical structure and, when absent, the required NUTS region(s) have to be created artificially.
4. Casellas and Galley (1999) demonstrate how, by bringing together regions of extreme diversity, the NUTS classification exaggerates the frequently noted existence of greater regional inequalities in Europe than the USA, although reclassification by no means eliminates the difference.
5. Some countries, such as the UK, have functional regions based upon travel-to-work areas rather than local administrative boundaries as the spatial basis for EU and national regional policies.
6. Its recommendations will enter into force at the end of 2001 (see Official Journal C 180 E/108, 26 June 2001).
7. Once again, where no administrative units of a suitable scale exist in a member state, the NUTS level shall be constituted by aggregating an appropriate number of smaller entities. If the population of a whole member state is below the maximum threshold for a given NUTS tier, the whole country will be one region at this level.
8. Of course, all policies, regional or not, tend to have differential spatial impacts.
9. Three meetings of the European Council in 1988 introduced the relevant changes. Thus, in February of that year, it was agreed that the commitment appropriations for the Structural Funds by 1993 should be doubled in real terms compared with the 1987 level. A June Regulation then specified the tasks of the Funds (Official Journal L 185, 15 July 1988), while a December Regulation laid down the provisions for coordinating the activities of the different Funds (Official Journal L 374, 19 December 1988).
10. Table 8.3 is taken from CEC (1989).
11. Other regions could also achieve Objective 2 status if they satisfied certain adverse unemployment and/or industrial employment criteria.
12. Full details of the reforms are contained in CEC (1989).
13. However, the major beneficiaries of such assistance (Greece, Ireland and Portugal) were allowed to submit plans drawn up at the national level.
14. There was also a complex set of financial provisions under which the Funds operated, each embodying the principle of co-financing. For the most significant funds (ERDF and ESF),

as these applied to Objective 1 areas, the Commission would donate a maximum of 75 per cent of the total cost and a minimum of 50 per cent of the total public expenditure.

15. Cohesion countries were those with a GDP of less than 90 per cent of the EU average. To date, these have been Greece, Ireland, Portugal and Spain. In fact, at the time of their original designation, all regions in these countries were Objective 1.
16. Derogations are laid out in Council Regulation (EEC No 2081/93).
17. Further detail on the rules governing the allocation of the Structural Funds is given in CEC (1999).
18. The possible impacts of the reduction in aid to regions previously receiving EU support are discussed further in McQuaid (2000).
19. Further details on the 2000–06 Objective designations can be found in CEC (1999a).
20. Countries from the CIS are eligible for funding from TACIS (Technical Assistance to the Commonwealth of Independent States).
21. The emphasis on establishing links with TEN is problematic insofar as the evidence for transport networks suggests that they tend to weaken the position of peripheral regions relative to the core (Vickerman et al., 1999).
22. However, the Commission has earmarked additional, temporally increasing finance for accession from 2002 (CEC, 2001a).
23. Although the Report embellishes the raw figures with detail such as the fact that the GDP per capita of the three poorest Cohesion countries (Greece, Portugal and Spain) increased from 68 per cent to 79 per cent of the EU average between 1988 and 1999 (CEC, 2001b), which goes some way towards correcting the deficiency, it still does not meet with acceptable statistical practice.
24. The papers in Armstrong and Vickerman (1995) provide a useful introduction to more extended concepts of convergence.
25. The reforms introduced at the beginning of the following year reduced the number of voivodships to 16.
26. Although justifiably cautious in the interpretation of the results, Armstrong (1995) found evidence that the convergence between European regions observed from 1950 to 1970 slowed somewhat thereafter. As he warns, however, the trends may have as much to do with general world integration as EU integration.
27. The number of observations for the EU GDP and unemployment data differs because France does not report unemployment rates for its overseas departments, while Ireland only reports GDP at the national level.

REFERENCES

Armstrong, Harvey (2001), 'Regional Policy', in Ali El-Agraa (ed.), *The European Union: Economics & Policies*, 6th edition, Harlow: Pearson Education Limited, pp. 388–413.

Armstrong Harvey (1995) 'An Appraisal of the Evidence from Cross-Sectional Analysis of the Regional Growth Process within the European Union', in Harvey Armstrong and Roger Vickerman (eds), pp.40–65 .

Armstrong, Harvey and Roger Vickerman (eds) (1995), *Convergence and Divergence Among European Regions*, London: Pion.

Bachtler, J. and R. Michie (1994), 'Strengthening Economic and Social Cohesion? The Revision of the Structural Funds', *Regional Studies*, **28** (8), 789–96.

Barro, R. and X. Sala-i-Martin (1992), 'Convergence', *Journal of Political Economy*, **100** (2), 223–51.

Barro, R. and X. Sala-i-Martin (1991), 'Convergence Across States and Regions', *Brookings Papers on Economic Activity*, **1**, 107–82.

Begg, I. and D. Mayes (1993), 'Cohesion, Convergence and Economic and Monetary Union in Europe', *Regional Studies*, **27** (2), 149–55.

Bernat, G. (1996), 'Does Manufacturing Matter? A Spatial Econometric View of Kaldor's Laws', *Journal of Regional Science*, **36** (3), 463–77.

Blazyca, George (2002), 'EU Accession: The Polish Case', this volume, pp. 205–21.

Casellas, A. and C. Galley (1999), 'Regional Definitions in the European Union: A Question of Disparities?' *Regional Studies*, **33** (6), 551–8.

CEC (Commission of the European Communities) (2001), 'Proposal for a Regulation of the European Parliament and of the Council on the Establishment of a Common Classification of Territorial Units for Statistics (NUTS)', COM(2001) 83 final, Brussels: CEC.

CEC (Commission of the European Communities) (2001a), *Regular Reports from the Commission on Progress towards Accession by each of the Candidate Countries*, available at http://europa.eu.int/comm/enlargement/report2001/index.htm.

CEC (Commission of the European Communities) (2001b), *General Budget of the European Union for the Financial Year 2001*, Brussels and Luxembourg: CEC.

CEC (Commission of the European Communities) (2001c), *Enlarging Solidarity, Uniting Europe: Second Report on Economic and Social Cohesion*, Brussels and Luxembourg: CEC. Available at http://www.inforegio.cec.eu.int/wbdoc/docoffic/official/report2.

CEC (Commission of the European Communities) (2000), *Regular Reports from the Commission on Progress towards Accession by each of the Candidate Countries*, available at http://europa.eu.int/comm/enlargement/report_11_00/index.htm.

CEC (Commission of the European Communities) (2000a), *General Budget of the European Union for the Financial Year 2000*, Brussels and Luxembourg: CEC.

CEC (Commission of the European Communities) (1999), 'Reform of the Structural Funds 2000-2006: Comparative Analysis', June, Brussels: CEC.

CEC (Commission of the European Communities) (1999a), 'Council Regulation (EC) No. 1260/1999 of 21 June 1999 laying down general provisions on the Structural Funds', Official Journal of the European Communities, L 161/1, 26 June 1999, Brussels: CEC.

CEC (Commission of the European Communities) (1997), 'Agenda 2000: For a stronger and wider Union', available at http://europa.eu.int/comm/agenda2000/overview/en/agenda.htm.

CEC (Commission of the European Communities) (1989), 'Guide to the Reform of the Communities Structural Funds', Luxembourg: Office for Official Publications of the European Communities.

Chatterji, M. (1993), 'Convergence Clubs and Endogenous Growth', *Oxford Review of Economic Policy*, **8** (4), 57–69.

Chisholm, Michael (1990), *Regions in Recession and Resurgence*, London: Unwin Hyman.

Chisholm, Michael (1982), *Modern World Development: A Geographical Perspective*, London: Hutchinson.

Comfort, A. (1988), 'Alternatives to Infrastructure? Possible Ways Forward for the ERDF: A Perspective from Luxembourg', *Regional Studies*, **22** (6), 542–51.

Croxford, G. and M. Wise (1988), 'The European Social Fund: Retrospect and Prospect', *Regional Studies*, **22** (1), 65–8.

Dewhurst, John and Hernando Mutais-Gaitan (1995), 'Varying Speeds of Regional GDP Per Capita Convergence in the European Union, 1981–91', in Harvey Armstrong and Roger Vickerman (eds), pp. 22–39.

Guersent, O. (2001), 'The Regional Policy of the European Union: A Balance and an Outlook', *Regional Studies*, **35** (2), 163–7.
GUS (Główny Urząd Statystyczny) (2000), *Rocznik Statystyczny Województw 2000*, Warsaw:GUS.
GUS (Główny Urząd Statystyczny) (1999), *Registered Unemployment in Poland I–IV Quarter 1998*, Warsaw: GUS.
GUS (Główny Urząd Statystyczny) (1995), *Registered Unemployment in Poland I–IV Quarter 1994*, Warsaw: GUS.
GUS (Główny Urząd Statystyczny) (1992), *Registered Unemployment in Poland I–IV Quarter 1991*, Warsaw: GUS.
Ingham, Hilary and Mike Ingham (2002), 'EU Expansion to the East: The Problem of Agriculture', this volume, pp. 110–33.
Kennard, Ann (2002), 'The Changing Role of Border Regions in Central and Eastern Europe', this volume, pp. 188–204.
McQuaid, Ronald (2000), 'Implications of European Union Expansion for Peripheral Regions', in Hirotada Kohno, Peter Nijkamp and Jacques Poot (eds), *Regional Cohesion and Competition in the Age of Globalization*, Cheltenham, UK and Northampton, MA, USA: Edward Elgar, pp. 284–308.
OECD (Organisation for Economic Cooperation and Development) (1992), *Poland 1992*, Economic Surveys, Paris: OECD.
Read, Robert (2002), 'Monetary Union and Eastward Expansion of the EU', this volume, pp. 23–49.
Romer, P. (1990), 'Endogenous Technical Change', *Journal of Political Economy*, **98** (5), S71–S102.
Swann, Dennis (1995), *The Economics of the Common Market*, 8th edition, Harmondsworth: Penguin.
Vickerman, R., K. Spiekermann and M. Wegener (1999), 'Accessibility and Economic Development in Europe', *Regional Studies*, **33** (1), 1–15.
Williams, Allan (1994), *The European Community*, 2nd edition, Oxford: Basil Blackwell Ltd.

9. The Changing Role of Border Regions in Central and Eastern Europe

Ann Kennard

INTRODUCTION

Cross-border cooperation schemes were seen as an oddity in the 1960s and 1970s when the Iron Curtain was regarded as the main dividing line in Europe and dabbling in low politics was not thought likely to have any long-run impact (Christiansen and Jørgenson, 2000). Subsequently, they have achieved much greater prominence, have multiplied in number and have attracted dedicated funding from the European Union (EU). Fresh impetus to their operation and scope was provided by the demise of the historic division of Europe and the desire on the part of many former communist states to accede to membership of the Union and finally unite the continent. While the widening of the EU has long been a stated policy goal, expansion to the east confronts the drive for cohesion with its strongest challenge to date and cross-border cooperation represents an important means by which the Commission is attempting to ensure that it is not undermined.

Notwithstanding expansions, proposed or past, the first cross-border initiatives were internal arrangements between contiguous regions of the founding members of the Union, most notably the Dutch and the Germans. The events of 1989 and 1990 in the former Soviet satellite states coincided with the commencement of explicit, internal cross-border funding programmes within the EU. However, the softening of common east–west frontiers and the coincidence of concerns between member and non-member states led quickly to an expansion of cross-border cooperation to include Europe's newly liberated neighbours. These developments are discussed in detail in the following section of the chapter.

While the inclusion of the aspiring new members in EU initiatives is now regarded as an important step in preparing them for accession and in ensuring that pre-existing development differentials do not widen to an unbearable degree prior to enlargement, the efficiency of the means by which they have been enabled to participate in cross-border schemes can be questioned. This applies in particular to the separate and rather incompatible funding arrangements available to members and non-members, respectively. Furthermore, the ongoing lack of administrative competence at sub-national level in the transition states is problematic in terms not only of local self-determination but also for their successful cooperation in international, multi-regional initiatives. These concerns are addressed in the third section of the chapter. Whatever the impediments, east–west cross-border ventures have proliferated, at least in numerical terms. Amongst the most successful, and the most wide-ranging, have been those along the German–Polish border, which have included cultural, economic, environmental and social projects. These, along with the particular problems with which they have been confronted, are considered critically in the fourth section.

Despite the implementation problems encountered with the early east–west collaboration initiatives, the notion of cross-border cooperation has now been extended on a grand scale with the creation of seven extremely large, multinational virtual regions as engines of spatial development. Two of these, one covering the Baltic territories and one stretching across central and south-east Europe, include transition states in their membership, although the terms upon which they participate differ considerably across the two organisations. Furthermore, EU member and non-member countries are once again subject to distinct funding arrangements. The emergence of, and prospects for, these super regions as catalysts in the enlargement process are considered in the fifth section. A series of concluding remarks completes the work.

THE EVOLUTION OF CROSS-BORDER COOPERATION

Cross-border cooperation is not new in Europe, with such ventures taking place on the Dutch–German and Franco–German frontiers for more than thirty years. The former, established in 1965, gave rise to the shorthand term EUREGIO (or Euroregion) to denote formal cross-border collaboration arrangements between municipalities involving a council, a presidency, a secretariat and subject-oriented working groups (Perkmann, 1999).[1] In part due to the efforts of the Dutch and German governments, these early experiments led to the foundation of the Association of European Border Regions in 1971. This body influences European debates on regional policy and, more specifically, policies that target regions across both the EU's internal and external borders (Scott, 1999). Its work has been aided by the actions of the Council of Europe in putting in place the legal framework for sub-national governments to cooperate across borders and by the creation of the single market (Anderson and O'Dowd, 1999).

Economic, political and spatial cohesion are viewed as essential in maintaining an effective and internationally competitive Union and, under the auspices of the structural policies, various programmes and initiatives have been launched with the aim of 'opening up new spatial perspectives for cooperation between cities and regions in various areas of economic development and regional policy. ... [This] serves not only to instil a sense of European identity, but also to diffuse innovations in, among other areas, economic promotion, job-creation schemes and revitalization strategies' (Scott, op. cit.:607). Since 1970, the Council of Europe's Conference of Ministers of Spatial Planning has been working intermittently on a European spatial development plan and EU ministers responsible for spatial development met to discuss the development of a European Spatial Development Perspective (ESDP) in 1993, although it took until 1999 for the final document to be published (CEC, 1999). The ESDP espouses three overall ambitions: a balanced and polycentric urban system, parity of access to infrastructure and knowledge, and prudent management and development of national heritages and cultures.

The availability of inter-regional funding programmes has, at least in part, driven enhanced cooperation between member states and the first INTERREG initiative (INTERREG I) was launched in 1990 with four aims.[2] First, to help areas on the Community's external and internal borders overcome development problems linked to their remoteness from the centres of national economic activity. Second, to encourage the development of cross-border cooperation networks. Third, to help areas adjacent to non-member states adjust to their role as border regions of the single market. Fourth, to promote cooperation with non-member countries situated on the Community's external borders. Funding was made available to NUTS 3 level regions that had been designated as Objective 1, 2 or 5(b), although payments were restricted to Community member states.[3] External border regions in Greece and along the Portuguese–Spanish frontier were major recipients and they applied the funding to initiatives that ranged from large-scale infrastructure projects to education and training and the promotion of small and medium-sized enterprises. Later evaluations found that projects were more likely to be successful when undertaken by partners with a tradition of, and structure for, cooperation and that few became operational on the periphery of the Community (CEC, 1997).

INTERREG II was launched in 1994 and, beyond amendments to render it compatible with the Maastricht Treaty, had the same objectives as its predecessor and remained available only to existing member states. Over its programmed five-year lifetime, the new initiative was allocated 2,900 million ECU from the Structural Funds, of which almost 83 per cent was designated for cross-border cooperation projects.[4] If to this figure are added the co-finances required from national and local sources, the total amount of monies earmarked amounted to almost 4 thousand million ECU. In the case of those regions adjacent to Central and Eastern European (CEE) countries, and also those on the Spain/Portugal border, projects were most often development orientated, while in other regions they were geared more to the promotion of economic and social integration.

Participants in INTERREG II were encouraged to establish cross-border cooperation structures. These have come to perform a wide variety of functions, including coordinating cross-border processes, promoting networks and trade between partners, informing their citizens about developments towards European integration, promoting cross-border cooperation at the regional and local levels, supporting working groups on issues such as the economy, education and culture and representing the general interests of their participants. Certain of the Euroregions have evolved to the point where they are involved in the preparation of INTERREG programmes and projects and, in some member states, in their implementation.

Phare–CBC was introduced at the same time as INTERREG II with the explicit aim of fostering EU–CEE trans-border cooperation.[5] The programme was earmarked for 1,035 million ECU over the period 1994–1999, although only countries that share a common border with an existing EU member state were eligible for funding. The objectives of Phare–CBC were broadly consistent with those of the INTERREG initiative.[6] First, it sought to support transformation and facilitate integration. Second, it was designed to promote economic development and increased competitiveness on both sides of the EU border. Third, Phare–CBC addressed environmental problems and the difficulties that border regions face due to their lack of infrastructure. Finally, the programme targeted the effects of peripherality, improvements in the quality of life and the formation of cooperation networks. In pursuit of these objectives, a wide range of projects attracted funding. Infrastructure improvements were achieved through the upgrading of energy, communication and transport and water networks. Monies were allocated to improve waste facilities, environmental protection and promote cooperation on health related issues. Projects were also undertaken to foster tourism and cooperation in agriculture and business, as well as general employment and training measures. In addition, initiatives to overcome the administrative and institutional obstacles to development within the border areas attracted support.

The Euroregion concept has been adopted on both sides of the external border and there are now in excess of sixty in existence, although not all are eligible for EU funding. Those that are not contiguous with the EU, such as regions on the Polish border with Belarus and those in Carpathia, which includes Poland, Slovakia, Ukraine, Romania and Hungary, were formed because the partner countries recognised that they face mutual problems, particularly as those relate to the environment and over-burdened border crossings. As certain of these states come closer to their goal of accession, they hope for additional financial assistance for their peripheral regions that are not adjacent to the EU. At least in part, this desire was satisfied by the launch of a new cooperation programme (CREDO) in 1997, which has the specific purpose of funding regional programmes across borders between CEE and the Newly Independent States. That is, initiatives without active EU member state participation.

The guidelines for INTERREG III were approved in April 2000, stating: 'The overall aim of the INTERREG initiatives has been, and remains, that national borders should not be a barrier to the balanced development and integration of European territory' (CEC, 2000:2). They also proclaimed explicitly that due attention will be paid to the external borders of the Community, particularly in view of the enlargement process (ibid.). The programme has been allocated 4,875 million euro for the period to 2006, divided between three implementation heads. Strand A is for cross-border cooperation to promote integrated regional development and will receive 50-80 per cent of the total budget allocation. Strand B, which is to receive 14-44 per cent of the budget, is for transnational cooperation between large groupings of European regions to promote balanced development and higher territorial integration, including with candidate and other neighbouring countries.[7] However, as described below, non-member states must still acquire funding for their participation from other sources. Strand C is to receive 6 per cent of the allocated funds and is available for initiatives throughout the territory of the Union and its neighbouring countries that aim to foster interregional cooperation to improve cohesion and development.

Phare–CBC was also continued, with unchanged objectives, but with a shorter time horizon and a budget of 480 million euro to end 2002. Notwithstanding the goals of the other strands, Phare–CBC is linked explicitly only to Strand A of the INTERREG programme (Shotton, 2000). The participation of applicant countries in Strands B and C is to be encouraged through effective coordination with other policy instruments, including the general Phare and TACIS initiatives, ISPA and SAPARD.[8] In contrast to the arrangements for existing member states, the Phare–CBC budget is to be allocated according to the financial size of the projects it supports. No more than one-fifth of the total can be used for small ventures costing less than 300,000 euro and remaining undertakings will normally be required to have budgets in excess of 2 million euro.

ADMINISTRATIVE IMPEDIMENTS

A recent evaluation study for the Commission found that the significant delays in the implementation of the Phare–CBC programmes were due both to the design of the funding vehicles themselves and a dearth of administrative capacity within the CEE countries. Thus, while the juxtaposition of the INTERREG and Phare–CBC initiatives can be viewed as an imaginative approach to funding trans-border projects, the manner in which they function leads to considerable tensions that do not assist the preparations for enlargement. INTERREG is financed from the Structural Funds, which are designed to promote sub-national policy making and, at the margins of Europe, where there is a need to encourage economic, cultural and political regeneration, they would appear to be an ideal instrument. Funding for cross-border cooperation by the CEE countries on the other hand is drawn from the separate Phare programme. The presence of two parallel, but totally separate, arrangements leads to institutional complications that hinder cooperation. In particular, problems arise because of differences in programming methods, decision-making procedures, competencies of the bodies involved and the different lead times for approval and implementation of projects (Roch et al., 1998; Kennard, 2000).

There are four major differences between the INTERREG and Phare–CBC initiatives. First, the funds emanate from different Directorates General in Brussels; the former is the responsibility of DG Regional Policy, while the latter is administered by DG External Relations. Friction between these two agencies has undoubtedly hampered cross-border cooperation in the past and the arrangements put in place in 2000 mean that the funds will not be merged into a single initiative in the near future. Second, the funding mechanisms of the two schemes differ: INTERREG is a programme financing system, while Phare–CBC is project oriented and 'This difference hampers a close common management of both programmes, but also the implementation of common projects. It can be an important source for programme delays' (CEC, 1998:10). Third, Phare–CBC operates with yearly financial decision-making procedures whereas INTERREG financial planning runs on a multi-annual basis. Finally, responsibility for the allocation of funding to projects under INTERREG rests with member states, but in the case of Phare–CBC it lies with the Commission, once it has obtained the opinion of the Phare management committee.

It is also important to note that there is an asymmetry between the administrative arrangements in the EU and CEE partner countries. In particular, regional policy within the Union tends to be decentralised whereas it tends to remain a central government responsibility in CEE. Taking the case of German–Polish cooperation as an example, the federal government of the former has no competence in regional or spatial planning, which is devolved to the Länder. In contrast, responsibility for these functions lies with the central government in Poland. While the decision-making process for INTERREG funding in Germany can be prolonged due to the involvement of a large number of ministries at Land level, in Poland the parallel mechanism suffers from all of the problems associated with remoteness. Phare–CBC funding flows from Brussels to the Phare implementation authority in Warsaw and is only distributed after a lengthy process of project selection.

Nevertheless, a policy that fails to deliver its expected output is not in itself necessarily flawed: it may be the implementation that fails. Under the original Phare–CBC scheme, there were no formal mechanisms for smaller municipalities to submit projects for consideration, although they have since been able to do this within the Small Project Funds (SPFs) component that was introduced in 1996. While this accounts for only a small proportion of the total available finance, the experience has had positive learning effects on local planning capacities. The existence of the SPFs should not, however, 'be seen as a mechanism to exclude local and regional authorities from other elements of the CBC programme, as these bodies should also play an increasingly pivotal role in relation to specific priorities and measures' (ibid.:6). In fact, the Commission expressed a general concern that Phare–CBC was not integrated into overall national regional policies and that the selected projects did not form part of a coherent strategy. It also noted that, with funds targeted on entire CEE–EU borders, they lacked any precise regional focus. Furthermore, CEE governments were criticised precisely for failing to draft their plans in partnership with either regional and local authorities or the relevant social partners.

The problems identified by the Commission were not, however, confined to central governments: the ability of local and regional administrations throughout CEE to prepare, select and implement projects was questioned. Its evaluation of Phare–CBC noted 'the poor quality and the low capacity of the local, regional and national government institutions' (ibid.: iii).[9] This raises concerns about the ability of any new entrants to the EU to manage the complete range of funding instruments to which they would have access upon becoming members and suggests that programmes to increase local competencies must be a priority policy concern.

POLISH–GERMAN COOPERATION

Of all CEE–EU border partnerships that between Poland and Germany can be argued, perhaps surprisingly, to have been the most successful. The adjacent Polish and German border regions have faced similar problems in the aftermath of the events of 1989. Thus, in addition to their location on the periphery of their respective countries, their industrial structures were both mono-central and technologically obsolete. Furthermore, the partnership is unique in so far as it brings together two former communist territories.[10] East German industry suffered the more severe collapse and Brandenburg lost three-quarters of its manufacturing jobs between 1990 and 1995; a decline that was not matched in the Polish border regions (Krätke, 1999:633–4). When Germany first suggested cooperation to the Poles there were understandable reservations in certain quarters, fuelled by fears that the hidden agenda was the development of the Polish border region as an extension of Germany.[11] In contrast, others viewed the political change in CEE as a unique opportunity to promote and develop a new region transcending the Polish–German frontier and it was they who championed the two initial agreements between the respective governments. The first was a treaty, signed on 14 November 1990, that confirmed the legal status of the border in international law and the second was the Treaty on Friendship and Cooperation, ratified on 17 June 1991.[12] From these roots emerged the four Euroregions that cover the entire German–Polish border from the Baltic Sea to the Czech Republic. Furthermore, such is the level of Polish enthusiasm for collaboration that almost all of Poland's border areas are now members of international regional consortia.

One important factor behind the growth of German–Polish cooperation was the unexpectedly rapid and intense response of local actors to the opening of the long-closed frontier. Small-scale trans-border trade developed rapidly as bazaars were established in Poland that had a turnover in excess of 7 billion US dollars by the middle of the 1990s, or 29 per cent of the country's total export value, according to the Polish Ministry of the Economy.[13] Between 1988 and 1992, the number of people crossing the border increased from 12.2 to 84 million (Lijewski, 1994:190) and this figure continues to increase year on year. In consequence, there is general agreement that the transport and communication systems in the trans-border areas can no longer cope with the volumes of traffic. It must be recognised, however, that the provision of EU funds to help solve these problems via the

INTERREG and Phare–CBC initiatives has also been an important factor motivating the creation of Euroregions, both on the Germany–Poland border and elsewhere.

Although Phare–CBC programmes have fallen seriously behind schedule, Poland has recently been more successful in spending its allocation than many other countries within CEE. For example, by the end of 1998, Poland had only managed to disburse slightly over half of its 1994 monies but had spent 14 per cent of its 1995–96 funding allocation, whereas the corresponding figures for the Czech Republic were 94 and 4 per cent, respectively (CEC, op. cit.:v). In addition, an impressive array of cross-border institutions has been assembled. There are inter-governmental commissions at both national and regional levels, an environmental working group and several inter-agency bodies dealing with specific issues. Furthermore, numerous municipal associations have been formed at the local level (Scott, op. cit.).

One of the most notable achievements is the founding of a cross-border university in the Pro Europa Viadrina Euroregion, the Europa-Universität Viadrina/Collegium Polonicum (EUV/CP) in Frankfurt (Oder) and Słubice. The EUV was opened in Frankfurt in 1991 on the condition that a Polish institution would be established in Słubice, on the other side of the Oder bridge, as a branch of the Poznań based Adam Mickiewicz University. Notwithstanding funding problems, the CP was opened finally in 1998 and there are now about three thousand students, one-third of them Polish. The latter have to offer two foreign languages, usually German and English, while German students are also beginning to see the potential advantage of learning Polish (*Der Tagesspiegel*, 17 July 1998). The three faculties within the university are law, economics and cultural studies and the emphasis throughout the teaching programme is on inter-disciplinarity and cultural understanding. With enlargement in prospect, it is anticipated that the graduates, but perhaps those from Poland in particular, will prove to be attractive to western firms with branches in CEE countries.

Although the potential political significance of the university was immense, given the message that it would convey about the future path of German–Polish relations in an enlarged Europe, it did not emerge easily. In the early stages of the venture, the Polish government was either unable or unwilling to devote any money to the project, although the town council did make an offer to provide land on the bank of the Oder for the Słubice campus at no cost. Later, circuitous methods had to be adopted to attract EU funding for the undertaking. Under Phare–CBC rules, a project of this size had to be 'infrastructural' and therefore it was presented as essential construction work in the development of Słubice. The same strategy was not, however, available under INTERREG rules and the venture had to be presented in Germany as falling under the auspices of European Social Fund on account of its cultural, educational and employment potential.[14]

Rehabilitation and future care of the environment represents a critical area for cooperation. Bi-national water treatment plants have been set up at Guben/Gubin in the Spree-Neisse-Bober Euroregion and on the island of Usedom in the Pomerania Euroregion. In general, however, progress has been slow, as indicated by the fact that a report detailing the environmental problems on both sides of the Oder was commissioned in 1994 but not completed until some five years later.[15] This notwithstanding, cross-border efforts are underway to develop the potential for tourism and to create integrated ecological areas. Encouraging signs of the enthusiasm of the inhabitants of the border regions for partnership have emerged from the success of a number of EU-funded trans-border cultural and social projects, such as the teaching of the partner language in schools and the staging of music and sports festivals.

Nevertheless, there are those who are sceptical of the achievements of German–Polish cooperation. Scott (op. cit.) points to the fact that it has failed in its regional development aspirations insofar as inward investment has largely not materialised. The Kostrzyn–Słubice Special Economic Zone that planned to create ten thousand jobs is one example of this failure: by the end of 1998, only one foreign firm had established itself in the zone and this company was from Croatia (Krätke, op. cit.).[16] The same author also highlights a number of cultural factors that are impeding economic development. He contends that Germans and Poles have still not developed an understanding of each other and there is currently a strong fear of competition in the region. The unease felt by Polish Eurosceptics concerning their border regions was highlighted by the Warsaw correspondent of the Stuttgarter Zeitung: 'Silesia is gradually draining towards Germany, the Kłodzko valley towards the Czech Republic, Suwałki will become a colony of Berlin and Germans will establish whole settlements as they did in Alsace, and after a while the region will demand autonomy or even integration into the Land Brandenburg' (quoted in Cielemęcki, 1998: 2). Krätke (op. cit.) also emphasises the basic mistrust between the two nations and the fact that anti-foreign attitudes are commonplace, while racist attacks are considered a normal occurrence. Indeed, he cites the results of one survey that found that only 3 per cent of Poles and Germans could accept an individual of the opposite nationality becoming a member of their family (ibid.:639). This social milieu is claimed to have reduced the attractiveness of the borderlands for potential investors and to have hampered development.

TOWARDS EUROPE-WIDE PLANNING REGIONS?

Whatever the shortcomings of the attempts to establish joint planning strategies in the promotion of cross-border cooperation, the EU has also sponsored an initiative under which collaboration on a much larger scale has begun to occur. Multi-country cooperation programmes have been established for the purpose of regional and spatial planning and a budget of 412.84 million ECU was made available for them under INTERREG IIC for the period 1994 to 1999. They came about as a result of increasing economic integration and interdependence between member states and regions and because of new common challenges resulting mainly from major economic trends, such as the globalisation of the economy. The trend is consistent with the view that 'a new map of Europe will emerge, which will show Europe as an interwoven, multi-layered and multi-faceted network' (Nijkamp, 1993:150). The transnational cooperative ventures funded under this initiative are designed to implement the objectives identified in the ESDP. Seven overlapping virtual regions have been created on the basis of contiguity and the principle that each has at least three member states within it. The initiative encourages the involvement and participation of non-EU neighbouring countries and two of them, the Baltic Sea Region (BSR) and the Central, Adriatic, Danubian and South-East European Space (CADSES) have CEE partners. For the first of these, the projected Community investment from INTERREG IIC over the period 1997–99 was 47.5 million ECU and for the latter the figure was 36.8 million ECU. It should be noted, however, that CEE participants cannot be funded from this budget.

BSR was established in December 1997, led by Denmark, Finland, Germany and Sweden, but including from the outset the Norwegian, Polish, and Russian Baltic coast areas, Belarus and all of the Baltic States. CADSES was first of all a joint action between Germany, Austria, Italy and Greece, approved by the Commission in August 1997, which has since expanded to fourteen other countries, ranging from Poland and the Ukraine in the north to Albania and Macedonia in the south. The inclusion of aspirant member states in these initiatives was recognised as part of the pre-accession programme in the final version of the ESDP in order to ensure that different policy measures do not counteract or neutralise each other. It also stated explicitly that 'The accomplishment of the enlargement, especially the integration of Central and Eastern Europe into the Union, is a new central task for European spatial development policy' (CEC, 1999:50).

The nature of the involvement of non-member states in the management structures of BSR and CADSES differs. In the former, they have full voting rights in both the Monitoring and Steering Committees and it is hoped that this will increase their commitment to the programme. There are six CEE states in the initiative, all of which have access to Phare–CBC funding. Conversely, although the participating CEE countries within CADSES are included in all discussions, they are primarily there as observers and not as full members. Nevertheless, as the process aims to be consensual it is unlikely that a project would go forward if any of the CEE countries harboured reservations, even though they have no formal resort to a veto.[17] Hungary is the single exception to this, having been a fully enfranchised member with a national secretariat since September 1998. The country undoubtedly sees this as beneficial to its accession endeavours and both the Czech Republic and Poland aspire to the same status. This notwithstanding, CADSES faces problems insofar as its membership is composed of only four EU member states and 14 CEE countries, not all of which are eligible for Phare–CBC or TACIS funding.

Aims, objectives and good intent are one thing, but is there any economic or political logic behind these groupings or is the desire to collaborate driven simply by the financial benefits offered by the EU? The search for an answer renders it necessary to consider whether the trans-national areas are coherent entities, with members that face common problems that are best solved via joint studies, policies and actions (Nadin and Shaw, 1998:287–8). In the case of the BSR regions there is a long history of cooperation between countries. The Nordic Council was founded in 1952, followed by the Nordic Council of Ministers in 1971, in order to promote cooperation between the parliaments and governments of Denmark, Iceland, Finland, Norway and Sweden. Since the reorientations of 1989–90, there have been parallel developments in the new partner countries from CEE. Thus the Baltic Assembly was established in 1991 and the Baltic Council of Ministers was formed in 1994, thereby providing equivalent bodies for the parliaments and governments of Estonia, Latvia and Lithuania. In addition, there have been regular summit meetings of the Heads of State since 1990 and of the Council of Baltic Sea States since 1992.

The new political geography of the region has certainly led to an intensification of cooperation since the beginning of the 1990s and the relevant ministers from each of the Baltic States met in 1992 to discuss the possibilities and perspectives for the future spatial development of the area. The resulting report 'Visions and Strategies around the Baltic Sea 2010', (VASAB) delivered wide-ranging recommendations. It considered the entire Baltic Sea region as an integrated whole, in a way not previously encountered in any trans-national area in Europe. In view of the burgeoning desire for enhanced economic links between the countries of the area since the removal of the Iron Curtain, it recognised the importance of improved communications to link cities and their infrastructures, the need for a trans-national approach to environmental problems and the desirability of encouraging a sense of regional identity that crosses national boundaries. Accession to the EU could be argued to be a logical continuation of this process. The report was accepted finally at the Third Conference of Ministers of Spatial Planning and Development in Tallinn in 1994.

With the Baltic Sea as a linking and unifying factor, it might be that the countries in this region have found it easier to identify with each other, even after decades of division, than have other groups of countries. The number of cooperation initiatives that have emerged since the collapse of the Iron Curtain certainly indicates a will to develop a common profile and thus to create 'a masterpiece for sustainable, environmentally sound development' (VASAB, 1994:4). As recognised in the Report, a reliable planning framework is a necessary prerequisite to galvanise investors and other key actors and spatial policies will be a vital component of the social and economic development process.

Agenda 21 was adopted by the foreign members at the Council of the Baltic Sea States meeting in 1998 as a cooperative blueprint for their countries. This aimed to steer the BSR down a path of sustainable development along its environmental, social and economic dimensions. It was heralded as a complement to international, national and local initiatives and focuses on seven sectors of crucial importance to the area: agriculture, energy, fisheries, forests, industry, tourism and spatial planning (Baltic 21 Secretariat, 1999).[18] For each sector, goals and scenarios were elaborated and action programmes drawn up specifying timescales, actors and financing. The Agenda was constructed in the context of a democratic, open and transparent process involving the participation of nations, international organisations, business, other non-governmental bodies and international finance institutes.[19]

The same degree of cohesion is not evident in CADSES, which is located in central and south-eastern Europe, whose members are heterogeneous and plagued by ethnic tensions. As such, the area does not have such a clear *raison d'etre* as the Baltic Sea grouping. CADSES emerged from an informal meeting that took place in Rome between Italy, Germany and Austria in 1996, convened because cooperation would open up the possibility of accessing EU funds. Initially, Austria and Italy favoured limited cooperation in the Alpine space, whereas Germany was interested in the Danube area. Italy then proposed extending cooperation to the Adriatic and including Greece in the plans. At a further meeting, held later in the same year in Bonn, an even wider ranging plan was accepted that sought to secure the participation of a large number of CEE countries in order that broader common interests could be pursued.[20]

The objectives of CADSES are linked directly to the ESDP and can be grouped under four general themes. First, it aims to create a network of cities to promote the development of a balanced and polycentric urban system. Second, it seeks to develop a compatible information system covering transport and the environment. Third, it wishes to promote sustainable development, while ensuring the prudent management of national and cultural heritage. Finally, it looks to promote research and development and to maximise the dissemination and utilisation of the results. Enlargement, albeit in stages, permeates the CADSES planning document.

This initiative prompted the study of numerous problems faced in common throughout the regions of central and south-eastern Europe. These include a water management scheme on the Danube, the creation of a main railway line from western Germany to Budapest, the development of urban networks to secure competitiveness, social balance and sustainable development, and the consideration of regional planning issues along the EU's eastern border in preparation for enlargement. However, the most ambitious venture to date is 'Vision Planet', a strategy for spatial integration involving the entire central and Danubian region. This project involves eleven of the eighteen CADSES countries and includes Bulgaria and Croatia, who are not in the first group of countries acceding to the EU. However, whether any of the plans come to fruition depends on whether CADSES can overcome its inherent weaknesses. At the heart of the problem is the fact that the organisation is dominated numerically by very poor CEE states that have minimal access to EU funds and who therefore have little say over which projects are finally approved.[21] Thus they have very little incentive to participate actively in the discussions of the group. As such, one must question whether CEE commitment to enhanced cooperation within the area can be sustained.

CONCLUSION

It is evident that the nature of borders throughout Europe is going to change. Notwithstanding Schengen, cooperation across boundaries is softening historical divides and fostering joint approaches to development problems. With accession now an early prospect for certain of the CEE countries, it is important that cooperation programmes such as INTERREG and Phare–CBC emit appropriate messages about the future of inter-state relationships. Economic and cultural links that have already been established successfully are a practical expression of the political will on both sides of the EU's boundary to engage in dialogue and to collaborate in building the new Europe.

Nonetheless, problems remain. First, the separate funding arrangements for INTERREG and Phare–CBC cause difficulties for trans-border and trans-national projects and it is disappointing that further steps were not taken to overcome the systemic inadequacies for the current funding period (2000–06). Furthermore, non-uniform approaches to regional policy across the EU and CEE hinder the formulation and implementation of initiatives. Within the Union, the Structural Funds are the major instrument of regional policy and they incorporate the concept of subsidiarity, which promotes local level decision-making. However, regional governance structures are either weak or absent in CEE, leaving regional planning as a central government function. Even within Poland, which has a new administrative structure designed to increase regional financial autonomy and promote the involvement of local actors, spatial issues remain primarily within the central government's portfolio. In less advanced CEE countries, multi-tiered governance does not yet exist. To promote the sustainable development of their territories, central governments must grant greater autonomy to regional bodies in order that they have the same powers as their EU partners. Such a move is essential if the aspirant member states are to convince the Commission that they would be able to administer successfully any Structural Fund monies they might attract upon accession. But this raises the issue of whether central governments are simply unwilling to relinquish power or whether they are unable to do so because of the absence of administrative competence at the local level. In either case, it will be important for the EU in its turn to further rationalise the trans-border cooperation framework so that it can provide a single template within which regional authorities on either side of the borders of CEE can work together.

NOTES

1. See Gabbe (1992) for further detail on the Dutch-German collaboration.
2. INTERREG is a Community Initiative of the Structural Funds and stands for 'international regions'.
3. The terms referred to here are defined in Ingham et al. (2002).
4. Although insignificant in economic terms, accounting for less than 1 per cent of the EU's structural operations, INTERREG has great political significance (Church and Reid, 1999).
5. Phare stands for Poland, Hungary, Assistance to the Restructuring of the Economy and CBC for Cross-Border Cooperation.
6. TACIS (Technical Assistance for the Commonwealth of Independent States) was introduced in 1996 to complement Phare in covering EU borders with countries of the former Soviet Union. This currently only applies to Finland/north-west Russia. In the following, Phare–CBC will be assumed also to include TACIS.
7. Member states themselves can decide on the allocation of monies between Strands A and B beyond the prescribed minima.
8. ISPA stands for Instrument for Structural Policies for Pre-Accession and SAPARD for Special Accession Programme for Agriculture and Rural Development.

9. The Commission noted that Poland had either experienced the problems to a lesser extent or had managed them better.
10. In all other cases, poor CEE border regions abut much richer EU ones: the Czech–Austrian border region is one such example.
11. The unsuccessful Stolpe Plan, named after the Prime Minister of Brandenburg, was an early attempt to foster trans-border cooperation with Poland. Unfortunately the Poles thought that the plan was primarily in Germany's interest. For instance, it included the reduction of intensive agricultural activity in Poland and the building of weekend dwellings there, presumably for Germans. It also included plans to establish German economic areas in Szczecin and in the Polish part of Usedom.
12. For the texts of these treaties, see Bulletin des Presse- und Informationsamts der Bundesregierung, Nr. 134, 16 November 1990 and Bulletin des Presse- und Informationsamts der Bundesregierung, Nr. 68, 18 June 1991, respectively.
13. See Stryjakiewicz and Kaczmarek (1997:4).
14. An interview with Bettina Morhard of EUV Frankfurt and a member of Pro Europa Viadrina Euroregion Council in January 1999 revealed that when Germany applied initially for INTERREG funding the bid was unsuccessful because the Brandenburg Land government refused to contribute the required 5 per cent of co-financing.
15. The 1997 floods also exacerbated this delay, as was noted in an interview with Alois Zimmermann of the Environment Committee of Frankfurt City Council and a member of Pro Europa Viadrina Euroregion Council.
16. Special Economic Zones offer firms generous tax concessions and are causing continuing difficulties in Poland's accession negotiations.
17. Interview with Ulrich Graute of the German national secretariat of CADSES, January 1999.
18. By 1999, numerous spatial planning projects had been developed and funded by INTERREG IIC.
19. This list is taken from the minutes of an informal meeting of the region's environment ministers (Baltic 21 Secretariat, 1999) and it might be noted that it excludes reference to local level consultations.
20. Interview with Rossella Rusca of the Italian national secretariat of CADSES, January 1999.
21. The EU has, however, provided some monies to enable the CEE representatives to attend meetings.

REFERENCES

Anderson, J. and L. O'Dowd (1999), 'Borders, Border Regions and Territoriality: Contradictory Meanings, Changing Significance', *Regional Studies*, **33** (7), 593–604.

Baltic 21 Secretariat (1999), 'Agenda 21 for the Baltic Sea Region', Stockholm: Baltic 21 Secretariat, available at http://www.www.ee/baltic21/document/minist_rep.htm.

Christiansen, T. and K.E. Jørgensen (2000), 'Transnational Governance "Above" and "Below" the State: The Changing Nature of Borders in the New Europe', *Regional and Federal Studies*, **10** (2), 62–77.

Church, A. and P. Reid (1999), 'Cross-border Co-operation, Institutionalization and Political Space Across the English Channel', *Regional Studies*, **33** (7), 643–55.

Cielemęcki, M. (1998), 'Przyczółki Unii' (Bridgeheads of the Union), *Wprost*, 10 May.

CEC (Commission of the European Communities) (2000), 'Communication from the Commission to the Member States', Official Journal 2000/C143, Brussels: CEC.

CEC (Commission of the European Communities) (1999), 'The European Spatial Development Perspective', Brussels: CEC.

CEC (Commission of the European Communities) (1998), 'An Evaluation of Phare Cross-Border Co-operation Programme', Final Report, November, Brussels: CEC.

CEC (Commission of the European Communities) (1997), 'Co-operation Between Regions', *European Dialogue*, Jan-Feb, Issue 1, available at http://europa.eu.int/comm/dg10/eur_dial/97i1a0s0.html.

Gabbe, J. (1992), 'Grenzüberschreitende Netzwerke', *Stadt und Gemeinde*, **3**, 92–8.

Ingham, Mike, Hilary Ingham and Ronald McQuaid (2002), 'Regional Development and EU Enlargement', this volume, pp. 162–87.

Kennard, A. (2000), 'The Role of Central and Eastern Europe in the EU's Regional Planning Agenda for the New Millennium', *Journal of European Area Studies*, **8** (2), 203–19.

Krätke, S. (1999), 'Regional Integration or Fragmentation? The German-Polish Border Region in a New Europe', *Regional Studies*, **33** (7), 631–41.

Lijewski, Teofil (1994), 'Voraussetzungen für bessere Verkehrsverbindung zwischen West-und Osteuropa', in *Materialien zu den räumlichen Entwicklungen in Europa aus polnischer und deutscher Sicht*, Hannover: ARL, pp. 189–97.

Nadin, V. and D. Shaw (1998), Transnational Spatial Planning in Europe: The Role of INTERREG IIC in the UK', *Regional Studies*, **32** (3), 281–99.

Nijkamp, P. (1993), Towards a Network of Regions: The United States of Europe', *European Planning Studies*, **1** (2), 149–68.

Perkmann, M. (1999), 'Building Governance Institutions Across European Borders', *Regional Studies*, **33** (7), pp. 657–67.

Roch, Isolde, James Scott and Astrid Ziegler (1998), *Umweltgerechte Entwicklung von Grenzregionen durch kooperatives Handeln*, Dresden: IÖR-Schriften 24, Institut für ökologische Raumentwicklung e.V.

Scott, J.W. (1999), 'European and North American Contexts for Cross-border Regionalism', *Regional Studies*, **33** (7), pp. 605–17.

Shotton, R. (2000), 'Co-ordination Between INTERREG III and Phare–CBC – How It Works', Brussels: CEC.

Stryjakiewicz, T. and T. Kaczmarek (1997), 'Transborder Cooperation and Development in the Conditions of Great Economic Disparities: The Case of the Polish–German Border Region', paper presented at the European Urban and Regional Research Network Conference, Frankfurt an der Oder, Germany, September 20–23.

VASAB 2010 Secretariat (1994), *Vision and Strategies around the Baltic Sea 2010*, Gdańsk: Committee on Spatial Development of the Baltic Sea Region.

10. EU Accession: The Polish Case

George Blazyca[1]

INTRODUCTION

As the first of the Warsaw Pact countries to reject communism and armed with an economic reform programme of a distinctly liberal flavour (the Balcerowicz Plan), Poland has long been regarded as a leading contender for accession to the European Union (EU) in its next wave of expansion. Following the initial transition shock, Poland's case has seemingly been strengthened by a relatively healthy macro-economy, albeit one confronted by some major outstanding sectoral restructuring issues (agriculture, steel and coal) and a democratic political system that has matured rapidly. This chapter considers the history and character of the country's relationship with the EU beginning, in the next section, with a review of the development of formal links up to the position in early summer 2001 when the parties were engaged in formal membership negotiations.

Joining the EU means unequivocal acceptance of the *acquis communautaire*; the only matter for negotiation being temporary derogations in particular spheres while speedy adjustments are made in order that the relevant requirements can be implemented. The prize is an entitlement to share fully in the 'four freedoms' that lie at the heart of the operation of the Union – the freedom of movement of goods, services, capital and people – in a, hopefully stable, single market that will foster growth, investment, employment and prosperity. At this stage in its evolution, however, Poland finds both the rights and the obligations implied by these freedoms problematic, matters that recur throughout this chapter.

Whatever the rhetoric, an EU that was preoccupied in the 1990s with internal developments had little interest in speedy enlargement to the east: there was, and remains, no clamour for enlargement. If opportunities existed following the collapse of communism for radical measures to build a new Europe, they were not taken. It has been suggested, for example, that leading reforming countries may have been able to obtain membership of a distinctly political hue in the early to mid-1990s, although Poland, at least, rejected such proposals for fear that they would lead to a kind of second-class EU membership. Nonetheless, whether viewed either as accession or expansion, widening the membership of the Union is an intensely political step. Recognition of the fact that enlargement will ultimately be a political act means that it cannot take place, in a context of democratic governance and with leaders who are ultimately accountable to their citizens, without a reasonable body of public support, another troublesome matter explored later.

The next section reviews Polish–EU relations in the 1990s. This leads to a discussion of the major accession problems in the context of the four freedoms. There then follows a consideration of some of the political aspects of the accession process and a review of public opinion on enlargement in both Poland and the EU-15. The conclusion summarises the discussion, restates the current position and examines future accession prospects future.

POLAND-EU RELATIONS POST-1989

The first step towards the integration of Poland with the west European economy was a very fast and dramatic shift in trade, facilitated by the Europe Agreement (EA) of 16 December 1991 which helped the country establish its place near the head of the accession queue. Although it did not enter into force until 1 February 1994, the associated Interim Agreement containing the crucial commercial provisions was effective from 1 March 1992. Its aim was to foster free trade in industrial products within a maximum of ten years. This objective was to be pursued asymmetrically. The EU removed all non-agricultural quotas immediately, as were tariffs on non-sensitive products, while those on sensitive goods were to be eliminated in a period not exceeding five years. Poland, on the other hand, was permitted to stage tariff reductions over seven to ten years and to maintain protection for restructuring industries (CEC, 1993). It is significant, however, that the country had signed a trade and economic cooperation agreement with the EU in September 1989 and was granted the Generalised System of Trade Preferences as of January 1990. These two measures had in fact already extended to the country many of the trade benefits that were to be embodied, and afforded great prominence, in the EA.

Increasingly, however, Polish leaders became disenchanted with association and the evident reluctance of the EU to commit itself fully to enlargement. In the eyes of the aspirant members, the latter required not only a clear timetable for accession, but also that this be buttressed by recognition of the need for profound institutional reform within the Union itself in order to accommodate new members. In short, they perceived the need for a transition to take place on both sides and that the adjustment strategy should not simply be viewed as a unilateral imposition of existing EU legislation. Whatever the strategic disagreements, Poland submitted its formal application for full membership on 8 April 1994 in the hope that accession negotiations would start immediately after the inter-governmental conference in 1996. In the event, EU heads of government decided at the Amsterdam European Council of 16–17 June 1997 to open accession negotiations with Poland with effect from 31 March 1998. Notwithstanding the delay, it is worth noting that, at the time of its initial application, the country's constitution did not permit it to accept the full obligations of membership. Poland's new constitution, which opened up the possibility of ceding certain sovereign powers to international communities, was only ratified in a national referendum in May 1997.

The detailed business of accession preparation was to begin through 'screening' Polish law for its adaptability to EU norms across 29 different 'Chapters' or subject areas. In order to expedite matters, however, the European Commission soon agreed that screening and negotiation could take place in tandem rather than sequentially. By April 2001, Poland had negotiated and temporarily closed 15 chapters. This pace was not the fastest among the candidate countries. Slovenia and Estonia had closed 18 chapters, Hungary 17 and the Czech Republic, like Poland, 15 (*Rzeczpospolita*, 16 May 2001). Much more important was the fact that the difficult areas remained substantially open to negotiation, but this too was as designed.

From 1998, the Commission has reviewed the accession performance of the applicants each autumn and, in general, Poland has been praised for macroeconomic achievement, but criticised for microeconomic failure. Other international agencies and business observers have tended to a similar view: credit for fast GDP growth and policy makers' care with overall macroeconomic stability is tempered with criticism of the slow pace of structural change, lags in privatisation and the liberalisation of key sectors (such as energy, telecommunications and insurance). In the November 1998 Regular Report, the Commission noted that Poland and Hungary had made noticeable progress in transformation generally and in adapting to EU norms, in particular, whereas the Czech Republic, the one-time 'star reformer', and Slovenia had slipped back.[2] During 1999, one of the main general criticisms of Poland was the poor pace of legislative activity, a point readily accepted in Warsaw and one that stimulated new efforts to build stronger cross-party political support for accession legislation, as described below; efforts that evidently paid off according to the Commission's 2000 review.

Nevertheless, it is widely regarded that the EU has dragged its feet over enlargement and that this has been made all the easier by lukewarm popular support (with some exceptions) across the EU-15. At the same time, certain issues have generated the impression in the Commission that Poland is especially troublesome, at times souring the Warsaw–Brussels relationship. One particularly sore point was the mid-1990s Polish regime of duty free motorcar assembly. This offered the Korean producer Daewoo a route into the European market on preferential terms via Poland's EA but, as those tariff exemptions have been phased-out, that problem has all but vanished as has Daewoo, but for different reasons. Steel industry restructuring, or more accurately the lack of it, and the maintenance of duties for longer than was originally planned was also greeted badly in Brussels. Another continuing dispute centres on the existence of some 17 special economic zones whose competition-distorting tax holidays are greatly disapproved of by the Commission. Finally, one of the most acrimonious of recent disputes was over the duties suddenly imposed by Warsaw on agricultural products in late 1999, although matters were later resolved, with Poland signing a 'double zero' agricultural trade agreement with the EU in September 2000 (Ingham and Ingham, 2002).

ACCESSION PROBLEMS AND THE FOUR FREEDOMS

The major hurdles confronting Poland's accession can be divided into two groups: those relating to certain sectors of the economy, whose outputs fall into the list of products classified by the EU as 'sensitive', and those that render the country's compliance with the *acquis* problematic. Agriculture is widely and rightly regarded as the most serious obstacle to membership because of its potential to drain the Common Agricultural Policy (CAP) budget. Heavy industry follows closely in the sensitivity league. Poland did eventually remove its steel tariffs in January 2000, but the country's output (8.85 million tonnes in 1999 (GUS, 2000)) is too great for a painfully restructured EU sector to contemplate. Concern focuses on the dangers of post-enlargement over-capacity in the industry, but in other sectors of the economy, such as telecommunications, banking and insurance, liberalisation is the issue: and Poland well knows that it is market size and the prospects offered by privatisation programmes that interest EU members.

Turning from specific economic sectors to *acquis* related problems, two of the most controversial issues are labour mobility and land sales to foreigners, both of which are explored more fully below. In these and other areas compromises must be reached or enlargement will stumble. Poland may get some transition concessions over land sales (not uncommon in previous enlargements) and may be pushed to yield something on labour mobility.[3] But, as one German journalist put it, this would be a very 'un-European' solution to the problem, and one that would be out of line with integrationist sentiment.[4] Other difficulties include Polish access to regional support and the country's need to meet EU environmental standards.

The EU's single market rests on the free flow of goods and services. With regard to the former, the EAs of the early 1990s achieved a great deal in a short period with relatively few hiccups. A free trade area in industrial products was created quickly. It was one where, as might be expected, the much more competitive enterprises of the EU found it easy to conquer thirsty new markets. Central and Eastern European (CEE) countries, or at least the Visegrád group, switched their trade from a Moscow to a Brussels–Berlin orbit remarkably quickly and the huge trade deficit that emerged was ample testimony to the imbalance in competitiveness that followed (Blazyca, 2001). But this snapshot of immense trade imbalance may be somewhat misleading. The trade deficit may also reflect active industrial restructuring in CEE. In the case of services, trade barriers to free trade are much greater than for goods and take longer to overcome, but pose few fundamental problems. Schedules for the liberalisation of the most important services (such as banking, insurance, telecommunications and transport) exist and are as likely to be met by Poland as by many existing members, many of which continue to have trouble in implementing EU regulations.

Agriculture

Agriculture was always going to be a difficult accession issue for Poland. The asymmetry between the much more efficient EU farming industry, albeit one underpinned by a complex system of subsidies whose main beneficiaries are nationally and regionally concentrated, and the inefficient, now hardly subsidised and highly fragmented Polish agriculture could not be starker. Poland expects to have access to a reformed CAP reasonably quickly. Meanwhile the EU naturally worries about the cost.[5] Poland is hardly a competitive threat to the EU, but the fact that it is a major producer of pork and dairy products means that there is enormous potential to add to the food mountains amassed under existing CAP incentives.

The difficulties surrounding agriculture should diminish as the EU pares support in line with World Trade Organization commitments, but that process is likely to be lengthy. Time is the problem. The Polish government's target in the late 1990s was to join the EU in 2003 and its opening negotiating position was that there should be no 'second-class' membership: its farmers should be entitled to full income support within the CAP, just like existing members. The Commission's position was initially equally robust: such a formulation was unthinkable, could not be sustained financially and there was no provision for it in the EU budget arrangements to 2006, which represents the end of its current financial planning horizon.

To make matters worse, the two sides became embroiled in acrimonious agricultural trade disputes even before negotiations started. During the 1990s, the EU imposed restrictions of various sorts on farm exports from Poland; including the declaration of the country as a 'swine fever' area, a capricious imposition of tariffs on Polish cherries after a particularly good harvest and failing its dairy industry on grounds of hygiene. Then, in late 1999, the Poles raised the stakes by imposing new tariffs on food produce imports from the EU, although that problem was later resolved, with Poland's 2000 'double zero agreement' providing for free trade in most agricultural products (CEC, 2000). Despite the inauspicious start, the contours of Polish access to the CAP became clearer in 2000 and rest on two issues: who precisely should be the recipients of support and when should it start to flow? If the former group is defined more narrowly than the headline 2 million farms that are said to operate in Poland and if access to support is in some way staged then agreement might be reached. As the Polish foreign minister began to talk in early 2000 about the 20 per cent of Polish agricultural units that had a real future as farms and also about a potential restructuring aid package for rural development that would embrace the other 1.6 million so-called farms, agreement even on agricultural matters did not look impossible to reach.[6]

Labour Mobility

The issues raised by the free flow of labour are among the most contentious and highly politicised of all, even though there is an overwhelming economic case in favour of this basic freedom. While fears exist that Polish membership of the EU will lead to job losses, particularly in Germany and Austria, they seem to be exaggerated. First, the experience of previous enlargements (Spain vis-à-vis France is the case most often cited) shows that labour remains relatively immobile, even in a wider Union. Second, estimates produced recently for the Commission suggest that the post-enlargement emigration from the ten accession states will be modest in relation to the EU workforce: around 335,000 per annum in the early years, but then falling off as incomes are equalised (Wagstyl, 2000). Third, demographic trends suggest that new pools of labour are, in any case, exactly what the EU needs. Finally, even if it was the case that some local 'cross-border' problems did emerge, the scale of the bigger venture at stake – the historic bringing together of east and west – implies that it would be sensible to commit additional resources to assist areas experiencing difficulties and so forestall unwelcome political developments.

Capital Flows and Land Sales to Foreigners

Opening central European markets to the free flow of capital is a delicate matter that, in the case of Polish public discussion, has been distilled into fears that some foreigners (by which is usually meant Germans) will thereby be able to purchase land cheaply. The country's negotiating position, drawing in part on Danish experience, has been to demand an eighteen- year transition period in which to allow for price equalisation before the freedom to purchase land is implemented in full. The Commission has dismissed that position, but there is plenty of room for compromise and, perhaps in return for more favourable structural/regional aid, that transition time scale will probably be reduced to a much more digestible figure of around seven years. Poland and the other candidates may still need to be able to control the flow of short-term speculative capital, should the need arise, at least until such time as their domestic currencies are merged into the euro. But this aspect has excited relatively little interest.

POLITICAL DEVELOPMENTS

One striking feature of the Polish political landscape over the period since the 'post-Solidarity' AWS–UW government was formed in November 1997 was the way in which EU accession suddenly emerged from the shadows of political life to dominate domestic politics, at least for a time.[7] The diversity of views on Europe (and much else besides) represented within the ruling coalition and indeed within AWS alone created the conditions for Europe to emerge as a major political issue. Thus, while UW was avowedly pro-European, AWS included decidedly Eurosceptic groups, such as the relatively strong Christian National Alliance Party (ZChN).[8] Fortunately for the governing coalition, both the well-disciplined SLD opposition and President Kwaśniewski were committed to speedy Polish accession and a potentially dangerous politicisation of the EU was easily contained, albeit following a few awkward months.

In early 1998, the new Polish government faced an epidemic of uncomfortable accession related events. First, but ultimately not so important, finding a chief negotiator for EU talks took longer than most observers expected, a fact that was contrasted at the time with the speed and smoothness of the process in both the Czech Republic and Hungary. Second, and much more damaging, a local 'turf war' broke out between ministers over which government department should be responsible for EU aid funds, with some in AWS suspecting that the UW leader and coalition finance minister Balcerowicz wanted to take total control over EU aid flows. Those internal political struggles between different factions led to a situation where in 1998 the European

Commission rejected 34 million ECU of Poland's Phare applications on the grounds of poor quality. This of course cast the country's EU ambitions and preparations in a particularly unfavourable light, generating a glare of damaging international publicity. [9] The political temperature was raised even more a few days later when the Warsaw newspaper *Życie* published a story on its front page claiming that a Polish government minister had telephoned his congratulations to Brussels after Poland had suffered the loss of its Phare allocations. According to the account, that minister was Balcerowicz.[10] Embarrassingly, all of this was happening as Prime Minister Buzek was making his first official visit to Washington and only on his return did he assert his authority, restructure his cabinet and restore some order to the government's management of EU affairs. Thus, in its first months in office, Europe commanded the domestic political scene and buffeted the ruling parties in a way that had not happened, openly at least, throughout the entire life of the previous post-communist SLD–PSL administration. [11]

While those early problems were solved, others emerged. By the summer of 2000, the Polish authorities became increasingly disappointed that EU members were not doing more to promote the enlargement case within their own borders. More frustrating still was the proposal to devote most resources for a promotional campaign on enlargement to the year 2003, by which time, according to the Polish government's ambitions, the country would already be a member.[12] Finally, Romano Prodi, the EU President, immediately reacted to the Haider problem in Austria by suggesting that the EU would be forced into a tougher stance in the enlargement negotiations in order to hold the Union together, which sent a shiver of alarm to Warsaw.

The Polish government acknowledged that some problems, particularly the tardy way the Sejm was dealing with adapting laws to conform to EU standards and the accumulating delays in getting legislation through, were entirely home grown. The collapse of the ruling AWS–UW coalition in June 2000, as its clearly Europhile element (the UW party) withdrew, did nothing to help. The election cycle, with the presidential contest of October 2000 and a parliamentary election in 2001, threatened to make matters worse still. Openly anti-European candidates in the race for the state presidency put growing pressure on the Solidarity candidate, Marian Krzaklewski, to deviate from the AWS's official 'pro-EU' position and to adopt a harder line on accession. But this had little impact on the final result. These developments took place just as the most sensitive Chapters in EU accession negotiations were about to be opened. Thus, while the Commission seemed to be hardening its position, the Polish side began to look distinctly shaky. Even if a brave face was put on events in Warsaw, in other candidate country capitals, especially Prague, the alarm was sounded in 2000 that Polish frailty might lead to generalised accession delays: a notion stoutly rejected by the

Commission as it reaffirmed its stance that 'candidates may join when they are ready'.

If 2000 was another turbulent year in Polish politics, it turned out to have little impact on Poland's accession preparations. As the November 2000 Regular Report showed, Poland seemed to make up any ground that looked lost during earlier political in-fighting (CEC, 2000a). In part, this was probably due to the fact that earlier adverse reports, particularly in 1999, created a powerful incentive encouraging the Polish political elite, or most of it, to pull together in an effort to demonstrate to Brussels that, despite local difficulties, there was no fundamental weakening of the strategic aim of gaining EU membership as quickly as possible. That was the backdrop to the suggestion that an above party coalition for entry could be created. The original proposal came from the independent journalists of the *Unia&Polska* magazine. In May 2000, it launched its 'Bristol Appeal', inviting all seven of the 1990s prime ministers to sign a public declaration of willingness to work together on Europe (Bobiński, 2001). Only two found it expedient to stay away: Jan Olszewski from a right wing Solidarity splinter party and Waldemar Pawlak of the PSL peasants' party. Pawlak seemed eager to forget that he had submitted Poland's membership application in April 1994.

Shortly after, Jan Krzysztof Bielecki, a former prime minister from the Solidarity camp, urged the serving (also Solidarity) Polish premier, Jerzy Buzek, to engage the opposition post-communist SLD in the EU negotiating team. This, he said, would ensure there could be no slippage of valuable negotiating time should Brussels show signs of stalling and claiming the need to wait for the result of the September 2001 general election in Poland before firming up any of its own accession proposals. The idea was quickly taken up by the influential *Gazeta Wyborcza* newspaper in its appeal for a domestic political 'pact for Europe'.[13] The one concrete result of this activity was that parliament agreed to establish a powerful 'grand committee on European legislation' to speed its passage through the Sejm. That committee came into being in July 2000 under the chairmanship of the outgoing, and staunchly pro-EU, foreign minister, Bronisław Geremek, who later became the leader of the Freedom Union party following the departure of Leszek Balcerowicz to head the National Bank of Poland.

It seems that, post-1997 and as negotiations got under way in 1998, EU issues have become a subject of intense political debate, at least sporadically. None of this altered Polish fundamentals in the sense that membership has remained a prime concern of the political elite throughout. It may be, however, that the political class and its EU ambitions are very far from the day-to-day concerns of most Poles, a consideration that leads to a consideration of public opinion on such matters.

PUBLIC OPINION

The views of the elites in Warsaw, Brussels or other west European capital cities on EU accession are one thing, those on the street, in the factory and on the farm are quite another. While opinion polls have consistently revealed a high level of popular support for joining the EU, Euroscepticism within the country seems to have increased in recent years, with farmers being particularly nervous (Gołębiowski, 1998). A referendum on joining the EU may not be a foregone conclusion. At the same time, such enthusiasm as existed in the EU for the eastern expansion seems to be waning, especially in Germany and Austria. Neither of these developments augers well for the cohesion and integration of an enlarged Union or for the further evolution of a European identity and sense of citizenship.

Views in the EU

An evident lack of momentum or popular enthusiasm for enlargement within the EU has been apparent for some time: as the head of the Polish government's Committee for European Integration (KIE), Jacek Saryusz-Wolski, put it in mid-2000, 'the general level of support from [EU] elite and society is below our expectations'.[14] In the mid-summer of 2000, only 27 per cent of EU citizens thought that welcoming new members, irrespective of who they might be, should be an EU priority, one point down on six months earlier and a figure that can be contrasted with the 90 per cent who felt that fighting unemployment should be an urgent concern (CEC, 2000b:43). Indeed, 60 per cent stated explicitly that enlargement should not be a priority and it attracted by far the lowest level of support from a list of twelve potential EU concerns (ibid.).

More revealing still are the answers to a question that probed views on the admission of specific new EU members. As Table 10.1 shows, less than half support enlargement and only three CEE countries (the Czech Republic, Hungary and Poland) attract more support than opposition.[15] Rich countries get most support as potential new members, 70 per cent are in favour of Norway joining and 69 per cent in favour of Switzerland, despite the fact that those countries are not in the accession queue.

Predictably in a club of 15, the figures in Table 10.1 conceal a good deal of variation across current member states. Averaged across the 13 actual applicant countries, the highest levels of support for enlargement are to be found in Sweden (61 per cent), Denmark (58 per cent) and Greece (55 per cent). At the other end of the spectrum, only 34 per cent of Germans, 30 per cent of Austrians and 26 per cent of the French look favourably upon the

*Table 10.1 EU citizens' support for new member countries (%), 2000**

Country	In favour	Against	Balance
Bulgaria	36	39	-3
Cyprus	44	32	+12
Czech. Republic	41	35	+6
Estonia	36	38	-2
Hungary	46	31	+15
Latvia	36	38	-2
Lithuania	35	38	-3
Malta	50	26	+24
Norway	70	13	+57
POLAND	44	34	+10
Romania	34	42	-8
Slovakia	37	38	-1
Slovenia	34	40	-6
Switzerland	69	14	+55
Turkey	30	47	-17

Note: * 'don't knows' excluded.

Source: CEC (2000b:54).

admission of new members. In the particular case of Poland, Table 10.2 indicates popular support in 2000 of nearly 70 per cent in Denmark and Sweden, both countries with high net balances in favour and with strong interests in the Baltic region, to less than one-quarter in Austria. The division of opinion between east and west Germany over Poland's potential membership is also worthy of note, with the latter being considerably less enthusiastic. It is tempting to conclude that, with the exception of the Baltic, support varies inversely with proximity. Furthermore, care must be taken with the 'don't knows', which exceed 30 per cent in three countries and could, in the Polish case, change the balance of support in no fewer than nine countries.

Lukewarm public support for enlargement in the key EU countries is a major brake on expansion and one that led Romano Prodi, to remark in early 2000, following the election of the right-wing Haider government in Austria, that the EU would have to take the most stringent care to ensure that enlargement only took place when all sides were prepared. As noted earlier, this caused great consternation among headline writers in Warsaw. The low

Table 10.2 EU citizens' views on Polish membership (%), 2000[*]

Member State	In favour	Against	Balance
Austria	23	60	-37
Belgium	41	46	-5
Denmark	67	20	+47
Finland	52	31	+21
France	35	45	-10
Germany	37	46	-9
East	45	37	+8
West	34	48	-14
Greece	55	28	+27
Ireland	48	16	+32
Italy	50	29	+21
Luxembourg	38	47	-9
Netherlands	62	24	+38
Portugal	43	26	+17
Spain	52	18	+34
Sweden	69	16	+53
UK	40	28	+12

Note: * 'don't knows' excluded.

Source: CEC (2000b:B.44).

level of public support for enlargement, particularly in France and Germany, the countries that drive EU integration, is a matter of some concern in CEE.

CEE Views

It is often assumed that citizens of the countries of CEE have an unambiguous enthusiasm for closer western links. There is much truth in this, but the over-simplification is evident from the preceding discussion. The Polish government seems likely to hold a referendum prior to acceding to the Union and this, coupled with the normal requirement that policy enactments require a certain minimum level of popular support in order for them to be accepted, highlights the fact that politicians cannot be too cavalier in their interpretation of public opinion regarding EU membership. While there was evident euphoria over developments in 1989, the mood tempered quickly once the costs of transition became clear (Kolarska-Bobińska, 1994) and fear of further impositions is one of the factors undermining support for accession (Skotnicka-Illasiewicz, 1998).

By 2001, some stability appeared to have emerged in the regular surveys of the Polish population's voting intentions in any referendum on EU membership. From a high point of enthusiasm in May 1996, when 80 per cent said they would vote yes, support fluctuated in a narrow range from 55–59 per cent between May 1999 and March 2001. Meanwhile, the opposing block has grown from only 6 per cent in May 1994 until it now seems to have hardened at about one-quarter of the population, although a recent survey hints at a further increase to 30 per cent in March 2001. The undecided element of the population account for almost another 20 per cent of those polled, which on the most negative interpretation could imply a narrow majority in favour of accession to the EU (CBOS, 2000, 2000a, 2001). Many Polish officials and political leaders view this decline in support for EU entry as a natural development and one that reflects the lack of realism that characterised unbridled EU passion in the early 1990s. The fall in the pro-membership majority is moreover by no means alarming in a comparative context and the Poles remain, after the Hungarians, the staunchest supporters of membership in the region.

It is little surprise to discover that farmers are the most sceptical group in society, while the young and the better educated are already won over. Yet, even among farmers, views appeared to change radically in 1999–2000. In November 1999, 58 per cent of farmers said they would vote against EU entry, with only 34 per cent in favour; but by May 2000 the balance was almost even, with 41 per cent against entry and 40 per cent in favour (CBOS, 2000). If these proportions were to remain steady in the excited Polish election season of 2000 and 2001, the struggle to win people over to the integrationist idea might look almost over. However, a poll in July 2000 by the Demoskop market and social research agency found that 39 per cent of farmers would vote against and only 27 per cent in favour of Poland's EU membership (*Warsaw Voice*, 29 October 2000). Furthermore, the May 2000 poll highlighted the fact that six out of ten people believe that integration with the EU will have a 'rather unfavourable' influence on Polish farms (CBOS, 2000). This doubtless reflects a growing realisation that the EU has expressed its unwillingness to admit farmers from new entrant countries into a reformed CAP designed to operate on the basis of income supports.

More generally, it is perhaps surprising that a majority of the Polish population (62 per cent in March 2001) have favoured the option of 'economic modernisation before entry' since late 1998, with only 27 per cent supporting 'speedy entry then modernisation' (CBOS, 2001). This casts a different light on the Polish government's claim that it needs EU commitment to an entry date for reasons of 'social mobilisation'. It seems to leave open room for the promotion of an alternative view based on longer preparation before entry, an option that appears to have been excluded on domestic political grounds. Despite that, the population looks ready to accept entry even later than the official target of 2003. One recent survey showed that less than 20 per cent expected Poland to enter the Union by 2003 (TNS, 2000). The same source also constructed an index of readiness for membership based on respondents' views on their country's ability to satisfy the accession criteria in ten key policy areas. With its possible value ranging from zero to unity, the aggregate Polish score was only 0.4, which ranked it fifth amongst the ten CEE applicant states. While the Polish population seems ready to wait, the politicians could still be right in arguing that losing 'mobilisation momentum' poses severe dangers.

On the distribution of the gains from the closer relations established between Poland and the EU during the past decade, some 54 per cent of those polled in March 2001 believed that the EU had gained most, with only 6 per cent taking the opposite view. A further 25 per cent of respondents thought that the benefits had been shared equally (CBOS, 2001).[16] In fact, the view that the EU has done best from the existing association arrangement is held more fervently in Poland than in the other candidate countries for which comparable evidence exists. Nevertheless, the suggestion that Polish politicians with anti-EU instincts digging for a seam of similar sentiment may not need to go too deep was tested in the November 2000 presidential election in which avowedly anti-EU candidates performed extremely poorly. Only the leader, Andrzej Lepper, of the radical farmers' union Samoobrona gathered more than 1 per cent of the vote, and even his tally was only just over 3 per cent.[17]

CONCLUSION

From the Polish official viewpoint, concern over the date of entry has clouded the accession process from the outset. Despite almost continuous pressure, Brussels steadfastly refused to make any firm commitment on timing. This left the AWS government with little choice but to devise its own target date for accession (1 January 2003), by which time the country was to be 'ready' for entry. The emphasis on timing appears on occasion to have irritated the EU enlargement commissioner, Günther Verheugen, and by mid-2000 there was some sign that the Polish authorities were ready to relax their demands in return for a commitment along the lines that 'it is expected that countries may be ready to join the EU from …'. In the event, the December 2000 Nice summit did succeed in producing the statement that the 'EU would be ready to welcome new members from 2003', although this is still well short of Polish hopes. After a crushing political defeat in the September 2001 general election, the AWS was left on the political sidelines. It was succeeded yet again by a coalition of SLD and PSL, with the new Prime Minister, Leszek Miller, adopting 2004 as his government's target date for EU entry, despite PSL's mild Euroscepticism.

Most often mentioned in the context of difficult and sensitive issues are agriculture, labour and capital mobility, and regional and environmental matters. Yet in each of these cases, the usual negotiating 'give and take' should ensure that compromises are struck – the major unknown being simply the length of time it will take to get to jointly agreed positions. Given that the EU is in no hurry to close negotiations and is by far the strongest partner, that time period could be long. Working in the opposite direction, on the other hand, are the urgency with which accession is treated by the candidates and the growing awareness of the damage that could be done by delaying entry. The hunch is that this will encourage compromise and that a mid-decade enlargement is most likely.

Nevertheless dangers remain. The low level of support for enlargement in the EU is one. It is easy to sympathise with former Prime Minister Mazowiecki's concern that Poland is too often viewed in the EU as a problem. Poland's potential to contribute to a constructive EU 'eastern policy' is not much recognised in an EU that, even after all these years, still lacks any strong lobby for expansion. Worse still, the requirement that the candidate countries introduce tighter frontier controls risks creating the next division across Europe. Moreover, an EU that fails also to appreciate the costs of transformation already borne in countries like Poland in the 1990s risks demanding too much and appearing as inflexible and overbearing. Public opinion on both sides could harden and it is conceivable, even if unlikely, that the membership negotiations might stall. That would be a dangerous outcome; and one in which it is not hard to imagine groups in a hard-pressed central Europe voicing growing demands for increased protectionism leading, in the worst case, to an unravelling of the integrationist gains so far achieved. It is most likely, however, that common sense will prevail. This will not solve the economic problems of the accession states and it will also create a real risk of new economic and political frontiers emerging between 'ins and outs', but any other outcome is likely to have far more dangerous consequences.

NOTES

1. The author is grateful to Mike and Hilary Ingham for comments and suggestions in preparing this chapter but takes full responsibility for the views expressed.

2. See 'Kto przyspiesza, kto spowalnia' (Who is speeding up, who is slowing down), *Rzeczpospolita*, 5 November 1998, also 'European Union looks outwards', *Financial Times*, 10 November, 1998.
3. Poland's chief negotiator, Jan Kułakowski, appeared to accept that this would be the eventual outcome, see *Gazeta Wyborcza*, 12–13 December 1998.
4. Klaus Bachman, 'Ziemia za spokój' (Land for peace), *Wprost*, supplement to no. 47, 22 November, 1998, p.19.
5. In a speech at the opening of the membership negotiations, the Polish foreign minister outlined what he saw as Poland's strong case for increased aid allocations to modernise the agri-food sector, restructure the countryside and upgrade rural infrastructure in the pre-accession period. He also reaffirmed the demand to participate in the CAP on an equal footing. The EU's position at the opening of the negotiations was vague on this issue, as on much else (Kawecka-Wyrzykowska, 1999).
6. See 'Dopłaty dla co piątego gospodarstwa' (Subsidies for every fifth farm), *Rzeczpospolita*, 19 January,2000.
7. AWS (*Akcja Wyborcza Solidarność*), Solidarity Electoral Action, was the united front of most of the post-Solidarity parties and was headed by the leader of trade union Solidarity, Marian Krzaklewski. By early 2001, the group had all but collapsed and, in May, trade union Solidarity withdrew from it. UW (*Unia Wolności*), Freedom Union, was the other leading post-Solidarity party headed by Leszek Balcerowicz, deputy prime minister and finance minister in the AWS–UW coalition until December 2000 when he was appointed President of the central bank. In 2001, the Freedom Union struggled for continued survival.
8. For full details of the composition of AWS see Szczerbiak (1998).
9. Phare (Poland, Hungary, Assistance to the Restructuring of the Economy) and other assistance channelled through the European Commission for the countries of CEE.
10. See 'Zadzwonił Balcerowicz' (Balcerowicz Rang), *Życie*, 8 July 1998.
11. SLD (*Sojusz Lewicy Demokratycznej*), The Alliance of the Democratic Left, a united front of left-wing parties and trades unions with antecedent links to the Polish Communist Party (headed since late 1997 by Leszek Miller) and PSL (*Polskie Stronnictwo Ludowe*), the Polish Peasants' Party. Some argue that SLD-inspired governments have a more professional approach to concealing awkward differences on matters like Europe. If the SLD had some success in this regard with Europe there were notable failures too – especially over privatisation.
12. According to Jacek Saryusz-Wolski, chief of the Committee for European Integration, while the Commission was preparing an enlargement promotional campaign 'it disturbs us however that most resources are expected to be used on it in 2003–04, in other words at a time when we would like to be already in', *Gazeta Wyborcza*, 15 June 2000.
13. 'Zróbmy pakt dla Europy' (Let's make a pact for Europe), *Gazeta Wyborcza*, 28 June, 2000.
14. As reported in *Gazeta Wyborcza*, 15 June 2000.
15. It might be noted that only half of the respondents regard their own country's membership of the EU as a good thing (CEC, 2000b:7).
16. As reported in CBOS (2000), farmers again appear clearly as the group most strongly of the opinion that the EU has done better (69 per cent of respondents in May 2000).
17. The September 2001 general election caused surprise when Samoobrona jumped to third place with 10.2% of the vote. This development startled the Polish political elite who immediately began to ponder its significance for EU accession.

REFERENCES

Blazyca, George (2001), 'Poland's Place in the International Economy' in George Blazyca and Ryszard Rapacki (eds), pp. 249–73.

Blazyca, George and Ryszard Rapacki (eds) (2001), *Poland into the New Millennium*, Cheltenham, UK and Northampton, MA, USA: Edward Elgar

Bobiński, Chris (2001), 'Can Polish Politicians Work Together on EU Accession?' in George Blazyca and Ryszard Rapacki (eds), pp. 296–306.
CBOS (Centrum Badania Opinii Społecznej) (2001), 'Opini o integracji Polski z Unią Europejską', March, CBOS: Warsaw.
CBOS (Centrum Badania Opinii Społecznej) (2000), 'On the Way to the European Union', available at http://www.cbos.pl.
CBOS (Centrum Badania Opinii Społecznej) (2000a), 'Czechs, Hungarians and Poles on the European Union', available at http://www.cbos.pl.
CEC (Commission of the European Communities) (2000), 'Breakthrough in farm trade liberalisation talks with Poland', IP/00/1065, Brussels: CEC.
CEC (Commission for the European Communities) (2000a), *Regular Report from the Commission on Poland's Progress Towards Accession*, Luxembourg: Office for Official Publications of the European Communities.
CEC (Commission of the European Communities) (2000b), 'Eurobarometer Report Number 53', Brussels: CEC.
CEC (Commission of the European Communities) (1993), 'Europe Agreement establishing an association between the European Communities and their Member States, of the one part, and the Republic of Poland, of the other part', Final Act, JOL1993/348-2EN, Brussels: CEC.
Gołębiowski, Janusz (1998), 'Political Developments in Poland', in Marek Lubiński (ed.) *Poland: International Economic Report 1997/98*, Warsaw: World Economy Research Institute, pp. 9–17.
GUS (Główny Urząd Statystyczny) (2000), *Statistical Yearbook 2000*, Warsaw: GUS.
Ingham, Hilary and Mike Ingham (2002), 'EU Expansion to the East: The Problem of Agriculture', this volume, pp. 110–33.
Kawecka-Wyrzykowska, Elżbieta (1999), 'First Phase of Accession Negotiations with European Union', in Marek Lubiński (ed.) *Poland: International Economic Report 1998/99*, Warsaw: World Economy Research Institute, pp. 179–89.
Kolarska-Bobińska, Lena (1994), *Aspirations, Values and Interests*, Warsaw: IFiS Publishers.
Szczerbiak, A. (1998), 'Electoral Politics in Poland: The Parliamentary Elections of 1997', *Journal of Communist Studies and Transition Politics*, **14** (3), 58–83.
Skotnicka-Illasiewicz, E. (1998), 'Poland on its Way Towards Membership of the EU and NATO: Hopes and Anxieties in a View of Public Opinion Polls', *Yearbook of Polish European Studies*, **2**, 243–63.
TNS (Taylor Nelson Sofres) (2000), *Eastern Europeans Keen to Join the EU*, November, TNS: Warsaw.
Wagstyl, S. (2000), 'Moving targets', *Financial Times*, 16 June.

11. Enlargement to the East: Romania

David Phinnemore

INTRODUCTION

Full involvement in European integration has been a key foreign policy aim of Romanian governments since the overthrow of the Ceauşescu regime in December 1989. With a 'return to Europe' included in the ten-point programme issued by the National Salvation Front (FSN) in that month, Romania's relations with the European Union (EU) have developed considerably and seemingly at a rapid pace. A trade and cooperation agreement and a Europe Agreement (EA) have been signed and in the mid-1990s Romania was involved in the EU's 'structured relationship' with the Central and Eastern European (CEE) states.[1] Inclusion in the EU's accession process came in 1998 and in March 2000 formal negotiations on EU membership were opened. It should be emphasised, however, that EU–Romania relations have evolved more slowly than those between the EU and most other CEE states: it lagged behind the Visegrád countries in concluding an EA in the first half of the 1990s and was later omitted from the first group to open accession negotiations in 1998. Nevertheless, this has not decreased the commitment of Romanian governments to integration and the ultimate goal of EU membership.

The intention here is to chart the development of the country's relations with the EU, highlighting how it has benefited from the EU's tendency to deal with CEE states in a similar manner. There will also be an examination of the significance of Romania's application for EU membership for those relations and how these have developed since, noting in particular the contents of the Commission's 1997 *avis* and its 1998 and 1999 Regular Reports on readiness for accession. The final two sections of the work analyse Romania's membership prospects and examine possible implications of the country's exclusion from the eastwards enlargement.

1989–1995: TOWARDS A EUROPE AGREEMENT

As with other CEE states, Romania's relations with the EU have developed considerably since 1989, progressing through the hierarchy of arrangements that the Union has put in place to manage its dealings with its eastern neighbours. In 1990, Romania and the EU signed a trade and cooperation agreement, followed three years later by an EA. Since then, Romania has concluded an Accession Partnership (1998) and has been working closely with the EU to satisfy the criteria for membership. However, relations have not developed as rapidly as those between the EU and other CEE states and the country is often viewed as lagging behind in the integration process (Linden, 1992).

Trade and Cooperation Agreement

Relations between Romania and the EU developed only hesitantly in the post-Ceauşescu period, despite the fact that the country was the CEE state with most experience of dealing with the European Community. Refusing to be constrained by the Council for Mutual Economic Assistance disciplines in the 1970s and 1980s, it had concluded various agreements with the Community: minor textile and steel agreements were signed in 1978, to be followed in 1980 by a more general industrial trade agreement (Dijmarescu, 1989). Also, unlike its CEE neighbours, Romania benefited from the Community's General System of Preferences. The familiarity implicit in such ties did not, however, guarantee the country an automatic upgrade of its 1980 agreement at the time when other CEE countries were negotiating trade and cooperation agreements in the years 1988–90. Although talks began in 1987, they were suspended in 1989 due to the country's failure to meet its existing obligations towards the Community and its deteriorating human rights record (Senior Nello, 1991). Developments after the overthrow of the Ceauşescu regime in December 1989 did not improve the situation. Concerns over the limited progress being made with reform in 1990 by the government of Petre Roman led to Romania's initial exclusion from the Phare programme. The government's approach towards the country's Hungarian minority and its reaction to the inter-ethnic violence in Târgu Mureş in March 1990, which left five dead and hundreds injured, also caused considerable concern abroad. Confidence in the commitment of the ruling FSN to democracy and multi-partyism was further undermined by the one sided nature of the contest preceding the presidential and parliamentary elections of May 1990. The government-backed descent of the miners on Bucharest in the following month was more significant still. This clearly heightened concerns about the FSN's democratic credentials and respect for human rights and was roundly condemned by the Community, the North Atlantic Treaty Organization and the Council of Europe, leading to a delay in both the signing and entry into force of the trade and cooperation agreement. The miners' episode also contributed to Romania's exclusion from the first group of CEE states with which the Community was about to negotiate EAs.[2] As Linden (op. cit.:220) notes, 'Western policy towards Romania went from cool to cold'.[3]

The agreement on trade and commercial and economic cooperation was, however, signed in September 1990.[4] This provided for the removal of quantitative restrictions on Romania's trade with the Community as well as cooperation in various fields including agriculture, research and the environment. It also led to the creation of a new European Community–Romania Joint Committee, which met for the first time in May 1991. For the Romanian government, the agreement was not the end of the road towards integration: an upgrade of relations to the level of association was openly desired. However, this did not necessarily reflect keenness on integration per se.[5] The government appeared to be more interested in domestic affairs. Indeed, Gallagher (1998) questions whether the political elite, too engrossed with internal matters, actually understood integration. Moreover, foreign policy seemed more concerned with perceived threats from Hungary and the development of ties with Yugoslavia and the USSR.[6] On the former, one senior presidential policy advisor noted that Hungary, despite being 'one of [Romania's] former allies, ... has transformed herself openly into a potential enemy' (Pascu 1992:279).[7] A supportive attitude was shown towards the Miloševíc regime in Yugoslavia, with Belgrade being the destination of Iliescu's first visit abroad as president. Further, a Romanian–Soviet Treaty was signed in April 1991 committing the parties to refrain from joining any alliance seen as hostile. This suggested pro-Soviet sympathies and only a limited enthusiasm for integration with the west. As such, it is easy to regard Romania's request for an EA as reflecting a desire not to be left out of developments in the Community's relations with CEE states. Fearing differentiation, the government was keen to ensure that its country would enjoy the same relations as the Visegrád states and, in particular, as the country's immediate neighbour, Hungary.

The reaction of the Community to Romania's desire for an EA was cautious. Concerns about the leadership's commitment to democracy and political reform persisted even though a new constitution received popular approval in December 1991 and a second set of presidential and parliamentary elections were held in September 1992. Certainly, the European Parliament (EP) was reluctant to advocate the conclusion of an EA. Oritz Clement (1993), for example, argued that even the two sets of elections since 1989 had 'failed to confirm beyond a doubt the credibility of Romania's process of transition towards full democracy'. Moreover, academic assessments did not dismiss entirely the possibility of authoritarianism reasserting itself in the country (Dellenbrant, 1994; Gallagher, 1995a). With regard to the Hungarian minority, concern over the level of inter-ethnic tension in the Transylvanian city of Cluj and the government's refusal to guarantee minority rights resulted in Romania's entry into the Council of Europe – widely regarded as a prerequisite for closer ties with the EU – being delayed until October 1993 (Gallagher, 1995:127–33).

Negotiating a Europe Agreement

Events in 1990 and the failure of Iliescu and the Roman government to implement adequate economic and political reforms ensured that Romania was not among the first group of CEE states to negotiate EAs (the former Czechoslovakia, Hungary and Poland). Negotiations were, however, opened in May 1992, although this had little to do with developments within Romania. External factors were of greater importance; in particular, security concerns. First, there was an emerging consensus in the west that ties between the Community and Romania should be strengthened in the light of developments in Yugoslavia. Disintegration had begun in June 1991 with Slovenia and Croatia announcing their independence leading to fears that the resultant instability could spread. Making the prospect of an EA more explicit could prevent any potential Romanian involvement in events on its western border. Second, and of greater significance, was the attempted *coup d'état* in the USSR in August 1991 and the subsequent fragmentation of the Soviet Union. This threatened the security of the region and encouraged the Community to deepen its ties with all CEE countries. In the case of Romania, there was also a desire to ensure that the country did not become embroiled in developments in troubled Moldova. Hence, during the few days of the *coup* and immediately afterwards, the Commission began to consult member states on the possibility of opening negotiations with Romania and Bulgaria, seeking authorisation to open talks within weeks.[8] By implication, the two countries were deemed to be politically and economically fit in the Commission's eyes for association. The Council agreed in the case of Bulgaria and authorised exploratory talks. However, concerns over the political situation prevented support for talks with Romania emerging until December 1991 (Jørgensen, 1993). Another factor that undoubtedly influenced the moves to start negotiations was the widespread criticism of the Community's emerging *Ostpolitik*. This, it was argued, was providing insufficient support for the economic and political reform processes in CEE countries. Hence, there was pressure on the Community to establish closer ties with the non-Visegrád states to help secure their transitions.

Once negotiations opened, the Romanians were keen to conclude them quickly. Arguably this reflected the fact that the government had before it a rare window of opportunity to repair the country's international image and promote its integration with the Community.[9] Not surprisingly, the Romanians appeared willing to accept almost anything the Commission laid before them, although they did seek and gain some limited concessions regarding market access for textile and agricultural goods (*Agence Europe*, 8 October 1992). Negotiations proceeded relatively swiftly and were concluded on 4 November 1992, with the EA being signed on 1 February 1993.

Romania's EA was not dissimilar to those signed with the first set of CEE states. The main elements were the introduction of free trade on an asymmetrical basis and the establishment of a new and more developed institutional structure for relations, political dialogue and cooperation in a wide range of areas.[10] The wording of the Agreement did, however, contain at least one indicator of Romania's tardiness in implementing political reform, with the preamble noting as one of its objectives support for the country's efforts 'to consolidate its democracy': a clear indication that the political reforms were not as advanced as in Bulgaria and other CEE states. In addition, the agreement, unlike those signed in 1991 with the Visegrád group, highlighted the signatories' respect for 'democratic principles and human rights' and contained a reference to the 'rights of persons belonging to minorities'. Accompanying the EA was an interim agreement containing the trade provisions, which entered into force on 1 May 1993.[11]

The conclusion of the EA represented a significant step for Romania. Despite concerns about the government's commitment to democracy and human rights being expressed at the time the agreement was signed (Ionescu, 1993; Balfe, 1993), the country was now being treated on a par with the Visegrád states. This would be underlined by developments at the European Council's Copenhagen Summit in June 1993. The significance of these developments were not lost on the country's Foreign Minister, Teodor Meleşcanu, who openly welcomed what he regarded as a new era of non-discrimination in the Community's relations with the CEE countries and the start of a new phase of increased cooperation (*Le Soir*, 21 September 1993).

Copenhagen, the Structured Relationship and Pre-Accession Strategy

Once signed, the EA took two years to be ratified before entering into force on 1 February 1995. In the meantime, the Copenhagen Summit heralded a new era in EU–CEE relations, with two key announcements being made. First, the European Council (EC) declared that 'the associated countries (i.e. including Romania) enter into a structured relationship with the institutions of the Union within the framework of a reinforced and extended multilateral dialogue'. This would include regular meetings at the level of Commission and Council Presidents, as well as joint meetings of all heads of government and advisory meetings at Council level (CEC, 1993:point I.26). Romania would therefore enjoy the same treatment as the Visegrád states. Second, Community leaders announced that:

> the associated countries of Central and Eastern Europe (i.e. those with Europe Agreements) that so desire shall become members of the European Union. Accession will take place as soon as an associated country is able to assume the obligations of membership by satisfying the economic and political conditions required. Membership requires that the candidate has achieved stability of institutions guaranteeing democracy, the rule of law, human rights and respect for and protection of minorities, the existence of a functioning market economy as well as a capacity to cope with competitive pressure and market forces within the Union. (CEC, 1993: point I.23)

On the basis of such a commitment, Romania seemed set for membership, provided that it could meet the criteria.

Tangible evidence of the new 'structured relationship' between the EU and the CEE states came in September 1993 when the Troika of foreign ministers – those from the past, present and next holders of the council presidency – met their counterparts from both the Visegrád countries and, for the first time, Romania and Bulgaria.[12] Then, in March 1994, the Council reached agreement on formalising cooperation at international conferences and on involving all six CEE associates in 'joint foreign policy actions' and *démarches*. A first 'historic' meeting between all EU foreign ministers and their counterparts from the associate countries was held in October 1994. Later, as part of this new relationship, the leaders of the associated countries, including Iliescu, attended the Essen Summit in December 1994. This occasion launched the 'pre-accession strategy' for CEE states and called on the Commission to draw up a White Paper on preparing them for integration into the internal market. Following the publication of the relevant document in May 1995 (CEC, 1995), the Romanian government adopted a national strategy designed to prepare the country for membership (Prisăcaru, 1996).

However, the EU's decision to include Romania alongside the Visegrád countries in its approach to eastern enlargement had little to do with internal developments. Although some progress had been made with economic reform, concerns about the position of the Hungarian minority had been heightened by the inclusion of the ultra-nationalist Party of Romanian National Unity (PUNR) and the Greater Romania Party (PRM) in the governing coalition in 1994–95. Their presence and vociferous opposition to the proposed Treaty of Friendship with Hungary were not received favourably in the west and Romania's inclusion in the structured relationship and pre-accession strategy once again reflected the wider interests of the EU. First, logistical considerations were significant: fewer human and financial resources would be needed if the implementation of the EU's *Ostpolitik* could be handled within a multilateral framework. Second, there was still a clear need for the EU to respond to criticism and be seen to be more supportive of the reform processes in all CEE countries. Third, with CEE countries applying for membership, there was increased pressure on the EU to set out its agenda for enlargement eastwards. A reluctance both to do this explicitly and to prioritise candidates encouraged less differentiation in the EU's *Ostpolitik*.

The Europe Agreement in Force

Romania's increased involvement with the EU was underlined on 1 February 1995 when the EA finally entered into force. As a consequence, new institutional relations were established. The Association Council, bringing together ministerial representatives from the EU and Romania, met for the first of its annual meetings on 10 April 1995. This was followed on 12–13 October 1995 by the first meeting of the Association Committee in Bucharest, which duly established both Association Sub-Committees and an Association Parliamentary Committee. However, the EA involved more than simply new institutions and Romania also had to assume the obligations of its new relationship with the EU. It was now committed to legislative approximation and the adoption of EU rules governing competition. This was duly recognised by the Parliament in a declaration timed to coincide with the entry into force of the EA.

Domestically, the EA led to new administrative bodies being established to promote the coordination of activities designed to further the country's integration with the EU. The key piece of legislation in this regard was Decision 140 of 9 March 1995, which established the Inter-ministerial Committee for European Integration, chaired by the Prime Minister and composed of cabinet ministers and heads of government agencies with responsibilities of relevance to integration. The Decision also confirmed the role of the Department for European Integration, responsible to the Prime Minister's office, which had been created in February 1993. The Department's main task was, and remains, to coordinate preparations for accession. In addition, special units were established within all ministries to supervise, monitor and control activities relating to integration. A parliamentary level joint Commission for European Integration consisting of senators and deputies, was charged with monitoring legal approximation and promoting relations with the EP, was also created in 1995. Finally, a Legislative Council responsible for monitoring the approximation of national laws with the *acquis communautaire* and their compatibility with the EA was brought into being. Such institutional and administrative developments suggested a clear commitment on the part of Romania to fulfil its obligations vis-à-vis the EU.

THE QUEST FOR MEMBERSHIP

The entry into force of the EA heralded a new phase in the development of EU–Romania ties. However, as was the case with other CEE states, the country did not regard the agreement and the association it created as ends in themselves, rather they were viewed very much as steps towards the goal of membership. This was made apparent on 22 June 1995 when Foreign Minister, Teodor Meleşcanu, submitted the country's formal request for accession, making it the third CEE state so to do. Officially, the application represented a firm statement of Romania's commitment towards integration and the government's apparent sincerity was underlined by the two documents which accompanied the application. The first of these was the so-called Snagov Statement, a unanimous agreement supporting the membership application signed by representatives of the government and of all political parties represented in parliament. The second was the recently adopted National Strategy for the Preparation of Romania's Accession to the European Union (Government of Romania, 1995).[13] This contained Romania's response to the pre-accession strategy, launched by the Community at Essen the previous December, and included a programme of legislative harmonization for integration into the EU's internal market.[14] It was also anticipated that 'through consistent efforts, Romania will be able, similarity [sic] to other associated countries, to fulfil the essential conditions for accession by the year 2000'.

Such a date was clearly optimistic. The ambassador to the EU, Constantin Ene, acknowledged as much when he noted that Romania was unlikely to be among the first CEE countries to gain full membership (CEC, 1995a:35). Yet the National Strategy did contain various statements indicating the government's apparent commitment to closer ties. Reference was made to the EA and to the EU's recently adopted pre-accession strategy as bases for the development of closer relations. Romania's desire to accede was reinforced in December 1995 when the government adopted 'The National Programme of Legislative Approximation regarding the Internal Market' (Gabanyi and Zamfirescu, 1996). A necessary follow-up to the Commission's White Paper earlier in the year, the National Programme committed the Romanian government to align domestic legislation with that of the EU.

Preparing for Membership

Since 1995, Romanian governments have, formally at least, remained committed to preparing the country for EU membership and this has particularly been the case since the elections of November 1996. These saw the defeat of Iliescu and his Party of Social Democracy of Romania (PDSR) and their replacement by Emil Constantinescu as President and the Democratic Convention of Romania (CDR) at the head of a coalition government committed to accelerating the pace of economic reform and furthering preparations for accession. The challenge though was daunting given the country's deteriorating economic situation (Smith, 2001). The new government's commitment to rapid economic reform, including price liberalisation and privatisation, appeared to be sincere and was received eagerly abroad. The government made it clear that one of its main goals was 'the creation of conditions ... for negotiating Romania's integration to the European Union', with fulfilment of the conditions for entry scheduled for around the year 2000 (Government of Romania, 1996). To this end, the 1997–2000 programme of the government noted that it would 'speed up the process of *harmonizing* ... Romanian legislation with that of the Community', with special attention to be paid to free competition and enforcement.

In addition, the incoming government of Victor Ciorbea committed itself to addressing some of the more political concerns of the EU regarding Romania's eligibility for membership. In particular, efforts were made to improve the position of ethnic minorities and to develop more friendly relations with the country's neighbours, notably Hungary. Hence representatives of the Hungarian minority were included in the government and the right to be schooled in Hungarian and to use Hungarian in education, courts of law and administration was granted. In foreign policy, relations with Hungary were intensified beyond the Basic Treaty signed in 1996 by a strategic regional partnership involving economic and military cooperation. Also, relations with Ukraine were improved via the Treaty of Friendship and Good Cooperation signed in June 1997. All this was warmly welcomed within the EU. It did not, however, prove sufficient to close the gap between Romania and most other CEE states in their attempts to gain admission: as enlargement eastwards loomed closer, it became increasingly clear that Romania was not viewed as a prime candidate.

THE EU AND ROMANIA'S APPLICATION

Since 1995, there have been various occasions when the EU has welcomed Romania's application and indicated that the country will join provided that it meets the membership criteria. However, it has only been since July 1997 and the Commission's publication of Agenda 2000, which contained the much awaited *avis* on Romania's membership application and its prospects, that progress towards accession has been made. The *avis* was favourable in several respects. It noted, for example, that the country was 'on its way to satisfy the political criteria' for membership. For the most part, however, it was less positive about the immediate prospects. Although progress in creating a market economy was deemed to have been 'considerable', it was argued that Romania 'would face serious difficulties to cope with the competitive pressure and market forces within the Union in the medium-term' (CEC, 1997:Conclusion). The *avis* was also critical of the country's limited progress in promoting legislative harmonization. Citing figures provided by the Romanian government, the Commission indicated that 426 measures had been adopted which had some degree of compatibility with the corresponding White Paper measures, but this represented little more than 47 per cent of the required list (ibid.:Annex). As a result, the Commission's conclusion was not encouraging:

> despite the progress that has been made, Romania has neither transposed nor taken on the essential elements of the *acquis*, particularly as regards the internal market. It is therefore uncertain whether Romania will be in a position to assume the obligations of membership in the medium term. In addition, considerable efforts will be needed in the areas of environment, transport, employment and social affairs, justice and home affairs as well as agriculture. More generally, substantial administrative reform will be indispensable if Romania is to have the structures to apply and enforce the *acquis* effectively. (ibid.:Conclusion)

Officially, the overall conclusions confirmed the Romanian government's view that the economy was not yet ready for accession (Geoana, 1997). Government ministers admittedly raised objections about several 'inaccuracies, outdated assessments, and misplaced emphases' (Severin, 1997–98:35), but the broad conclusions were deemed to be a relatively fair reflection of the situation. The government naturally shared the view that the 'current improvement in Romania, following the arrival in power of a new government, indicates that Romania is on its way to satisfy the political criteria' (CEC, 1997:Conclusion). It also welcomed the conclusion that the country had made 'considerable' progress in creating a market economy. It took less readily, however, to the concerns raised regarding guarantees for fundamental rights and the integration of the Roma. Similarly, there was only a reluctant acceptance of the view that Romania 'would face serious difficulties to cope with the competitive pressure and market forces within the Union in the medium-term'. That the country had neither 'transposed nor taken the essential elements of the *acquis*, particularly as regards the internal market', could not be blamed on the present government, although it would clearly have to undertake the 'considerable efforts' noted above.

While many of the substantive conclusions drawn in the *avis* were accepted, officials in Romania could barely conceal their disappointment at the Commission's overall assessment that their country should not be invited to negotiate membership at the present time. To proceed with enlargement in waves as the Commission was proposing was described as being 'artificial and discriminatory' (RFE/RL Newsline, 16 July 1997). Concern was also expressed as to whether the proposed pre-accession strategy would guarantee an inclusive enlargement process. Hence, a key aim of Romanian policy was to ensure that the EU would ultimately adopt 'non-discriminating solutions' to enlargement (Severin, op. cit.). The government lobbied EU governments to ignore the Commission's recommendation in favour of a so-called 'regatta' approach to enlargement whereby all CEE states would start accession negotiations simultaneously, with each set of negotiations proceeding at a speed appropriate to the readiness for membership of the country concerned (Severin, 1997; Stan, 1999).

Partial success came when the EU, at its Luxembourg Summit in December 1997, agreed not only to open negotiations with five CEE countries (the Czech Republic, Estonia, Hungary, Poland and Slovenia), but also declared that the accession process would be all-inclusive. Romania would not be left out of the enlargement plans: indeed, the country became part of an enhanced strategy intended to enable all applicant states 'eventually to become members' and involved new Accession Partnerships being negotiated with each. In addition, regular reviews of progress in meeting the criteria for membership would be carried out, with a positive review possibly leading to the opening of accession negotiations. Finally, the establishment of an annual European Conference involving the EU and applicant states was announced, which would 'address questions of general concern to the participants and ... broaden and deepen their cooperation on foreign and security policy, justice and home affairs, and other areas of common concern, particularly economic matters and regional cooperation' (EC, 1997:5). Hence, with the launch of the accession process in March 1998 and the establishment of an Accession Partnership (AP), Romania appeared to be moving closer towards membership.

1998 Accession Partnership

Romania's AP, like those of the other CEE applicants, sets out the areas to which it must give priority if it is to meet the criteria for membership. Among the short-term objectives were economic reform, the reinforcement of institutional and administrative capacity, the internal market, justice and home affairs and the environment. These were to be achieved by the end of 1998, with EU financial assistance being conditional on progress in meeting them, the obligations under the EA and further progress in satisfying the accession criteria (CEC, 1998:point 6). As for medium-term priorities, the AP included detailed objectives on which work should begin in 1998, which covered the same areas as the short-term objectives plus the political criteria for accession, economic policy, agriculture, fisheries, transport, employment and social affairs, and regional policy and cohesion. Particular emphasis was placed on the *acquis*:

> incorporation of the *acquis* into legislation is not in itself sufficient; it will also be necessary to ensure that it is actually applied to the same standards as those which apply in the Union. In all areas listed ... there is a need for credible and effective implementation and enforcement of the *acquis*. (ibid.:point 4)

With regard to the four freedoms – the free movement of goods, services, capital and people – Romania was informed that 'efforts to accelerate the approximation of legislation need to be intensified'. A call was also made for more effective enforcement of anti-trust legislation (ibid.:point 3.1).

The appropriateness of the priorities and objectives was recognised implicitly by the Romanian government in its National Programme for Accession to the European Union (Government of Romania, 1998). Published in October 1998, this confirmed the government's wish to assume an active part in the process of European integration 'by accepting and meeting the obligations due to it by participating in assimilating, developing and preserving the *acquis communautaire*'. It acknowledged, however, that although 'significant progress' has been made in absorbing the *acquis*, efforts must be intensified in order to fulfil the Copenhagen criteria. To this end the government also adopted a National Programme for the Adoption of the *Acquis Communautaire*, which has since been updated (ibid.:171–519; Government of Romania, 1999:59–256).

1998 Progress Report

Involvement in the accession process did not, however, guarantee that progress towards the goal of membership would be realised and Romania's leaders acknowledged their country's limited preparedness and the need to pursue rapid and far-reaching reform. Yet despite their avowed commitment, the necessary changes were not forthcoming and, even before its first Regular Report was released in November 1998, Commission officials were voicing concern about the pace of change. Romania, it was argued, risked being 'the only applicant state which instead of progressing, actually regresses' (CEC, 1998) and the report itself concluded that 'Romania has made very little progress in the creation of a market economy and its capacity to cope with competitive pressure and market forces has worsened' (ibid.). While improvements had been made in meeting the economic criteria for membership, it was noted that 'reforms have been far too hesitant and slow, complicated by legal and administrative uncertainty, as well as by frequent changes and delays in implementation' (ibid.). The Commission added: 'The economic situation in Romania is very serious. The new [Vasile] government must give absolute and urgent priority to restoring macroeconomic stability and establishing credibility in international financial markets' (CEC, 1998a:B.24). The Commission's overall conclusion made no better reading:

> Romania meets the Copenhagen political criteria. Much remains to be done in rooting out corruption, improving the working of the courts and protecting individual liberties and rights of the Roma. Priority should also be given to reform of the public administration ... Despite progress made in transposition of key parts of the *acquis*, Romania has a long way to go in terms of additional legislative transposition, implementation and enforcement before the country will be able to assume the obligations of membership. (ibid.:C)

Admittedly, the Commission did recognise that the pace of transition in agriculture, energy, transport, regional development and 'some areas' of the internal market had been accelerated. It was, however, critical of the government's unsatisfactory progress in fulfilling the short-term priorities of the AP. Furthermore, it concluded that substantial administrative reform would be 'indispensable' if Romania was to be able to apply the *acquis* effectively (ibid.:B3.10 and B.4).

Doubtless the Commission was disappointed with Romania's efforts and this could hardly have gone unnoticed in domestic government circles. As a result, renewed efforts were soon being made to ensure that the EU did not abandon the country and allow it to slip further behind the other CEE applicants. The government's priority became non-exclusion from the enlargement process (Phinnemore, 2000). At home, the prime minister and president continued to demand an end to political in-fighting within the coalition and renewed efforts to proceed with economic reform. Externally, they made calls for Romania to be invited to open accession negotiations at the Helsinki Summit in December 1999. Although the country was not yet ready to join and did not expect early membership, this would send an important political message that it was not being 'left outside' (O'Rourke, 1999) or forgotten by the EU.[15]

In the event, following the Kosovo crisis, the EU began to pursue a more pro-active policy of integration towards south-eastern Europe and to reconsider its approach towards enlargement. Hence, following high profile visits to Bucharest by the UK Prime Minister, Tony Blair, and Germany's Chancellor, Gerhard Schröder, the Commission recommended, in its 1999 Regular Reports on the applicant countries, that Romania should be invited to open accession negotiations (CEC, 1999:VI). This was duly welcomed at the Helsinki Summit and formal negotiations began in March 2000.

ROMANIA'S PROSPECTS OF MEMBERSHIP

Officially, Romania's participation in the accession process means that the country is on track for membership of the EU, although this cannot be guaranteed. Much will depend on the extent to which it is able to meet the accession criteria, with the Commission regularly expressing concern about the lack of progress. Indeed, although Romania was invited to start accession negotiations following the 1999 Report, its contents make depressing reading. While the situation regarding fulfilment of the political criteria laid down at Copenhagen remained satisfactory, concerns were expressed over a number of areas: the crisis in the country's childcare institutions; the government's increased use of ordinances to enact legislation; the independence and efficiency of the judiciary; progress in the fight against corruption and the situation of the Roma.[16] But such concerns were nothing compared to the conclusions regarding economic policy, where further attention and reform were seen to be needed regarding macroeconomic imbalances, privatisation, exports, economic growth, living standards, financial discipline, the restructuring of large loss-making public enterprises, the creation of a more transparent and business-friendly environment, transposition and implementation of internal market measures, the adoption of a law on public procurement, the banking sector and financial control, the commercialisation of former state monopolies, the low priority given to the environment, weak administrative capacity and public administration reform.

The concerns seemed endless and were underlined in the Commission's summary of its reports where it noted:

> All candidates except Slovakia, Lithuania, Bulgaria and Romania are considered to be functioning market economies ... The economic situation in Romania is very worrying and sustained efforts will be needed to put a functioning market economy in place ... Romania [does] not meet either economic criterion. Regrettably, the situation in Romania has, at best, stabilised compared with last year. (CEC, 1999)

The critical observations contained in the Commission's Report were unprecedented and that issued in 2000 drew similar conclusions, noting that Romania had made 'too limited progress' towards meeting the criteria (CEC, 2000). Thus, even though the country had received an invitation in 1999 to negotiate membership, accession remained at best a medium-term prospect. While the government was envisaging 2007 as a realistic date, domestic critics (e.g. Brucan, 1999) and voices within the EU predicted 2010 at the earliest.

The progress that Romania needs to make in completing the reform process appears considerable and is not facilitated by domestic constraints that have the potential to undermine its membership prospects in the medium-term. These include the reluctance of governments to push through microeconomic elements of the reform agenda (e.g. enterprise restructuring, closures and privatisation of large state-owned companies) and to tackle entrenched special interests. This much has been evident in the period of reformist government from 1996–2000 and is likely to remain the case following the success of former president Iliescu and the traditionally less reform-minded PDSR in the 2000 elections. Moreover, progress is often hampered by the institutional forces ranged against reformers (Gallagher, 1998) and the increase since 1998 in civil unrest and strike action, with the clashes between miners and the authorities in early 1999 being notable examples. Nonetheless, domestic support for integration remains high, even though popular concerns have become focused more heavily on the economic situation, with unemployment increasing, inflation remaining high and governments proving to be unstable. Hence, only 5 per cent of the population regard integration as a pressing need (Mungiu-Pippidi, 1998). In such circumstances, the commitment to reform speedily, and by implication to meet the accession criteria within the medium-term, could wane and thereby delay membership.

Yet it is not just the situation in Romania that will determine the country's membership prospects: accession will take place only if the EU is willing and able to admit more than just an initial wave of CEE countries (Phinnemore,

1999). Therefore, even if Romanian governments do succeed in implementing reform and meeting the membership criteria, admission is not guaranteed. First, there is the question of institutional reform. Left almost untouched by the Treaty of Amsterdam, this is regarded as a fundamental prerequisite for eastern enlargement, without which the EU's decision-making mechanism risks paralysis. Not surprisingly, the EU brought forward the Inter-Governmental Conference (IGC) on institutional reform envisaged in the Treaty of Amsterdam and, in March 2000, began the process of seeking solutions to key issues, including the redistribution of votes in the Council of Ministers, the extended use of qualified majority voting (modified or otherwise) and the size of the Commission. Although the Treaty of Nice agreed in December 2000 addressed some of these issues successfully, not all the reforms deemed necessary for successful enlargement were forthcoming. Without these, expansion beyond an initial wave or waves (i.e. excluding Romania) is hard to envisage. Hence, although the Treaty delivered reform sufficient to admit some states and provided a boost to the enlargement process, further change, whether in the context of the IGC called for 2004 or a later one, could be necessary before Romania might be allowed to join.

A second issue is the EU's commitment to eastern enlargement generally, and to Romania's accession in particular. Both are regarded as costly projects and the EU's current budgetary perspective, adopted in 1999, is predicated on the admission of no more than six new states. Hence a new round of budget negotiations and policy reforms, almost certainly with an enlarged membership, will have to be undertaken before Romania can enter and the decision reached in Nice to retain the need for unanimity in reforming the Structural Funds until after the 2006–13 budgetary perspective is agreed provides little room for optimism. The challenge for the EU in finding the political will to prepare itself financially, as well as institutionally, to admit Romania and other CEE states excluded from the first wave is considerable.

All this assumes of course that the EU wishes to admit Romania. Certainly there is the possibility that it could be distracted away from eastwards enlargement by renewed applications from richer states, such as Norway and Switzerland. Moreover, the EU has no experience of enlarging to include former communist countries and the impact of accepting an initial wave of countries with economies still in a state of transition could dissuade it from further expansion eastwards. Finally, there is the question of whether the strong public commitment to admit Romania, as evidenced in the opening of accession negotiations in March 2000, will be sustained. The number of member states openly supportive of Romania's accession may have increased in recent years, but not all governments are convinced of the merits of the case and neither are their populations. Among the ten CEE applicants, the country attracts the second lowest levels of support in opinion polls with only

Slovenia's application being viewed less favourably. Only 33 and 34 per cent of EU citizens were in favour of admitting Romania in 1999 and 2000, respectively (CEC, 1999a:B.50; CEC, 2000a:B.45). These figures were lower than in the two previous Eurobarometer polls, which found that 39 and 37 per cent, respectively, were in favour (CEC, 1998b:B.45; CEC, 1999b: B.63). Opposition to Romania's accession was as high as 71 per cent in Austria in 1999.

THE IMPLICATIONS OF NON-ACCESSION

Even though accession negotiations have been opened, it does not mean that Romania will necessarily become a member within the next decade. Indeed some in the country argue that membership is impossible given the economic distance the country is from the EU (*The Economist*, 10 June 2000). Perhaps, such views are unduly pessimistic and tend to ignore the EU's professed commitment to enlargement and the Romanian government's determination to join. All the same, the emphasis is very much on the country meeting the accession criteria before a final decision is taken on when it can take place and there can be no guarantee that the EU's resolve will suffice to ensure Romania remains on course for membership. As such, there is a need to consider the potential implications of non-accession.

It is certainly possible that non-accession could result in Romania becoming a less stable and less dedicated participant in the enlargement process. Indeed, there exists the possibility of a domestic backlash against integration if Romania does not accede to the EU within the next five to ten years, particularly if it remains committed to the full implementation of the onerous obligations under its EA and AP. Domestically, government failure to achieve membership is likely to prove unpopular. Assuming that the country implements the obligations that it has already accepted, it could find itself in a situation where it becomes a *de facto* satellite of the EU, obliged to continue the approximation of its domestic legislation with that of the *acquis communautaire* without having any say in its adoption (Phinnemore, 1999a). Admittedly, approximation cannot be assured, particularly in view of the country's record to date, although it is likely if Romanian governments remain committed to reform, since failure will only lead to further delays in membership.

If Romanian governments do not remain convinced of the EU's willingness to admit the country within a reasonable period of time, a key incentive to meet the accession criteria and promote legislative approximation and harmonization will cease to exist. Moreover, although the EU is providing assistance to meet the costs of the AP, the country is unlikely to be willing to spend money on meeting the criteria unless the goal of membership can be guaranteed. Domestically, the use of resources for this purpose may prove increasingly difficult to justify, leading to the conclusion that energies could be better channelled into more pressing economic and social concerns.[17] Also, it has been argued that an anti-western backlash cannot be ruled out if plunging living and health standards continue to be the lot of people at a time when the country is seeking to meet the accession criteria (Gallagher, 1999). Indeed, it has already been suggested that, in states such as Romania, there may come a point when the population realises that the EU does not want their country. One scenario would then be that the association agreements are revoked and self-interested economic, trade and industrial policies will be adopted (Podkaminer, 1999). There is also no guarantee that the domestic consensus among parties on European integration will hold once its requirements are seen to dictate the domestic policy agenda. This may lead Romanian governments to favour less intrusive forms of integration by which the country is left to choose the speed and the direction of economic reform (Hartwig, 2001).

Pressure in this direction will come not only from those traditionally opposed to speedy economic reform (e.g. successors to the former communists), but also from nationalists critical of externally prescribed reforms and policies. Of potential significance here are the results of the presidential and parliamentary elections held in late 2000. The normally less reform-minded PDSR won both, with the nationalist PRM emerging as the second largest party in parliament, gaining 19.4 per cent of the vote compared to the PDSR's 36.6 per cent (RFE/RL Newsline, 1 December 2000). The PRM's leader, Corneliu Vadim Tudor, was also runner up to the PDSR in the presidential contest. While the PDSR has emphasised its commitment to seeing Romania join the EU, it has still to prove its reform credentials. If it fails and the 2000 election result proves to be a genuine reflection of growing nationalist sentiment, then the threat to the country's membership prospects is real. Assuming that avowedly more reformist parties do gain power again in the future, the result could be a relationship similar to that often experienced between the EU and Turkey or the EU and Malta, in which periods of rapprochement have been interwoven with estrangement.

CONCLUSION

Romania, like all CEE countries, has seen its relations with the EU intensify considerably since 1989 and currently finds itself set for EU membership at some unspecified point in the future. This said, Romania has tended to lag behind its CEE neighbours in terms of economic and political reform during the first decade of post-communist transformation. Consequently, it is at the end of the queue of current applicants, ahead only of Turkey, and with the dynamics of eastwards enlargement yet to be experienced, this is not a favourable position. Without doubt, many of the reasons for this situation lie with Romanian governments. The EU nevertheless has a significant role to play in maintaining the prospect of membership. This must remain real, irrespective of the progress made in meeting the membership criteria: if it does not, Romania's full integration could be delayed significantly. The accession process launched in 1998 must therefore be seen to be evolutive and inclusive, as intended, and the negotiations started in 2000 need to be accompanied by appropriate preparation on the part of the EU to admit all CEE states, including Romania.

The launch of the Stability Pact for south-eastern Europe in 1999 means that the EU's attention has become more firmly fixed on the region and that the country is unlikely to become a forgotten partner in the integration process. Hungary's accession to the EU is also likely to ensure that Romania's candidacy for EU membership is not neglected. This should not, however, lead to complacency on the part of future Romanian governments. The EU's approach to enlargement is based on conditionality and membership prospects will be enhanced only through reform and the effective implementation of obligations. Progress in both areas is vital if Romania is to move towards accession. Also the EU must prepare itself for enlargement beyond an initial wave of CEE states. Assuming that Romania remains committed to reform, it is in this latter area that the major barrier to accession facing the country potentially lies.

NOTES

1. The CEE states are Hungary, Poland, the Czech Republic, Slovakia, Bulgaria, Romania, Estonia, Latvia Lithuania and Slovenia.
2. See, for example, EPC Statement Concerning Romania, Document 90/251 (Brussels, 18 June 1990) in which member states deplored 'the indiscriminate use of force by the Romanian Government and its supporters in putting down demonstrators ... The Twelve believe that acts of violence, by whomever they are committed, constitute a major obstacle on the road to democratic change'.
3. One notable snub came in October 1990 when Iliescu was the only leader of a CEE country not to be received by the US President, George Bush, when attending a meeting of the UN General Assembly (Gallagher, 1995).
4. See Official Journal L 79, 26 March 1991.
5. Arguably, the commitment of the FSN and of Iliescu to European integration was little more than rhetorical. In his 'political biography' Iliescu refers to his commitment to the creation of a 'united Europe', but scarcely mentions the EU (Iliescu, 1995).
6. For analyses of Romania's foreign policy in the early 1990s, see Socor (1990), Sturdza (1991) and Ionescu (1991)

7. Pascu continued: 'Because of irredentist claims among some Hungarians concerning the ethnic Hungarian minority inside Romania, and because of statements and actions that interfere in Romanian domestic politics, we must be concerned ... In a larger context, a new triangle of powers seems in the making on our borders, placing Romania once again in its traditional buffer-state role. Thus, on our western border, a bloc of Catholic states is taking place under the guidance of Budapest and Vienna backed by Berlin. The 'Slav bloc', consisting of orthodox Russia and the Ukraine, will dominate our northern and eastern borders, while Islamic Turkey - with which Romania maintains extensive and good relations and has concluded a treaty - is becoming more and more active close to our southern border ... [Romania's relationship with Bulgaria] could, too, deteriorate even to the point of potential Bulgarian territorial claims against Romania. Sofia's claims would be rejected but the presence of such views that Dobrudja 'belongs' only to Bulgaria is known to us and pursuing these would be unwelcome'.
8. The US also moved towards restoration of most favoured nation status for Romania and the G-24 announced US$ 125m worth of assistance as part of US$ 500m deal to help the country's balance of payments (Linden, 1992).
9. The view is advanced by Bulgarian sources, who also argue that the speedy conclusion of negotiations reflected 'the apparent Romanian approach of unconditional surrender' (Skak (1993, p. 161, note 5 and p. 164).
10. See Official Journal L 357, 31 December 1994.
11. See Official Journal L 81, 2 April 1993.
12. The meeting was followed in early December 1993 by a working lunch between the Council and ministers from the six CEE states (*Agence Europe*, 2 December 1993). The Visegrád-3 had become the Visegrád-4 following the disintegration of Czechoslovakia in 1993 and the creation of its two successor states: the Czech Republic and Slovakia.
13. The National Strategy was drawn up by an *ad hoc* committee, established in February 1995, of parliamentarians, government representatives, academics and representatives of youth organisations (see Prisăcaru, 1996).
14. In fact, Decision 140 of March 1995 had already required that all proposed legislation conform with the relevant EU equivalent.
15. See for example, President Emil Constantinescu's comments after the Kosovo crisis in 'How much is Enough', in *Review*, July/August 1999 and his accusations of western indifference as reported in *Le Monde* (édition électronique), 28 August 1999 (via www.lemonde.fr). See also his earlier criticism of the west and in particular Austria's presidency of the EU in the second half of 1998, in 'Österreich hat vergessen, daß es nicht das letzte westliche Land ist, sondern mitten in Europa liegt', *Die Presse*, 23 November 1998 (via www.diepress.at). For a critical analysis of the Romanian government's reaction to the EU's position in 1998, see Stan (1998).
16. A further issue not mentioned in the report is the criminalisation of homosexuality under Romanian legislation about which voices within the EU and the Council of Europe have long expressed concern. In June 2000, reforms decriminalising homosexual acts in private were adopted by the lower chamber of the Romanian parliament. Homosexual acts conducted in public remained classified as criminal and subject to up to five years' imprisonment (RFE/RL Newsline, 29 June 2000).
17. Such arguments have been raised with regard to Turkey's commitments towards the EU (Kramer, 1996).

REFERENCES

Balfe, R. (1993), 'Report of the Committee on Foreign Affairs and Security on Relations between the European Community and Romania', *European Parliament Session Documents*, A3-0128/92, Luxembourg: European Parliament.

Brucan, Silviu (1999), *Treptele Tranzitiei Spre Capitalism* , Bucuresti: Nemira.

CEC (Commission of the European Communities) (2000), *Regular Reports from the Commission on Progress towards Accession by each of the Candidate Countries*, Luxembourg: Office for Official Publications of the European Communities.

CEC (Commission of the European Communities) (2000a), *Eurobarometer 52*, April, Brussels: CEC.

CEC (Commission of the European Communities) (1999), *Regular Report from the Commission on Progress towards Accession by each of the Candidate Countries*, Luxembourg: Office for Official Publications of the European Communities.

CEC (Commission of the European Communities) (1999a), *Eurobarometer 51*, July, Brussels: CEC.

CEC (Commission of the European Communities) (1999b), *Eurobarometer 50*, March, Brussels: CEC.

CEC (Commission of the European Communities) (1998), *Accession Partnership - Romania*, Luxembourg: Office for Official Publications of the European Communities.

CEC (Commission of the European Communities) (1998a), *Regular Report on Progress towards Accession: Romania*, Luxembourg: Office for Official Publications of the European Communities.

CEC (Commission of the European Communities) (1998b), *Eurobarometer 49*, September, Brussels: CEC.

CEC (Commission of the European Communities) (1997), *Commission Opinion on Romania's Application for Membership of the European Union*, Luxembourg: Office for Official Publications of the European Communities.

CEC (Commission of the European Communities) (1995), 'Preparation of the Associated Countries of Central and Eastern Europe for Integration into the Internal Market of the Union', COM(95)163 final Brussels: CEC.

CEC (Commission of the European Communities) (1995a), 'Euro-East', Brussels: CEC.

CEC (Commission of the European Communities) (1993), *Bulletin of the European Communities*, **26** (6).

Dellenbrant, Jan Å. (1994), 'Romania: The Slow Revolution', in Sven Berglund and Jan. Åke Dellenbrant (eds), *The New Democracies in Eastern Europe: Party Systems and Political Cleavages*, 2nd edition, Aldershot, UK and Brookfield, US: Edward Elgar, pp. 203–18.

Dijmarescu, Eugen (1989) 'Trade Relations between Romania and the EC', in Marc. Maresceau (ed.), *The Political and Legal Framework of Trade Relations Between the EC and Eastern Europe*, Dordrecht: Martinus Nijhoff, pp. 39–49.

EC (European Council) (1997), 'Presidency Conclusions - Luxembourg European Council', Brussels: Council of the European Union General Secretariat.

Gabanyi, Anneli U. and Elena. Zamfirescu (1996), 'Romania', in Werner Weidenfeld (ed.), *Central and Eastern Europe on the Way into the European Union: Problems and Prospects of Integration in 1996*, Gütersloh: Bertelsmann Foundation Publishers, pp. 177–99.

Gallagher, T. (1999), 'Ceauşescu's Legacy', *The National Interest*, **56**, 107–11.

Gallagher, T. (1998), 'Romania's desire to be normal', *Contemporary Politics*, **4** (2), 111–25.

Gallagher, Tom (1995), *Romania After Ceauşescu: The Politics of Intolerance*, Edinburgh: Edinburgh University Press.

Gallagher, Tom (1995a), 'The emergence of new party systems and transitions to democracy: Romania and Portugal compared', in Geoffrey Pridham and Paul

Lewis (eds) *Stabilising Fragile Democracies - New Party Systems in Southern and Eastern Europe*, London: Routledge, pp. 206–28.

Geoana, M. (1997), 'Romania: Euro–Atlantic Integration and Economic Reform', *Fordham International Law Journal*, **21** (1), 12–23.

Government of Romania (1999), *National Programme for Accession to the European Union*, Bucharest: Government of Romania.

Government of Romania (1998), *The National Programme for Accession to the European Union*, Bucharest: Government of Romania.

Government of Romania (1996), *The Basic Programme for Romania's Macro-Stability and Development until the Year 2000: The 1997–2000 Governance Programme*, Bucharest: Government of Romania.

Government of Romania (1995), *National Strategy for the Preparation of Romania's Accession to the European Union*, Bucharest: Government of Romania.

Hartwig, Ines (2001), 'Romania and the Black Sea Economic Cooperation: Leaning towards the East or the West?' in Duncan Light and David Phinnemore (eds), pp. 207–87.

Iliescu, Ion (1995), *Aufbruch nach Europa: Rumänien - Revolution und Reform 1989 bis 1994* Köln, Weimar, Wien: Böhlau.

Ionescu, D. (1993), 'Romania Signs Association Accord with the EC', *RFE/RL Research Report*, **2** (10), 33–7.

Ionescu, D. (1991) 'Striving for a Better Image', *Report on Eastern Europe*, 20 December, pp. 27–31.

Jørgensen, Knud E. (1993), 'The European Community and Eastern Europe', in Ole Nørgaard, Thomas Pedersen and Nikolaj Petersen (eds), *The European Community in World Politics*, London: Pinter, pp. 77–97.

Kramer, H. (1996), 'The EU–Turkey Customs Union: Economic Integration amidst Political Turmoil', *Mediterranean Politics*, **1** (1), 60–75.

Light, Duncan and David Phinnemore (eds) (2001), *Post-Communist Romania: Coming to Terms with Transition*, London: Palgrave.

Linden, Ronald H. (1992), 'After the Revolution: A Foreign Policy of Bounded Change', in Daniel N. Nelson (ed.), *Romania After Tyranny*, Boulder, Colorado: Westview Press, pp. 203–38.

Mungiu-Pippidi, A. (1998), 'Identity Crisis', *Transitions*, **5** (4), 75–9.

O'Rourke, B. (1999), 'EU, East European Candidates Review Progress', *RFE/RL Newsline*, 06 May.

Ortiz Clement, L. (1993), 'Report of the Committee on External Economic Relations: Economic and Commercial Relations between the European Community and Romania', *European Parliament Session Documents*, A3-0132/92, Luxembourg: European Parliament.

Pascu, Ioan M. (1992), 'Romania's Response to a Structured World', in: Daniel N. Nelson (ed.), *Romania After Tyranny*, Boulder Co.: Westview, pp. 271–84.

Phinnemore, David. (2000), 'Romania and the European Union in the 1990s: Avoiding Exclusion or Seeking Inclusion?', in G. Cipăianu and V. Ţârău (eds) *Romanian and British Historians on the Contemporary History of Romania*, Cluj-Napoca: Cluj-Napoca University Press, pp. 57–85.

Phinnemore, David. (1999), 'The Problems of EU Enlargement: EU and CEE Perspectives', in Karen Henderson (ed.), *Back to Europe: Central and Eastern Europe and the European Union*, London: UCL Press, pp. 71–88.

Phinnemore, David. (1999a), *Association: Stepping-Stone or Alternative to EU Membership*, Sheffield: Sheffield Academic Press.

Podkaminer, L. (1999), 'EU Membership for the Transition Countries: A Moving Target?', *Vienna Institute Monthly Report*, **1**, 2–4.

Prisăcaru, G. (1996), 'The National Strategy Preparing Romania's Accession to the European Union', *Romanian Journal of International Affairs*, **2** (4), 31–55.

Senior Nello, Susan. (1991), *The New Europe: Changing Economic Relations between East and West*, London: Harvester Wheatsheaf.

Severin, A. (1997), 'L'Intégration de la Roumanie dans l'Union européenne et l'OTAN: un acquis pour la securité en Europe', *Studia Diplomatica*, **50** (2), 17–30.

Severin, A. (1997-98), 'Towards a New Foreign Policy Strategy', *Central European Issues*, **3** (3), 28–39.

Skak, Mette (1993), 'Bulgaria's Policy Towards the EC', in: Krassimir Nikolov (ed.), *Bulgaria and the European Community*, Sofia: Centre for European Studies, pp. 152–71.

Smith, Alan (2001), 'The Transition to a Market Economy in Romania and the Competitiveness of Exports', in Duncan Light and David Phinnemore (eds), pp. 127–49.

Socor, V. (1990), 'Foreign Policy in 1990', *Report on Eastern Europe*, 28 December, pp. 25–30.

Stan, V. (1998), 'Cu spatele la Europa ... ', *Sfera Politicii*, **65**, 16–20.

Stan, Valentin. (1999), *România şi Eşcul Campaniei pentru Vest*, Bucureşti: Editura Universităţii din Bucureşti.

Sturdza, M. (1991), 'The Politics of Ambiguity: Romania's Foreign Relations', *Report on Eastern Europe*, 5 April, pp. 13–20.

12. European Order, Global Governance and the Liberal Peace

Hugh Miall and Robert McKinlay

INTRODUCTION

Europe has always been a battleground of political theories. Liberalism, socialism and realism are European ideologies with the potential to act as organising principles on a global basis. In the early twentieth century, the battles were between the liberal democracies in Western Europe and authoritarian conservatism in Central and Eastern Europe (CEE). In the 1930s and 1940s, the clash between liberalism, fascism and socialism culminated in total war engulfing the continent from 1939 to 1945. In the second half of the twentieth century Europe was divided by the internecine struggle between liberalism and socialism. With the end of the Cold War, however, liberalism appeared to emerge triumphant, not only as the prevailing order in Europe but as a blueprint for a new order of global governance based on democratisation, free markets and human rights, promising a liberal peace.

The European Union (EU) now embodies these liberal principles in its treaties: 'the Union is founded on the principles of liberty, democracy, respect for human rights and fundamental freedoms, and the rule of law, principles which are common to the member States'.[1] No other institution comes so close to Kant's aspirations for a European confederation of republics with a juridical basis that aims at a state of perpetual peace among its members. The founders of the Community hoped to banish the spectre of war through shared control over iron and steel, the common market and ultimately the development of a political union.

In its original form, the Community of the six embraced former enemies (France, West Germany, Italy and Benelux) but scarcely spoke for all of Europe. It developed in the shadow of the largest military confrontation in human history, with permanent armies and nuclear forces facing each other across a divided continent. The liberal principle was in abeyance and the realism of nuclear deterrence in the ascendant. Like West Germany, the Community was an 'economic giant but a political dwarf'. Nevertheless, as it began to grow through successive enlargements, it came to embrace the most important remaining liberal democracy in Western Europe when the United Kingdom joined in 1973, along with Ireland and Denmark, and the nine became the world's largest trading bloc. Then, in the late 1970s, the second enlargement, including Spain, Portugal and Greece, signified the movement of formerly authoritarian dictatorships into the liberal fold. In 1986, the Single European Act laid the basis for the extension of the common market to the remaining EFTA-member countries of Western Europe; and the former neutrals, Austria, Finland and Sweden joined the Union after the end of the Cold War.[2] With the collapse of the communist governments in CEE, the unification of Germany and the end of the Soviet Union, the EU was left as the most potent economic and political structure in Europe. It was set to expand from a membership of 15.

The Union is a new kind of political organisation, which cannot be identified closely with previous models; it is neither a state, nor a federation, nor a confederation, nor merely a regime or an international association. Which political theory most closely explains it and what political form it should develop into is still contested. It is on the road to an 'ever closer Union' but its members disagree on the final form that this should take. The argument made here is that what is most significant about it is not that it represents a new superstate, but rather that it enshrines and represents a new form of emergent governance which is increasingly significant in the world under the conditions of globalisation: namely, a system of rules, relationships, networks and agreements between countries that provides governance without government. As such, it provides a framework for transnational cooperation between societies and the international pooling of powers, without necessarily specifying a permanent form for that cooperation. It is a forum for shaping outcomes in areas such as monetary policy, trade, economic management and environmental regulation, through mutual bargaining and agreements. This pattern of orchestration and harmonisation is becoming increasingly important not only as a means of governance affecting the 370 million EU citizens, who represent an enormous diversity of linguistic, cultural, religious and geographical backgrounds, but also for those in non-member European states and for the 95 per cent of countries in the world with which the EU has trade, cooperation or Association Agreements (Piening, 1997).

In its relations and agreements with other countries, the EU increasingly assumes that open markets, free trade, democratisation and human rights are to be the basis for cooperation. For example, the New Transatlantic Agenda, signed by Presidents Clinton, Gonzalez and Santer in Madrid on 3 December 1995, outlined four major goals for the partners: '1. Promoting peace and stability, democracy and development around the world; 2. Responding to global challenges; 3. Contributing to the expansion of world trade and closer economic relations; 4. Building bridges across the Atlantic'. These broad headings represent some of the main underpinnings of the project of global governance and liberal peace.

In large parts of the world, however, it is very clear that the historical conditions that gave rise to liberalism in Western Europe do not apply now and never have in the past. It is unclear to what extent the application of liberal principles as a basis for universal governance can be either assumed or imposed. Even in CEE, the assumption that the so-called 'transition countries' would make a rapid switch from communism to democratic systems and free markets has not been borne out. Although there has been significant change towards a market system, the transition in many countries has not been to liberal democracy but to 'post-communism', a type of politics that is democratic in form but undemocratic in substance. Moreover, the introduction of western-style liberal nationalism, which reflected western conditions in which states were largely dominated by a single ethnicity, proved disastrous in south-eastern and Eastern Europe where demands for ethnically-based statehood threatened to disintegrate multi-ethnic states.

The liberal peace operates on the assumption that democratic states do not make war on one another and that the spread of democratisation will lead to the enlargement of the sphere of the Euro–Atlantic security community. However, it has also been established that democratic states are more inclined to make war on authoritarian states than are other authoritarian states; a finding that reflects the greater tendency of democracies to join coalitions against authoritarianism. The recent war of the North Atlantic Treaty Organization (NATO) against Yugoslavia and the similar campaign against Iraq suggest the development of a new kind of war, in which, through the use of high-technology armaments which minimise casualties in liberal states, the liberal peace is imposed by force on those who breach its norms. This development has implications not only for the regulation of the international system at large, but for liberalism itself.

The end of the Cold War left Western Europe and the United States as the dominant, politically ascendant and economically most powerful group of societies in the world. It was natural that they used the principles on which their own success had been based to forge the basis for a new world order. But would the attempt to introduce these principles on foreign soils succeed? Are there seeds of future problems in the political and economic principles on which the west European order is based? Would the old problem of how liberal states should deal with illiberal regimes jeopardise the very basis of liberalism? This chapter seeks to elucidate the principles of liberal governance and liberal peace, assess their impact on CEE and draw conclusions for the wider extension of a liberal peace enshrined in a system of global governance.

THE LIBERAL RULES OF GLOBAL GOVERNANCE

Political systems, it is said, rest on the ideas of long-dead thinkers. The liberalism that the European order now encapsulates is certainly not new: it developed in the eighteenth century out of an agrarian, oligarchic society. Liberalism defined itself as opposition to absolutist government and it was the rising urban and middle classes who expressed the demand for popular representation and codified universal human rights, including property rights, freedom of belief, expression and assembly, as well as freedom from arbitrary arrest, excessive fines or cruel and unusual punishments. Liberalism was also an economic theory that asserted that social gains flow from the pursuit of private self-interest, that the invisible hand of the market has benign effects and that markets flourish best when governments do not intervene. This ideology is now dominant in a quite different world; a world of mass markets, interconnected cities and instantaneous communications. But, despite this change of context, the basic tenets of the liberal philosophy have survived and triumphed, albeit with significant changes in application, interpretation and implementation.

It is as well to note the achievements and the limits of eighteenth-century liberalism. It provided the basis for a flexible system of government that won a very wide degree of acceptability and has inspired generations living under tyranny. It has given a sense of community and purpose to people living under a wide range of constitutions and economic systems. At the same time, liberalism was a creature of its time. It was a doctrine upheld in the name of the people, but with no great respect for all the people, especially not the landless, the poor, the uneducated and the masses. Liberalism was careful to ensure that democracy was organised on a representative basis and therefore that the political classes, rather than the working classes, retained the initiative. It offered freedoms and protection to those with property, but no remedy for those who lacked property or the means of acquiring it. The remedy, to be developed through the nineteenth century, was equality of opportunity: the property qualifications and limitations of eighteenth-century liberty were gradually eroded by the extension of the suffrage and of the other liberal freedoms to the mass of the people. Even so, liberalism never fully accepted the case for social, as well as political and legal, rights and it certainly resisted the socialist demand for equality.

Two other developments in the nineteenth century profoundly influenced the development of liberalism. The first was the growth of industrial capitalism. Because capitalism used the market and liberalism defended the market, it was natural for liberalism to become a political theory of capitalism. But there was no inevitable link between the two. Capitalism has flourished in authoritarian societies and even in communist states. Capitalism has some inherently illiberal tendencies, as the activities of very large corporations have often indicated. For the executives and shareholders of these corporations, the preservation of liberty came to mean something not unlike the protection of the privileges of powerful groups in ancient empires (Hall, 1985:23). The marriage of liberalism and capitalism contributed to the spread and appeal of the former, but it also exposed liberal values to the vagaries and contradictions of the latter.

The second influence on the development of liberalism was its other marriage, to nineteenth-century nationalism. If the people were to be sovereign, it was necessary to define the people. In the large nation-states of Western Europe this was not too problematic, but in the fragmented principalities of central Europe and the Italian peninsula, and the multi-national empires to the east, existing states offered little guidance. The French Revolution had shown what a creative and destructive force this second marriage could be; and the Italian and German unifications showed also that it could be manipulated for non-liberal ends. While nationalism remained the dominant means of social identification and the basis for citizenship and identity throughout the nineteenth and twentieth centuries, the liberal principle would inevitably be shaped and interpreted in its shadow.

At the beginning of the twenty-first century, we are again witnessing profound changes in social and economic conditions. The industrial mode of production is being transformed by the digital mode of control. Knowledge creation is becoming the basis of wealth creation. The currency of information is taking over the currency of plant, machinery and fixed capital. The fluid movement of foreign direct investment and mobile capital has escaped the control of the state and states have been forced to accept that they cannot control their own economies by traditional national policy instruments. In a world of rapidly accelerating change, even the most advanced states face the risk that significant industries and sectors of the workforce will become redundant or uncompetitive. Yet to opt out of rapid change is to opt out of being an advanced industrial state. In this new world, therefore, liberalism has come to mean openness to globalisation, willingness to promote innovation and transformation, and acceptance of new scientific and technological changes of whatever kind. Together with capitalism and nationalism, it is taking a leap forward into a global 'network society', for whose governance it provides a convenient political and economic ideology (Castells, 1996).

NEW MODES OF GOVERNANCE IN EUROPE

Any organising principle in Europe has to cope with huge variations in linguistic, ethnic and geographical conditions, which have produced an immense diversity and richness of cultures and political systems. Over the historical landscape of Mediterranean coastlines, medieval villages, Renaissance towns and industrial conurbations, the late twentieth century has laid a fast-moving network of continental and intercontinental traffic, international financial and capital flows, and cross-national organisation of production. This phenomenon, partly regional integration, partly globalisation, has transformed the conditions of life on the continent. But the linguistic, cultural and political communities and cultures of Europe have enormous durability. There remain profound differences between northern and southern Europe, the Protestant, Catholic and Orthodox (and Muslim) parts, the west and the east, the unitary and the federal states, the very large states and the very small, the agricultural and the industrial, the land-locked and the ocean-going.

Finding a single economic or political dispensation to govern all this variety would be extremely difficult. Whenever the integration project has sought to impose too much unity, it has run into difficulties. What has emerged instead, more by adaptation than intent, has been a complex system of governance with different levels of integration on different issues, multiple layers, operating through a mixture of supranational law, inter-governmental arrangements, and informal understandings and practices. A body of European law exists side by side with a variety of national laws, providing a continuing influence on national regulations and a mechanism through which states influence one another's domestic jurisdictions.

A central aspect of the system is the *acquis communautaire*, the corpus of laws, treaties and regulations that the Community has already agreed. This is binding on new members and is effectively written into their national laws. It is as though members of the EU are obliged to buy an operating system, within which they can organise their own programmes, but which nevertheless impose a common 'look and feel' to their policy making. While new members negotiate derogations to ease their entry, the *acquis* influences even prospective members who have an incentive to adapt themselves to it in order to qualify for admission. As candidate countries must achieve 'stability of institutions guaranteeing democracy, the rule of law, human rights and respect for and protection of minorities', the Union has gained considerable influence over the domestic jurisdiction of applicants even before they join.[3] This is a force for common governance without common government. It also ensures that those who have been members of the Community the longest have the largest influence on the common rules.

Historically, the most important arm of Community policy making has been in the area of trade. It is the common market, the customs union and the common external trade policy that most powerfully stamps a common system of governance on exchange between member states and between them and the rest of the world. In practice, the implementation of the common market proceeded slowly, with non-tariff barriers and national promotion of domestic industries resulting in a market as fragmented in the 1980s as it had been in the 1960s (Church and Phinnemore, 1994). But the trends towards liberalisation and deregulation in the 1980s and 1990s established a new impulse towards a single market. This led to a wide range of harmonisation measures, a stronger competition policy and an incentive for companies outside Europe to locate investment within the Union in order to benefit from the lack of internal tariffs. Meanwhile, in external trade policy, the Commission assumed the responsibility for a common commercial policy that would determine trade rules not only for firms operating within its territory, but also for any firm wishing to import to it.

Since the EU has become the world's largest single market, its impact on the rules governing world trade has been crucial. These rules affect both the tariff and non-tariff barriers that traders have to face, as well as health and safety regulations, quality and environmental standards. With the EU playing a central part in the production of agreements by the World Trade Organization (WTO), Brussels is one of the hubs of a continuous system of negotiations involving multinational companies, European and non-European governments, WTO working groups, special interest groups of all kinds, and of course the political representatives of domestic electorates, both in Europe and elsewhere.[4] Given the size and influence of its market, this means that the European system of governance affects the production of everything from steel to bananas to services and indirectly shapes economies and societies around the world. Through its graded system of Association Agreements, Partnership and Cooperation Agreements, Trade Cooperation and Framework Agreements and Lomé Convention Agreements, the EU not only influences the terms of trade, but has also introduced an explicit system of conditionality linking human rights and democratic forms to the more preferential offerings. When concluding trading agreements and establishing special forms of association, the EU (together with other actors in global governance such as the World Bank, the International Monetary Fund and the Organisation for Economic Cooperation and Development) takes into account domestic economic performance, the freedom of elections, the soundness of the banking system, the extent of public debt, the size of the public sector and a wide range of other indicators of conformance with 'good governance' in the liberal model. Its market muscle thus spills over readily into influence on the domestic structure of other societies.

Naturally various groups within the EU have a strong interest in the rules of the system and attempt to set rules that favour themselves. Within a framework of commitment to openness, free trade and market transparency, EU governments have frequently sought to protect domestic producers, especially where these are powerful in domestic politics, such as those in the agriculture sector. The EU's trade agreements with third countries have tended to favour the interests of member states and where weaker societies are desperate for access to EU markets, as in CEE, the advantage has been overwhelmingly on the side of EU firms penetrating these new markets, especially in areas like agriculture or iron and steel which threaten protected interests. In principle, global governance and open markets provide opportunities for all, but those who are already strong benefit the most. Hence what some see as liberalisation is taken to be hegemony by others.

Nevertheless, it would be misleading to suggest that the EU is at the centre of European governance, or that this system is entirely based on laws and regulations. The real dynamics of European and global governance come from the interplay between governments, multinational corporations and international institutions, and between political, technological and market forces. Multinational companies play a vital role since they have a dominating impact on decisions about investment, production, product innovation and on the development of new technology. They now account for about two-thirds of world trade, one-half of which is intra-firm, between different branches of the same company.[5] Competition for inward investment has forced states to adapt their tax regimes and in some cases even their welfare systems to increase their attractiveness. The same pressure exists even more strongly outside Europe. Thus transnational companies shape market rules and influence the size and funding of public sectors. Of course, European electorates too have strong stakes in the emerging rules of the system and help to shape them through their individual governments. There are conflicts of interest between the governments, companies and interest groups involved and it is out of the bargaining between them that the system of governance emerges. This system, embracing rules, bargains, informal arrangements and technological imperatives has become more important than direct government in Europe, and an equivalent system at the world level is being advanced as the basis for global governance.

The national state is no longer sovereign in national issues, whether in the economic, security, environmental or international political realms. Enlarging the state to form a super-state capable of government over a wider area is not a credible alternative because of the variety of local and national political communities. This is why the European system of governance is more impressive, and more pervasive, than the EU's somewhat fitful efforts to form a political union. It has proved to be impossible to form a true political union, given the different aspirations of member states. This has forced the EU into increasingly complicated contortions, such as the pillar structure introduced at Maastricht, the *de facto* multi-speed system and, since Nice, the adoption of enhanced cooperation. The Nice Inter-Governmental Conference introduced the minimum changes required to enable the Union to proceed with expansion, but confirmed the drift towards a more powerful Council, in which the larger states have more power. The Union continues to accrue new powers and seems unlikely to disintegrate as neo-realists have suggested. But it lacks a clear constitution, blocking minorities can be easily formed, and it lacks transparent democratic accountability. As the hub of a system of governance and rules, the European Union is extremely influential. As a type of state, it is distinctly shaky.

THE LIBERAL PEACE

The Treaty of Rome expressed the hope that 'by creating an economic community' the founder members could lay 'the foundations of a deeper and wider community among peoples long divided by bloody conflict'. They have been remarkably successful in doing so. Bearing in mind the extremes of destruction to which Europe has been subjected, the repressive regimes, devastating wars and genocide its people have suffered, the transformation after 1945 has been exceptional. No wars have been fought since then between west European states. All of the formerly military regimes in Western Europe have been democratised. The Cold War was brought to a peaceful conclusion. The west European states have become members of a pluralistic security community in which war between one member and another is no longer plausible.

For neo-realists, the explanation for the 'long peace' in Western Europe lies in the discipline and cohesion imposed by the Cold War. Mearsheimer (1990) predicted that the end of the discipline it imposed might lead to a new era of instability, disorder and fresh conflicts in Europe, even within its western sector.[6] However, this prediction has not been borne out. Liberal institutionalists criticise the neo-realist view for failing to account for the mitigating effect of years of mutual accommodation and concerted decision-making (Keohane and Nye, 1993:6). There appears to be a link between the post-war peace in Europe and the strong empirical finding that democracies do not make war with one another. This is not to say that liberal states are unlikely to go to war, but rather that pairs of democracies are very unlikely to go to war with one another. Democracies are more prone than autocracies to join in wars against autocracies.[7]

There is an excess of possible explanations for this important phenomenon. 'Zones of peace' have been attributed to security communities, democratic governance, economic interdependence, trans-national transactions, strong states and membership of common institutions.[8] A lively research literature has yet to establish clear distinctions between these different explanations. There is no support for Kant's view that democracies would be more peace-loving than autocracies, since democracies are as prone to engage in wars as other regime-types; the finding holds only at the dyadic level. Nor do economic interdependence and mutual trade alone provide a satisfactory explanation, since there have been occasions when trade issues have been not only a source of civilised relations but also of disputes and even wars between states.[9] Before 1914, levels of mutual trade were at levels that have only recently been surpassed. But Rosecrance's (1986) argument that the rise of the trade-state has offered states previously tempted by militarism an alternative route to world power is convincing. Indeed, the weight of statistical evidence, although not uncontested, appears to support the proposition that trading relations between dyads that might be prone to fight (dyads which are contiguous or in which one of the states is a major power) have reduced their propensity to engage in militarised disputes.[10]

Arguing from a theoretical point of view, Keohane and Nye (1989) have suggested that under conditions of complex interdependence, states are likely to consult one another, develop coalitions between officials in different governments, act in predictable ways and avoid the use of force, since this is both costly and inappropriate when the interests of states are interrelated across a multiple set of issues. Even though we still have no clear guidance from the empirical studies, it appears that we are witnessing the emergence of conditions within significant areas of the world that constitute a 'liberal peace', in which certain states no longer find it appropriate or effective to resolve disputes with each other by the use of force (Adler, 1998). This complex of conditions includes democratic governance, trading relations, complex interdependence and membership of international institutions.

The implication of this finding is that further democratisation may extend the zone of liberal peace. If the conditions that have brought a liberal peace to European, North American and Australasian states can be spread to other regions of the world, then it is reasonable that the region of 'liberal peace' will be enlarged and militarised disputes would become incredible between increasing numbers of states. There are three caveats to this conclusion. Firstly, this whole body of literature applies to war between states, rather than to war within states, which have become a higher proportion of all wars in recent decades. There is less research on the relationship, if any, between the 'liberal peace' complex of conditions and internal war. Secondly, the tendency of liberal states to join other liberal states in fighting against autocracies is compatible with the possibility that attempts at democratisation and liberalisation may well lead to further warfare, especially if certain areas of the world prove resistant to liberal conversion. More liberal states could mean more wars or larger wars between liberals and the rest. Thirdly, the complex of conditions associated with the liberal peace may also contribute to a pattern of exclusion and mal-development in the parts of the world outside the liberal zone. This may make it more likely that wars take place within the non-liberal zone or between the liberal and non-liberal zones as a result.

But what if democracy, complex interdependence and global governance spread to the entire world? In this case, extrapolation from the findings about democracy and peace would suggest that a comprehensive liberal peace might come about. The number of democratic states in the world increased from 29 in 1920, 36 in 1945 to 66 in 1990.[11] According to the UN, some 120 countries now hold generally free and fair elections, the highest total in history (Annan, 1997). Trade interdependence and membership of common institutions is increasing. Will these developments, and the introduction of democratisation into new areas, extend and consolidate the liberal peace? We can get some idea by looking at the post-Cold War experience in CEE.

DEMOCRATISATION, GOVERNANCE AND THE LIBERAL PEACE IN CENTRAL AND EASTERN EUROPE

The introduction of liberal democracy and free markets in CEE has resulted in significant transformations, but the transition has been less rapid and less complete than was originally hoped. Some countries were more fertile ground for liberalism than others. Poland, Czechoslovakia and Hungary all formed part of the central European cultural area, sharing the experience of the Renaissance, the Reformation and the Enlightenment with other western and central European states. They made quite rapid strides towards western-style market economies, based on earlier market reforms and social movements in the 1980s. Others did not. The Orthodox areas of Europe and the post-Ottoman states had a very different historical experience, living under multinational empires until the early twentieth century, and then undergoing an incomplete form of modernisation under communism that built modernism from above in previously agricultural societies. 'Civil society' is much more of a western implant in the latter group.

The pace of economic reform and economic recovery has varied inversely with distance from Berlin (Wolf, 1999). While the central European countries and the Baltic States recovered their 1990 level of output by the end of the 1990s, the average transition economy shrank by a quarter during the decade and the economies of the Commonwealth of Independent States almost halved (ibid.). In Russia, Ukraine and other former republics of the Soviet Union, as well as in parts of the Balkans, a form of 'nomenklatura capitalism' came into existence in which industrial bosses, former state industries and the mafia monopolised economic resources, cannibalising the existing economic infrastructure and discouraging enterprise and investment. Overall, then, while some countries in CEE have been closely integrated into the western market, other more distant ones suffered, for some years, a sharp economic downturn. The weakness of their trading ties, capital investment and institutional participation would suggest that the conditions for a liberal peace were absent.

The transition from communism was not to liberalism but to 'post-communism', a form of society that was apparently transitional but increasingly seemed to characterise a new system. As described by Schöpflin (1994), post-communism implied strong presidents, weak parliaments, political parties based on personal networks and factions rather than any deep social roots, weakly developed or non-existent civil society, weak states and use of the resources of the state by dominant elites. Western and European institutions tried to introduce democratic reforms, for example by supporting non-governmental organisations, independent media and other organs of civil society, by extending the Council of Europe, and by trying to get modern protections for minorities written into constitutions. These had some successes, but also failures. The introduction of market reforms was also mixed. The Czech Republic and Slovenia for example rapidly became 'westernised', while in Bulgaria and Russia the market led to distortions such as state companies competing in markets, but operating large debts from national banks, and privatisations which spun off the profitable parts of businesses into the hands of their former managers, while leaving the unprofitable parts in the hands of the state.

One of the basic ideas that people in the CEE states have taken from western experience has been the idea of self-determination, that each nation should have its own state. This aspect of liberalism, which is not intrinsic to liberal philosophy but stemmed from the marriage between nationalism and liberalism, led to conflicts throughout the region between states and minorities. Hence not only did the Soviet Union break up, there were also the frequently violent conflicts between national groups within the newly independent states; most notably, the violent disintegration of Yugoslavia. A significant cause of these conflicts was exposure to western political models.

The liberal peace has had a violent periphery, exacerbated by the tendency of transitional democratising states to experience a relatively high incidence of destructive conflicts.

European diplomats tried as best they could to mitigate these conflicts, using institutions of global governance such as the Organisation for Security and Co-operation in Europe, the EU's Stability Pact, the NATO Partnerships for Peace and the lure of the EU's Europe Agreements and Partnership and Cooperation Agreements. In many cases new constitutions reflected western models and institutional innovations were introduced at the instigation of western states. These were not without successes. The national conflicts in the Baltic States were well managed and a potential showdown between the west and the Russian Federation was averted. In Estonia, for example, a single transferable vote system overcame the ethnic alignment of politics and cross-ethnic voting developed on the basis of regional and economic interests. The proximity to western markets and the high value placed on links with the rest of Europe induced the Baltic States, the Russian Federation and the Russian-speaking minorities to avoid a violent conflict.

In south-eastern Europe, too, there were significant examples of peaceful transition. The issue of the Hungarian minorities in Slovakia, Romania and Serbia was handled remarkably peacefully, in part because of Hungary's aspiration to join the EU; Bulgaria and Romania also largely avoided violent conflict with their minorities. This is not to say that tensions over minority issues do not persist. In the case of Slovakia's Law on the Use of Minority Languages (1999), for example, the ambiguous legislation failed to satisfy the Hungarian coalition party despite pressure and advice from western quarters. Notwithstanding a number of continuing problems in similar areas, the Commission, in its assessments of applicant countries on the basis of accession criteria, has judged that only one applicant state, Slovakia, fails to meet them on political grounds. However, the majority of the applicants do not yet meet the criteria on economic grounds or in their administrative and judicial capacities to apply the *acquis* (CEC, 1997).

Yugoslavia has been the harshest test of the liberal peace. Its destruction came as a shock, since it had been well regarded as a modern, sophisticated country, pursuing a decentralised, semi-market form of economy. Under President Miloševíc, Serbia was an autocracy, yet with democratic forms and multi-party elections: a classic post-communist state. Croatia was similar. The introduction of multi-party elections led to the rise of nationalist, ethnically-based parties in all the Yugoslav successor states, and European liberal influence contributed directly to the clash between the western states and Serbia. Of course, it was Miloševíc's mobilisation of the ethnic Serb communities that led to war. European diplomacy in this instance made things worse, as the Community first insisted on Yugoslav unity and then abruptly reversed course (Woodward, 1995). As Bosnia disintegrated, the European commitment to tolerance, human rights, pluralism and liberalism were placed in conflict with the norm of non-intervention and inviolability of borders. In an odd reversal, liberalism was no longer arguing for peace and realism was no longer arguing for war. The experience tarnished the liberal peace and when it was challenged again, over Kosovo, the European states (under changed governments) were more willing to intervene. When Miloševíc responded to their challenge by deporting the entire Albanian population, NATO member states joined in a Euro–American war against Serbia, a classic example of a liberal war. This marked a turning point in several ways: the first use of force by NATO and the first outside its borders, the first war by European powers against another European state since 1945 and the first war fought exclusively in defence of the principles of liberal governance and human rights. In return for their cooperation, other Balkan states were promised a more sympathetic hearing for their demands to join NATO and the EU.

The Yugoslav war showed the coercive side of liberalism: challengers who overstepped the mark could be met by overwhelming force. In the rest of CEE, and in Serbia itself after Miloševíc's electoral defeat, the liberal community of states held out a promise: if sufficient progress was made towards a form of democratisation, market economy and human rights observance that met western tests of acceptability, then states could join the western institutions and hence enter the zone of liberal peace.

In the meantime, this left an important grey area. Exactly how democratic did states have to be, to qualify?[12] In the grey area, while states were democratising and transitional, they were prone to both internal and external conflicts; their peaceableness could not be relied upon and whether states in the liberal zone were willing to step in and help them could not be guaranteed. In many post-communist countries, governments are centralist, administration is politicised, institutions are undeveloped, politics are polarised and political parties have weak roots (Kaldor and Vejvoda, 1997). Nevertheless, the judgements made by the Commission suggest that these are not regarded as significant obstacles to membership and that a degree of discrimination against minorities and political ethnic conflict will be accepted, so long as this does not spill over into open, violent conflict. Outside Europe, the emergent system of global governance rests on the same liberal principles. The offer to include liberalising states in western, or global, institutions is conditional on similar terms and the same implicit threat to illiberal challenges applies. This suggests that the advance of liberalism may be associated with an enlarging security community, but that this could come into sharper conflicts with regimes that resist its values. As it enlarges, violent conflicts will continue to be likely in the peripheral regions.

GLOBAL GOVERNANCE: PROMISES AND CHALLENGES

By extending a new system of governance to Europe, the European integration project had brought a liberal peace and the largest market in the world to a group of middle-sized economies previously divided by military confrontation. It has also produced a new form of polity that is neither exactly a state, nor exactly a federation or confederation, nor merely a regime. What can be learned from the experience in CEE to date? Are the liberal principles of a global trading regime, universal standards of human rights, democratic governance and a liberal peace the basis for a tranquil, stable and prosperous global order? Or will the efforts by European, North American and other partners to establish a system of global governance lead to further violence on the periphery of a stable zone of liberal peace and possibly even to resistance to what may be seen as a renewed bid for world hegemony?

It is clear that, under the pressure of globalisation, the world faces a much more dramatic set of challenges from its even more diverse peoples and states than Europe did in 1945. The rapid growth in the trans-national flows of capital, people, goods and ideas has in many respects outstripped the capacity of national governance and raises issues which require a large degree of international cooperation. The challenges include the regulation of increasingly turbulent and volatile global financial markets, the maintenance of an orderly trading system, the need for macroeconomic coordination of increasingly integrated economies which are undergoing structural change at a rapid pace and are subject to unpredictable shocks, the management of increasing migration flows, the control of trans-boundary pollution and the regulation of international climate change. Besides these global problems, there are the traditional security problems, exacerbated by the widening access to long-range missiles and weapons of mass destruction and the broader problems of insecurity and exclusion resulting from the gap between rapidly rising wealth in the richer parts of the world and spiralling poverty in the poorer parts. The need for some form of global governance is clear, as the Brundtland Commission argued (WCED, 1987).

The western response to these problems has been to establish institutions, practices and networks for financial, economic, trading, security and environmental issues, based on the practices that prevail in its area. The European Union and the major European states, together with the United States, have been at the forefront in developing them. The principles of global governance dominate the United Nations system and are exercised through institutions such as the G7, the Organisation for Economic Cooperation and Development, the International Monetary Fund (IMF), the WTO and the World Bank. In pursuit of development, liberalisation and political and economic reform, these global institutions have linked political conditionality explicitly to access to the trade, capital and services that the liberal industrial states offer and that developing states need. In Africa, for example, structural adjustment programmes in the 1980s were tied to conditions of good governance, budget discipline and multi-party elections. In some cases, the IMF effectively took over the running of the local economies. The G7's decision in June 1999 to relieve about half of the poorest countries' debt was tied to the condition that they sign up to an IMF structural adjustment programme for six years (Denny, 1999:17). In these ways, global governance is taking command of the states least able to govern themselves.

There is more resistance to global governance in the middle-ranking countries, especially in areas with long cultural traditions, which consider themselves equal or superior to the west. China is a particularly interesting and important case. China's economy is already as large as Japan's in purchasing power parities and it is expected to become the world's largest economy in a generation (Piening, op. cit.:155). It is therefore likely to be included in the WTO and in the world's other institutions of global governance. A question will arise as to whether global governance will succeed in exporting liberalism to China, or whether a compromise with Chinese practices and cultural assumptions will have to be made. Yet despite the pre-eminence of liberal institutions in global governance, liberalism does not have an exclusive claim as the basis for a global governance system, nor even as the basis for peace. ASEAN countries, for example, have their own 'Asian way' of managing complex interdependence, making government actions predictable and limiting the use of force. Where the European powers have overwhelming influence, as in CEE, the spread of liberal governance seems likely to succeed. Even there, however, the persistence of post-communist political characteristics leads to a reserved judgement over democratisation and the wars in Yugoslavia have indicated the limits of the liberal peace.

In the longer term, non-western cultures are likely to become the predominant powers in economic and political terms, as they are in population. In the short term, western-based global governance is in the ascendant. It is still gathering strength as globalisation proceeds. In the longer term, however, it seems unlikely that the extension and consolidation of liberalism will prove capable of underpinning a universal world order, unless the benefits derived from liberal systems are much more widely shared. This raises the question of whether a new system, or a compromise between systems, will have to be found. In the poorer countries, whose agricultural and primary produces are losing value relatively, capitalism as manifested in the world trading and financial system is arguably a cause of misery and conflict. Liberalism linked to capitalism encourages rapid growth in the interests of capital holders and ignores the social and environmental costs of production. A comprehensive liberal peace may require a reassessment of some of liberalism's bedfellows.

The economic and military superiority of the liberal powers encourages others to find ways to compete. One obvious strategy was to turn the Cold War tables on the west, developing nuclear weapons or other weapons of mass destruction to offset the west's conventional superiority. The 1990s saw a new phase in the proliferation of nuclear weapons and also of long-range missiles capable of delivering them. This is turn tended to support the arguments of realists and to undermine the prime condition of complex interdependence, as there are clearly areas of the world in which the use or threat of force remained a primary method for resolving disputes. As liberalism and global governance have advanced, the world, at the same time and in some respects, is becoming more disorderly and anarchic.

Within Europe, a liberal peace has been established and a form of global governance is making impressive strides. A more universal human rights regime has developed. An increasingly integrated world trading system is leading to widespread improvements in living standards. The practice of free elections has become much more common. Yet it is still unclear whether liberal democracy will take full root in cultures and societies with non-European traditions. Within Europe itself, there are calls to cut the link between liberalism and nationalism, for example through the development of a more cosmopolitan democracy, and to qualify the link between liberalism and capitalism by developing accounting systems that reflect social and environmental externalities. Perhaps a more universally acceptable basis for peace and governance will develop out of the encounter between different cultural traditions and civilizations. As we look forward to a new century in which the threats of armed conflict are manifest, but the basis for peace-building and peace-making is stronger than ever before, the quest for a form of governance that can provide a comprehensive peace remains as urgent for us as it was for Kant.

NOTES

1. This wording is from Article F.1 of the Treaty on European Union, adopted in the Amsterdam Treaty.
2. EFTA is the European Free Trade Association.
3. This requirement was laid down at the Copenhagen European Council in 1993.
4. For an account of how this complex system of negotiation and consultations operated in the Uruguay Round, see Woolcock and Hodges (1996).
5. Based on 1995 UNCTAD data, quoted in Held et al. (1999:236).

6. Mearsheimer (1990) expected that west European states would begin 'viewing each other with greater fear and suspicion, as they did for centuries before the end of the Cold War'.
7. See Raknerund and Herge (1997) and Russett (1993).
8. See Deutsch et.al. (1957), Holsti (1996), Keohane and Nye (1989) and Sorensen (1998).
9. For example in the case of the War of American Independence, which is counted as a war between near-democracies.
10. For a review of evidence for this proposition, see O'Neal and Russett (1999), while Barbieri and Schneider (1999) provide a critical perspective.
11. See Huntington (1991).
12. This relates to a grey area in the statistics of liberal peace: exactly how is a liberal democracy defined?

REFERENCES

Adler, E. (1998), 'Condition(s) of Peace', *Review of International Studies*, **24**, Special Issue, 165–91.

Annan, Kofi (1997), *Renewal Amid Transition: Annual Report on the Work of the Organization*, New York: United Nations.

Barbieri, K. and G. Schneider (1999), 'Globalization and Peace', *Journal of Peace Research*, **36** (4), 387–404.

Castells, Manuel (1996), *The Rise of the Network Society*, Oxford: Blackwell.

CEC (Commission of the European Communities) (1997), *Commission Opinion on Slovakia's Application for Membership of the European Union*, Luxembourg: Office for Official Publications of the European Communities.

Church, Clive and David Phinnemore (1994), *European Union and European Community: A Handbook and Commentary on the Post-Maastricht Treaties*, Hemel Hempstead: Harvester Wheatsheaf.

Denny, C. (1999), 'Mountain of Debts', *The Guardian*, 6 August.

Deutsch, Karl W., Sidney A. Burrell, Robert A. Kann, Maurice Lee Jnr, Martin Lichtermann, Raymond E. Lindgren, Francis L. Loewenheim and Richard W. Van Wagenen (1957), *Political Community and the North Atlantic Area*, Princeton: Princeton University Press.

Hall, John (1985), *Powers and Liberties: The Causes and Consequences of the Rise of the West*, London: Penguin.

Held, David, Anthony McGrew, David Goldblatt and Jonathan Perraton (1999), *Global Transformations*, Cambridge: Polity Press.

Holsti, Kalevi (1996) *The State, War, and the State of War*, Cambridge: Cambridge University Press.

Huntington, Samuel (1991) *The Third Wave: Democratisation in the Late Twentieth Century*, Oklahoma: Oklahoma University Press.

Kaldor, M. and I. Vejvoda (1997), 'Democratisation in Central and East European Countries', *International Affairs*, **37** (1), 59–82.

Keohane, Robert and Joseph Nye (1989), *Power and Interdependence*, 2nd edition, Harvard: Harper Collins.

Keohane, Robert and Joseph Nye (1993), 'The End of the Cold War in Europe', in Robert Keohane, Joseph Nye and Stanley Hoffman (eds), *After the Cold War: International Institutions and State Strategies in Europe 1989–91*, Cambridge, Mass.: Harvard University Press.

Mearsheimer, John (1990) 'Back to the Future: Instability in Europe After the Cold War', *International Security*, **15** (1), 5–56.

O'Neal, John and Bruce Russett (1999), 'Assessing the Liberal Peace', *Journal of Peace Research*, **36** (4), 423–42.

Piening, Christopher (1997), *Global Europe: the European Union in World Affairs*, London: Lynne Rienner.

Raknerund, Arvid, and Havard Herge (1997), 'The Hazard of War: Reassessing the Evidence for the Democratic Peace', *Journal of Peace Research*, **34** (4), 385–404.

Rosecrance, Richard (1986), *The Rise of the Trading State: Commerce and Conquest in the Modern World*, New York: Basic Books.

Russett, Bruce (1993), *Grasping the Democratic Peace: Principles for a Post-Cold War World*, Princeton, New Jersey: Princeton University Press.

Schöpflin, George (1994), *Politics in Eastern Europe*, London: Blackwell.

Sorensen, Georg (1998) 'IR Theory After the Cold War', *Review of International Studies* **24**, Special Issue, 83–100.

Wolf, M. (1999), 'Caught in the Transition Trap', *Financial Times*, 30 June.

Woodward, Susan (1995), *Balkan Tragedy*, Washington: Brookings.

Woolcock, Stephen and Michael Hodges (1996), 'EU Policy in the Uruguay Round', in Helen Wallace and William Wallace, (eds), *Policy-Making in the European Union*, Oxford: Oxford University Press, 3rd edition, pp. 301–24.

WCED (World Commission on Environment and Development) (1987), *Our Common Future*, Oxford: Oxford University Press.

Index